D0933413

Books by William H. Gass

IN THE HEART OF THE HEART OF THE COUNTRY
OMENSETTER'S LUCK
THE WORLD WITHIN THE WORD
ON BEING BLUE
WILLIE MASTERS' LONESOME WIFE
HABITATIONS OF THE WORD

FICTION AND THE
FIGURES OF LIFE

Fiction and the Figures of Life

Essays by

William H. Gass

Nonpareil Books

DAVID R. GODINE
Publisher · Boston

Acknowledgment is gratefully made to the following publications which first printed
these essays, some in slightly different form:
New American Review, #7—"The Concept of Character in Fiction"
New American Review, #10—"In Terms of the Toenail: Fiction and the Figures of
Life"
The New York Review of Books—"The Leading Edge of the Trash Phenomenon";
"Mirror, Mirror"; "Imaginary Borges"; "In the Cage"; "Cock-a-doodle-doo";
"From Some Ashes No Bird Rises"; "The Evil Demiurge"; "The Stylization of
Desire"
The New York Times—Vol. 119, No. 40811 "Pricksongs and Descants"
The Philosophical Review—"The Case of the Obliging Stranger"
Book Week Magazine, The Chicago Sun-Times—"Russell's Memoirs"; "A Spirit in
Search of Itself"
The New Republic—"A Memory of a Master"; "The Artist and Society"
The Nation—"The Medium of Fiction"; "The Bingo Game at the Foot of the Cross"
The Philosopher-Critic—"Philosophy and the Forms of Fiction"
South Atlantic Quarterly—"The Imagination of an Insurrection"
Reprinted by permission of The Duke University Press.
Accent—"Gertrude Stein: Her Escape from Protective Language"; and "The High
Brutality of Good Intentions"
Reprinted by permission of The University of Illinois Foundation.
Frontiers of American Culture—© 1968, Purdue Research Foundation "Even If, By All
the Oxen in the World"
Reprinted by permission of the Purdue Research Foundations.
—"The Shut-In"

This is a NONPAREIL BOOK first published in 1979 by David R. Godine,
Publisher, 300 Massachusetts Avenue, Boston, Massachusetts 02115

LC 78-58453

ISBN 0-87923-254-4

Manufactured in the United States of America.

Third printing, April 1989

to
Lynn Nesbit
and
David Segal
for believing

CONTENTS

vii

viii

ACKNOWLEDGMENTS

I WANT TO THANK THE EDITORS OF THE FOLLOWING PUBLICA-
tions for permission to reprint the pieces collected in this
book, although a number appear here in a somewhat different form: *The New York Review of Books* for "Cock-
a-doodle-doo," "The Leading Edge of the Trash Phenomenon," "Mirror, Mirror," "From Some Ashes No Bird Rises,"
"The Evil Demiurge," "In the Cage," "The Stylization of
Desire," and "Imaginary Borges and His Books"; *Accent*
for "The High Brutality of Good Intentions," and
"Gertrude Stein: Her Escape from Protective Language";
The New American Review for "The Concept of Character in Fiction," and "In Terms of the Toenail: Fiction
and the Figures of Life"; *Book Week* for "A Spirit in
Search of Itself," and "Russell's Memoirs"; *The Nation* for
"The Medium of Fiction," and "The Bingo Game at the Foot
of the Cross"; *The New Republic* for "A Memory of a
Master," and "The Artist and Society"; *The South Atlantic
Quarterly* for "The Imagination of an Insurrection"; *The
New York Times Book Review* for "Pricksongs & Descants";
the Southern Illinois University Press for "The Shut-In";
The Purdue University Press for "Even if, by All the Oxen

Acknowledgments

in the World"; *The Philosophical Review* for "The Case of the Obliging Stranger"; and Robert Scholes for "Philosophy and the Form of Fiction."

PREFACE

IT IS EMBARRASSING TO RECALL THAT MOST OF PAUL VALÉRY'S prose pieces were replies to requests and invitations, just as attendance at a wedding is. The card is from a couple you scarcely know perhaps, yet you dress and go, a decision which seldom springs from the deepest sources. Whether his were prefaces, lectures, addresses, or reviews, whether they appeared in journals or gazettes, in periodicals as different as *Art et médecine* and *La Nouvelle Revue française*, he enjoyed the challenge of his limitations; length, topic, audience, appropriate tone: he allowed each a seat at the center of his method and his method's meditations, and brought his clear and graceful mind to every occasion. He created, in himself, opinions—often fragile, momentary blooms, often ones as tough and as continuous as ivy. He dared to write on his subjects as if the world had been silent; and because he was so widely reflective, because he looked upon the arbitrary as a gift to form, he turned the occasions completely to his account, and made from them some of his profoundest and most beautiful performances—the *Eupalinos*, for which no praise will suffice, "Poetry and Abstract Thought," or "Man and the Seashell"—shaping subtle, elusive lines of thought like the silvered paths of fish, and with his calm, poetic style, robbing the reader of his breath.

The recollection is embarrassing because the reviews and essays gathered here are responses too—ideas ordered up as, in emergency, militia are. Though ill-equipt and ragged, the call comes, and they are sent out willy-nilly. Valéry's hands were so strong, he could hold his views lightly, offering his thought as he might offer feeling. Rarely was he cruel, defensive, or angry—never smart aleck. He spoke easily to widely separated minds—painters, dancers, doctors, poets, politicians, humanists, men of science—because he had their interests too, but none of their disunity. One of the more obvious characteristics of my essays, however, is the evidence of a struggle in them to find such a calm and confident single voice. Instead—strange spectacle—we observe an author trying to be both philosopher and critic by striving to be neither. Here is one who puts out his principles like flags, and then lowers the flags to half-mast; one whose views seem stretched like wet string between passion and detachment, refusal and commitment, tradition and departure. In another sense I see them as the work of a novelist insufficiently off duty.

If there is not, among these pieces, the promised community of the completed jigsaw, I have tried, with revisions and arrangements, to make it seem so. I don't believe I go back on my words very often, and I would suggest to any reader with the idleness and inclination to pursue it, that he will find shifts of emphasis, mainly, not basic alterations in ideas.

Ideas or themes? motifs? metaphors? I see that I circle around a good many without ever quite coming to grips, as though they all had cold hands. I notice, too, that some are regularly accompanied by a surge of feeling, while near others I find myself calm. Perhaps I am too suspicious of public speech, of the manufacture of opinions, the filling of orders for views. I ought to doubt my own reasons for accepting these invitations to lecture or review, then. It may be that one's thought should be carried out in the same privacy as good poetry and fiction is, in full indifference to daily hoopla, at a distance from every audience, and apart from any causing occasion, for its own sake only, just as the purest philosophy; but possibly Valéry himself, recognizing as he did that poetry was composition, refinement, silence, that it was not outcry, not communication, felt the nag of that lack as a man of words might, felt the need to write about his trade the way Flaubert wrote of his; and that stirred by this—perhaps no nobler itch than any—said in reply to yet one more request: Dear sir, I shall be happy to lecture to your group on the day you suggest; I shall speak on the subject . . . well, I shall speak on any subject that you like.

PART ONE

PHILOSOPHY AND THE
FORM OF FICTION

So much of philosophy is fiction. Dreams, doubts, fears, ambitions, ecstasies . . . if philosophy were a stream, they would stock it like fishes. Although fiction, in the manner of its making, is pure philosophy, no novelist has created a more dashing hero than the handsome Absolute, or conceived more dramatic extrications—the soul's escape from the body, for instance, or the will's from cause. And how thin and unlaced the forms of *Finnegans Wake* are beside any of the *Critiques*; how sunlit Joyce's darkness, how few his parallels, how loose his correspondences. With what emotion do we watch the flight of the Alone to the Alone, or discover that "*der Welt ist alles, was der Fall ist*," or read that in a state of nature the life of man is "solitary, poor, nasty, brutish, and short." Which has written the greater *Of Human Bondage*, or brooded more musically upon life's miseries, or dwelled more lovingly upon the outlines of its own reflection? Is it not exhilarating to be told that the "desire and pursuit of the whole is called love"? And if we wish to become critical we can observe that Descartes' recourse to a gland in the skull to account for our intercourse with ourselves is a simple failure of the imagination, and that for the philosophers, God is always in His machine, flying about on wires like Peter Pan.

Novelist and philosopher are both obsessed with language, and make themselves up out of concepts. Both, in a way, create worlds. Worlds? But the worlds of the novelist, I hear you say, do not exist. Indeed. As for that—they exist more often than the philosophers'. Then, too—how seldom does it seem to matter. Who honestly cares? They are divine games. Both play at gods as others play at bowls; for there is frequently more reality in fairy tales than in these magical constructions of the mind, works equally of thought and energy and will, which raise up into sense and feeling, as to life, acts of pure abstraction, passes logical, and intuitions both securely empty and as fitted for passage as time.

Games—yet different games. Fiction and philosophy often make most acrimonious companions. To be so close in blood, so brotherly and like in body, can inspire a subtle hate; for their rivalry is sometimes less than open in its damage. They wound with advice. They smother with love. And they impersonate one another. Then, while in the other's guise and gait and oratory, while their brother's smiling ape and double, they do his suicide. Each expires in a welter of its own surprise.

Philosophers multiply our general nouns and verbs; they give fresh sense to stale terms; "man" and "nature" are their characters; while novelists toil at filling in the blanks in proper names and at creating other singular affairs. A novelist may pin a rose to its stem as you might paper a tail to its donkey, the rose may blush at his command, but the philosopher can elevate that reddening from an act of simple verbal predication to an angel-like ingression, ennobling it among Beings. The soul, we must remember, is the philosopher's invention, as thrilling a creation as, for instance, Madame Bovary. So I really should point out, though I shall say little more about it, that fiction is far more important to philosophy than the other way round. However, the novelist can learn more from the philosopher, who has been lying longer; for novelizing is a comparatively new, unpolished thing. Though philosophers have written the deeper poetry, traditionally philosophy has drawn to it the inartistic and the inarticulate, those of too mechanical a mind to move theirs smoothly, those too serious to see, and too fanatical to feel. All about us, now, the dull and dunce-eyed stool themselves to study corners.

Souls, essences, the bickering legions of immortals, the countless points of view which religion and philosophy have shaped, are seldom understood as metaphorical, as expressions of our wishes and our fears, as desperate political maneuvers, strategies of love or greed, as myths which make a sense which some men may, at moments, need; for the celebrated facts of life, whatever they are, are not very forceful, and even the most stubborn and most brutish ones (that man must eat to live, for instance) allow an indefinite number of attitudes and interpretations, including vegetarianism or solemn pronouncements in favor of fish or stern edicts against pork and beans.

If games, then sometimes dangerous ones. Let us suppose for a moment that both our Russells and our Becketts are engaged in telling us *how it is*, that the novelist and the philosopher are companions in a common enterprise, though they go about it in different ways. The objects I see and sometimes label—pencil, paper, table, penny, chair—each seems solid yet is pocked with spaces, each seems steady yet is made of moving pieces: shape, steadiness, solidity, and color . . . are these illusions? I call the penny round, but I'm reminded I see an ellipse. I say the pencil's yellow, yet perhaps the yellow's painted in by eye, the yellow is the reading of a signal maybe, although the reading does not reside within the receiver, and possibly its actual home is in the mind. The what? The mind. Who, or what, is that? A character. Like Micawber. Going on in the firm belief that something will turn up. Hasn't he made my world strange, this philosopher? I find I have a body, then a mind. I find that the world I live in, the objects I manipulate, are in great part my constructions. I shortly come to believe in many invisible beings, gods and angels, wills and powers, atoms, voids. Once where I thought an anger "out there" like a demon, a color "out there" in an object, connections "out there" holding hands with things, I now think otherwise. Loose bundles of affections and sensations pass me like so many clouds of dust in space (and, dear heaven, who am I?).

Beckett tells us that we live in garbage cans; sit at the side of empty roads, in emptiness awaiting emptiness; crawl blindly through mud. My skin is the tattered dirty clothing of a tramp, my body a broken bicycle, my living space is earth to just beneath my shoulders, my speech the twittering of an unoiled pump. Hasn't he made my world strange, this novelist? No, of course our lives are not a muddy crawl— *apparently*. But that is mere appearance. We're fooled constantly. We think our emotions fine when they are coarse; we think our ideas profound when they are empty, original when commonplace; we think at first we are living richly, deeply, when all we possess is a burlap bag, unopened tins, dirty thoughts, and webby privates.

I cannot help my home still looks well furnished, or my

body trim; I cannot help the colors which I seem to come upon, or the unflinching firmness of my chair; I cannot help I glory in my sex or feel and think and act as one and not as a divided community; for I'm incurably naïve, incurably in love with deception; still, I can be taught, I can learn suspicion, learn that things aren't really what they seem; I can learn to hate my pleasures, condemn my desires, doubt my motives, deny my eyes, put unseen creatures in the world and then treat them with greater reverence, give them greater powers than those I innocently know—to bow and bow and bow in their direction; I can replace my love for people with a love for principle,[1] and even pursue a life beyond the grave as a program for the proper pursuit of this one. Bravo, novelists and philosophers; good show.

Save the appearances, Plato said. Then make them all realities. No better way. Yet without that splendid distinction, the novelist as philosopher and the philosopher as novelist would both be out of business.

2

The esthetic aim of any fiction is the creation of a verbal world, or a significant part of such a world, alive through every order of its Being. Its author may not purpose this—authors purpose many things—but the construction of some sort of object, whether too disorderly to be a world or too mechanical to be alive, cannot be avoided. The story must be told and its telling is a record of the choices, inadvertent or deliberate, the author has made from all the possibilities of language. Whether or not it was correct of Aristotle to rea-

---

[1] This point is developed at length in "The Case of the Obliging Stranger."

son, as he apparently sometimes did, from the syntax of the Greek language to the syntax of reality, the art of fiction consists of such reasoning, since its people and their destinies, the things they prize, the way they feel, the landscapes they inhabit, are indistinct from words and all their orderings.

The artist's task is therefore twofold. He must show or exhibit his world, and to do this he must actually make something, not merely describe something that might be made. This takes tremendous technical skill, and except in rare and highly favored persons, great labor.[2] Furthermore, he must present us with a world that is philosophically adequate, and this requires of him the utmost exercise of thought and sensibility. No one should mistake the demand. It is not for a comprehensive and correct philosophy. Truth, I am convinced, has antipathy for art. It is best when a writer has a deep and abiding indifference to it, although as a private person it may be vital to him. If the idea of truth is firmly defined and firmly held in line; if it is not, like Proteus, permitted to change its shape at every questioning, the very great difference between the theoretical formulations of the philosopher and the concrete creations of the novelist must make itself felt. The concepts of the philosopher speak, the words of the novelist are mute; the philosopher invites us to pass through his words to his subject: man, God, nature, moral law; while the novelist, if he is any good, will keep us kindly imprisoned in his language—there is literally nothing beyond.[3] Of course, if the philosopher has made up his subject, as I suspect he has made up God, sin, and sense data, then he is performing for us, at least in part, as the novelist

[2] For more on this, see "In Terms of the Toenail: Fiction and the Figures of Life."

[3] This is a recurrent theme—see especially, "The Concept of Character in Fiction"—though I qualify it in "In Terms of the Toenail: Fiction and the Figures of Life."

performs. Theology, it appears, is one-half fiction, one-half literary criticism.

A philosophy may be "adequate" without being true. If it answers, or shows how to answer, the questions its assumptions and its inferential laws allow, it is complete; if its conclusions follow from these assumptions as its rules dictate, it is consistent; and if the questions it permits are, in any degree, the same that everyday life puts to the ordinary man, it and its answers are to that degree significant; for the everyday questions of ordinary life are always addressed to those ultimate appearances which we remember must be saved. Any philosophy complete, consistent, and significant is, in the sense here used, adequate. It is adequate within its range, although its range may not be vast. A long and complex novel, or series of novels, however, may present us with a world complete through every principle and consequence, rivaling in its comprehensiveness the most grandiose philosophical systems; while a brief story may exhibit only an essential part from which we may infer, at our desire and leisure, much of the remainder. Finally, the artist is not asked to construct an adequate philosophy, but a philosophically adequate world, a different matter altogether. He creates an object, often as intricate and rigorous as any mathematic, often as simple and undemanding as a baby's toy, from whose nature, as from our own world, a philosophical system may be inferred; but he does not, except by inadvertence or mistaken esthetic principle, deem it his task to philosophize. A man who makes a thing that moves utilizes the laws of motion, although he may be unaware of their existence. All he cares about is the accomplishment of his particular design. The worlds which, in like manner, the writer creates, are only imaginatively possible ones; they need not be at all like any real one, and the metaphysics which any fiction implies is likely to be meaningless or false if taken as nature's own. The man who makes machines intuitively, the laws of heat and light and motion in his fingers, is inventive. Indeed, he may invent, in the principles of its running, what science knows nothing of. The writer, similarly, thinks through the medium of which he is the master, and when his world arises, novel and complete—sometimes as arbitrary and remote from real things as the best formal game, sometimes as searchingly advanced and sharp to the fact as the gadget of the most inspired tinker—his world displays that form of embodied thought which is imagination.

Nature is more than its regulations. Galileo follows the swinging Pisa Cathedral lamps with his dreadful eyes, but it is not the spill of light and shadow, the halo or the burning, that attracts him. It is the quantity in the action, the principle in the thing. So any maker, bent on rendering concrete the dominion of number, must find the qualities of sensation which will embody them.[4] Nor can he merely name the qualities over, for what he makes is a world, not a diagram, and what he makes must live. Swinging has a law, but before the law of swinging come the swings.

Writers whose grasp of esthetic principles is feeble, or whose technique is poor and unpracticed, or whose minds are shallow and perceptions dim, give us stories which are never objects for contemplation, but arguments; they give us, at best, dramatized philosophy, not philosophically significant drama; or, if they know they must exhibit or present, show us Bradleyan selves in Berkeleyan suits sitting down to Boolean tea.

The philosophy that most writers embody in their work, with those amendments and additions which any strong

---

[4] More on embodiment in "The Concept of Character in Fiction."

personality will invariably insist upon, since it can only identify itself with what it calls its own begetting, is usually taken unconsciously from the tradition with which the writer is allied. As a result, a writer whose work has little esthetic merit may retain an historical or a philosophical interest. He may have represented, in just the confused way it existed, the world his generation saw and believed they lived in; or he may have produced a model of some philosopher's theoretical vision; and since the philosopher's vision is as often as not blind at the last to the signals of reality, it may be as near to the sight of fact his theory will ever come. On such occasions the work is commentary. Some novels are of very great philosophical importance, as it is doubtless one test of a philosophy to imagine, more simply than the cosmos itself does, what it would be like to live under its laws— whether, in other words, with its principles it is possible to build something that will run. Such imaginative construction is particularly useful for the evaluation of moral and political systems. One wants to know what people, good according to Kant or Nietzsche or William James, are like, and how it feels to house the conscience of Saint Paul or guard with the eyes of Augustine the affairs of the city of God. An artist may precede the sciences in discovery, just as the inventor may, by incorporating in his work ideas which turn out true, but his success in this is not esthetic, and depends entirely on what science decides.

An idea must first be thought before it can be tested, but a principle encased in fiction has, most likely, not been thought of at all. It has been used. This may have been what Plato had in mind when he classified his citizens according to their nearness to the Forms. Certainly it is one thing to employ an idea, another to state it in a manner suitable to thought, while yet another to carry out the tests which make it true or false. It is a sadly limited view of the power of mind in man to suppose that only truth employs or pleasures it. It appears that any expression suitable to science must be quantitatively abstract, and that thought itself proceeds by quantities and extensions, yet one may contemplate the most purely abstract and most purely quantitative system for the values of the system's sake, and so far as this is done, and is the end of such pure systems, they, and the opposite pole of art, have the same appreciative aim, and are in value much akin; for creative thought and creative imagination are not so much stirred on by truth in any synthetic sense as by sublimity—a vision of absolute organization. It is really a moral insistence, this insistence that truth be first, whether it is the Platonist, who requires that Ideas do the work of things, or the Pragmatist, who demands that things perform the functions of ideas.

3

For the purposes of analysis we can regard the sentences of fiction as separate acts of creation. They are the most elementary instances of what the author has constructed. Wittgenstein believed for a time that a proposition, in the disposition of its names, pictured a possibly equivalent arrangement of objects. This is a pleasant fancy, and plainly must be true . . . of fictions; though sentences in stories should do more than simply configure things. Each should contrive (through order, meaning, sound, and rhythm) a moving unity of fact and feeling.

Before us is the empty page, the deep o'er which, like God, though modestly, we brood. But that white page, what is it? Perhaps it is the ideally empty consciousness of the reader—a dry wineskin or a *tabula rasa*. And if, as authors, we think this way, then what we want is a passive mind and, as in love, an utterly receptive woman. Thus our attitudes, before the first act of creation, make a philosophical difference. What shall we sail upon it first?

> All known all white bare white body fixed one
> yard legs joined like sewn,

Beckett's "Ping" begins. An audacious first term: all. The sentence isolates its words; they slowly fall, slowly revolve, slowly begin to group themselves. We are in the hands of an ancient atomist.

> All known all white bare white body fixed one
> yard legs joined like sewn. Light heat white floor
> one square yard never seen. White walls one yard
> by two white ceiling one square yard never seen.

Stately monotonous strokes, like measured beats of a gong, occur within, but do not fill, this void. Though here the gong sometimes emits a ping. Truly, nothing is previous. Groups first formed form the first connections, and are repeated.

> Bare white body fixed only the eyes only just.
> Traces blurs light grey almost white on white.
> Hands hanging palms front white feet heels to-
> gether right angle. Light heat white planes shining
> white bare white body fixed ping fixed elsewhere.

With what remarkable confidence, on the other hand, does Jane Austen reach for our responses. She does not form a chaos or create from nothing. Her pen moves through us; we part a bit and yield the paths of her design. How much we are expected to know already: manners, values, social structure. She thinks in far, far longer lengths; her silences are like the silences which occur in happy conversations; her spaces are interiors, tamed and quiet; she does not begin, she ends, in terror, and the metaphysical.

Let's descend into the sentence briefly, on a rope for our return. How amazing they can be, how strange. The shortest one can spell us back to infancy. ("A cow broke in tomorrow morning to my Uncle Toby's fortifications," for instance.) The meaning of a sentence may make a unity, comprise some whole, but inevitably its concepts are loosed one by one like the release of pigeons. We must apprehend them, then, like backward readers: here's a this, now a that, now a this. The sentence must be sounded, too; it has a rhythm, speed, a tone, a flow, a pattern, shape, length, pitch, conceptual direction. The sentence confers reality upon certain relations, but it also controls our estimation, apprehension, and response to them. Every sentence, in short, takes metaphysical dictation, and it is the sum of these dictations, involving the whole range of the work in which the sentences appear, which accounts for its philosophical quality, and the form of life in the thing that has been made.

In Beckett's sentences, quoted above, there is no subordination, but a community of equals—well, hardly a community either, though the primordial relationship of adjective to noun is not entirely suppressed. This is not the place to get lost in details, but we are all aware of the kind of influence Aristotle's subject-predicate logic had on his philosophy, and on all those which followed for quite a long time. The novelist's characteristic grammatical forms affect the building of his book at least as much, though we must be careful to notice not only his words' syntactical pasts, but their present syntactical functions. So some sentences are crowded with nouns; some contain largely connectives. Some sentences are long and tightly wound; others are as hard and blunt as a hammer. Some combine events of contrasting sizes, like a sneeze and the fall of Rome; others set dogs at bears, link the abstract and the concrete, quality and number, relation and property, act and thing. In some worlds the banjo and its music are two banjos, in others all the instruments dissolve into their music, that into a landscape or a climate, thus finally, through the weather, to an ear.

The Humean sentence will reduce objects to their qualities, maintain an equality between them by using nonsubordinating conjunctions, be careful not to confuse emotion and reflection with perception, but at the same time will allow their presence in the same onward flow. Everywhere, Hume makes his world out of lists and collections. Some novelists, like I. B. Singer, for example, drain the mental from their books as if it were pus in a wound. Thoughts are rendered as public speech; there is recourse to journals; incidents and objects are presented always as the public might see them; and even inner temptations—lusts, hates, fears—receive embodiment as visibly material demons.[5] Henry James's sentences are continuous qualifications, nuance is the core and not the skin;[6] and the average idealist, proceeding with a similar scrupulosity, treats his entire work as the progressive exploration and exposure of a single subject. It would suit him if there were no ordinary periods, no real beginning or real end, if every word were an analytic predicate of one ultimate Idea.

Imagine for a moment we are making up a man, breathing life into a clay lung.

> He stood in the mud: long, thin, brown in his doctor's gown of fur, with his black flapped cap that buttoned well under his chin and let out his brown, lean, shaven and humorous face like a woodpecker's peering out of a hole in a tree.

[5] This is a central concern of my essay on Singer, "The Shut-In."
[6] See "The High Brutality of Good Intentions" and "In the Cage."

What is the shape of Achilles' nose? what color were his eyes? Achilles is what Achilles does; he has no secret wishes, secret dreams; he has no cautiously hidden insides. Shall we make our man on that model, out of deeds? or shall we see him through his station: prince or clown, clerk or plumber, servant or secretary, general or priest? Shall we dress him in his features as Ford here puts Magister Nicholas Udal in his clothes? Whether a man has thick lips or thin, crafty ones or cruel, we can always count on Ford to tell us, though in other men's fictions many are lipless. The colon contrives to give the qualities which follow it to Udal's whole muddy standing, not to Udal and his form alone. Observe what happens if we remove it, and at the same time alter the order of our apprehension of these details:

> *He was long, thin, and brown in his doctor's gown of fur, with his black flapped cap that buttoned well under his chin and let out his brown, lean, shaven and humorous face like a woodpecker's peering out of a hole in a tree. He stood in the mud.*

The original passage is packed with possessives, the dominant relation is that of ownership, but the Magister need not own everything. Can we feel the effect of progressively loosening these ties, the clothing first, and then the features?

> *He stood in the mud: long, thin, brown in a doctor's gown of fur, with a black flapped cap that buttoned well under his chin and let out his brown, lean, shaven and humorous face like a woodpecker's peering out of a hole in a tree.*

> *He stood in the mud: long, thin, brown in a doctor's gown of fur, with a black flapped cap that buttoned well under a chin and let out a brown, lean, shaven*

and humorous face like a woodpecker's peering out of a hole in a tree.

Perversely, let us let him own his clothes but not his face.

He stood in the mud: long, thin, brown in his doctor's gown of fur, with his black flapped cap that buttoned well under a chin and let out a brown, lean, shaven and humorous face like a woodpecker's peering out of a   hole in a tree.

It is not simply that our understanding of Udal changes; our understanding changes because Udal has become a figure in a changed world.

We might at first be inclined to think that style is a form of perception; that each sentence reveals the way the writer looks at the world—

for example, observe the differences between (1) We walked through the woods. The trees had leaves. The leaves were newly green. (2) We walked through the woods. New leaves greened the trees. (3) We walked the greening woods. (4) It seemed the greening woods walked while we stood.

—but strictly speaking style cannot be, itself, a kind of vision, the notion is very misleading, for we do not have before us some real forest which we might feel ourselves free to render in any number of different ways; we have only the words which make up this one. There are no descriptions in fiction, there are only constructions,[7] and the principles which govern these constructions are persistently philosophical. The same, for that matter, is true of narration, dialogue, character, and the rest. Just as the painter's designs help make

[7] See "The Concept of Character in Fiction."

his object, the lines of the novelist offer no alternatives, they are not likely interpretations of anything, but are the thing itself.

4

Thus so many of the things which are false or foolish when taken to the world—in religion or philosophy—become the plainest statements of what's true when taken to fiction, for in its beginning *is* the word, and if the esthetic aim of any fiction is the creation of a world, then the writer is creator— he is god—and the relation of the writer to his work represents in ideal form the relation of the fabled Creator to His creation.

Once God was regarded as the cause of all, as the Great Historian with a plan for His people, the Architect, the Law-giver, the principle of Good; so that if Mary sickened, the cause was God, and if Mary died, it was God who called her Home, and if anything happened whatever, it was ordained by Him, indeed it was counted on, by Him, from the beginning. He saw things, all things, plain—plainer surely than any novelist ever saw his story before a word of it went down. So that really, in this created world, there are no necessary beings, there are no categorical creatures, and events do not follow one another out of the past, because of the past, but everlastingly out of God, because of God. In a movie, too, where everything is predestined, the illusion of internal structure is maintained, as though one part of the film explained the occurrence of another. However, the director had the scenes shot; had them spliced as he desired; and the sensation that the villain's insult has provoked the hero's glove is an appearance often not even carefully contrived. In the story of Mary, if Mary dies, the novelist killed her, her broken heart did not. The author of any popular serial knows, as Dickens did, that to the degree he makes his world real to his readers, to that degree they will acknowledge his authorship; hold him responsible; and beg him to make the world good, although evil seems present in it; beg him to bring all to a moral and materially glorious close, in clouds and hallelujahs. Though such appeals may cause smiles in the sophisticated, they are appeals more rationally directed to the actual power than those, exactly parallel, delivered by the faithful in their prayers to God. The novelist is uncomfortable. He may enjoy his alleged omnipotence, his omniscience and omnipresence, but with it, spoiling it, is responsibility. What about all that perfection? Can he take upon himself this burden? Can he assure his readers that his world is good, whatever happens? He can explain evil no better than the theologian; therefore shortly the novelist who assumes the point of view of the omnipotent, omniscient, and omnipresent narrator begins to insist upon his imperfection; apologize, in a gentle way perhaps, for his cutpurses, whores, his murderers, and in general surrender his position. "I'm sorry Becky doesn't seem as sweet as she should, but what can I do about it? That's just how she is." "Well, I'm terribly sorry about all this sordidness, as sorry as you are," he may say, "but that's how the world is, and what am I, poor fellow, but a dime-store mirror held to it?" This is a sly device. And the worlds which the novelist creates are shortly deprived of their deities. At last the convention seems acceptable only if it's all in fun. God snickers and pushes parsons into ditches. And when the novelist begins to explain that, of course, omnipotence is artistically vulgar; that one must limit oneself to a point of view, he is insisting, for *his* world, upon the restriction of knowledge to the human, and often only to a few of these, and finally only to rare moments occurring in the best minds. He gives up his powers to a set of principles. He allows himself to be governed by them, not to govern, as if God stepped down in favor of moving mass and efficient causes, so to say: "This is not mine; I do not this; I am not here." Novels in which the novelist has effaced himself create worlds without gods.

Even outside books time passes. These days, often, the novelist resumes the guise of God; but he is merely one of us now, full of confusion and error, sin and cleverness. He creates as he is able; insists upon his presence and upon his wickedness and fallibility too. He is not sure about what he knows; his powers have no great extension; he's more imperfect than otherwise; he will appeal to us, even, for sympathy. Why not? He's of his time. Are there any deities who still have size?

An author may make up his own rules, like the god of the Deists, or take them from experience where he thinks he finds them ready-made; but the control which these rules exercise is little like that exercised by the laws of nature, whatever they are. The star-crossed lovers in books and plays are doomed, not because in the real world they would be, but because, far more simply, they are star-crossed. Simple slum conditions, as we know, do not so surely produce a certain sort as in novels they are bound to, and no amassing of detail is sufficient to ensure a perfectly determinate Newtonian conclusion. Authors who believe they must, to move their fictions, hunt endlessly through circumstances for plausible causes as they might hunt for them in life, have badly misunderstood the nature of their art—an enterprise where one word and one inferring principle may be enough.

As in a dice race, when we move over the squares with our colored disks, the dice impel us and the ruled lines guide.

There are no choices. The position of each disk is strictly determined. We see the track, we know the throw, we can predict the new arrangement. Such a game is the simplest kind, and forms the simplest system. There is one rule of inference. Any principle that permits the rational expectation of some situation upon the occurrence of another is a principle of inference, and such a principle is called a rule when the conclusion to be inferred awaits an inferring power—a power that must be, therefore, ordered to its task—and is called a law when the inferring power acts, as it were, from within its premises. The form of the game, however, lies in number, the winner he who rolls the highest score; but this form is imaged out upon a table; disks describe the level of addition; and these are transmogrified by fancy into thoroughbreds, while the player, through this really peculiar evidence of the superiority of man, becomes the owner of a stable. The adding of the dice can be expressed in many ways. This simple system is the foundation of many more complicated ones. There are principles, one might call them, of embodiment, wherein the players are enjoined to treat the disks and the squared path as representing the units and the total of addition. There are yet other principles, here assumed, that call the squared-up path a track, the flat disks horses. The game may make these assumptions explicit, but if it does not, the player may imagine for himself any other suitable kind of linear contest.

When God abdicates, or at least sanctions a belief in the end of miracle, he gives over his rule to inference. For fiction, the rules can be as many as the writer wishes, and they can be of any kind he wishes. They establish the logic, the order, of his world. They permit us to expect one event will follow another, or one sentence another, or one word another. To the degree words, sentences, and, materially, things and happenings follow without rule, the world is a world of chance. Since no work can exhibit a conformity to principle so complete each word is, in its place and time, inevitable and predictable, all fictional worlds contain at least an element of chance, and some, of course, a very high degree of it. It is merely a critical prejudice that requires from fiction a rigidly determined order. Chance, too, is a kind of principle, and can be brought to the understanding of reason. In the natural realm, the principle of causality is often regarded as the inferring instrument. Causality, in general, makes out the possibility of predicting events from the evidence of others. Since the inferring power is thought to reside otherwise than in the observer, any particular expression of it is a law. When, as in the game above, it is impossible to predict the future organization of a system on the basis simply of its present state and its governing rules or laws, and when the prediction must await the unpredictable disclosure of further facts, for instance what the dice will read, then the system is a system based on chance. It must be borne in mind that the results of the game proceed inevitably from its nature, and that a system based on chance remains as beautifully systematic as any other. If what the fates decree must come to pass, chance can lie only in the way to it. Or each affair may be seen necessarily to unfold out of its past without anyone's being able to guess the ultimate consequences. Again, certainty and doubt about both end and means may be so shrewdly mixed, the reader is delightfully tossed between cruel suspense and calm inevitability. In the dice game, the players finger disks, but if the game, by its conventions, calls them horses, they are horses. However, to a fellow who, his disk dead even with the others, resolutely calls all disks, and only waits the adding up of his account, art must ever be a failure; for it can succeed only through the cooperating imagination and intelligence of its consumers, who fill out, for themselves, the artist's world and make it round, and whose own special genius partly determines the ultimate glory of it.

The causal relation itself may be logically necessary or psychologically customary, formal or final, mechanical or purposive. It may be divinely empowered or materially blind. Causality in fiction is usually restricted to the principle that controls the order of constructed events, considered separately from whatever rule may govern the placement of symbols, the dress of the heroine, the names of the characters, and so on, if any rule does govern them. An event, however, may be anything from the twitch of an eyebrow to the commission of adultery, and a cause, any event which leads beyond itself to another. The plot (to risk that rightly abused word) is composed of those events the novelist has troubled to freshly arrange as causes, as opposed to those he has thrown in for vividness, but which cause nothing, or those concerning which he has let nonfictitious nature have its way. Nonfictitious nature has its way about a good deal. If in a story it rains, the streets usually get wet; if a man is stabbed, he bleeds; smoke can still be a sign of fire, and screams can be sounds of damsels in distress. No novel is without its assumptions. It is important to find them out, for they are not always the same assumptions the reader is ready, unconsciously, to make. Hawthorne could count on more than Henry James, as James complained. Do we any longer dare to infer goodness from piety, for example, evil from promiscuity, culture from rank?

And has not the world become, for many novelists, a place not only vacant of gods, but also empty of a generously regular and peacefully abiding nature on which the novelist might, in large, rely, so to concentrate on cutting a fine and sculptured line through a large mass taken for granted, and has it now also seemed to him absent of that perceptive and sympathetic reader who had his own genius and would undertake the labor, rather easy, of following the gracious turns that line might take; so that, with all these forms of vacantness about him, he has felt the need to reconstitute, entire, his world; to take nothing, if he felt the spur of that conceit, for granted, and make all new, distinct, apart, and finally, even, to provide, within the framework of his vision, the ideal reader, the writer's words his mind and eyes?

5

The use of philosophical ideas in the construction of fictional works—in a very self-conscious and critical way, I mean—has been hastened by the growing conviction that not only do these ideas often represent conceptual systems of considerable complexity, they have the further advantage of being almost wholly irrelevant as accounts of the real world. They are, that is, to a great degree *fictional* already, and ripe for fun and games. Then, too, the novelist now better understands his medium; he is ceasing to pretend that his business is to render the world; he knows, more often now, that his business is to *make* one, and to make one from the only medium of which he is a master—language. And there are even more radical developments.

There are metatheorems in mathematics and logic, ethics has its linguistic oversoul, everywhere lingos to converse about lingos are being contrived, and the case is no different in the novel. I don't mean merely those drearily predictable pieces about writers who are writing about what they are writing, but those, like some of the work of Borges, Barth, and Flann O'Brien, for example, in which the forms of fiction serve as the material upon which further forms can be imposed. Indeed, many of the so-called antinovels are really metafictions.[8]

Still, the philosophical analysis of fiction has scarcely taken its first steps. Philosophers continue to interpret novels as if they were philosophies themselves, platforms to speak from, middens from which may be scratched important messages for mankind; they have predictably looked for content, not form; they have regarded fictions as ways of viewing reality and not as additions to it. There are many ways of refusing experience. This is one of them.[9]

So little is known of the power of the gods in the worlds of fiction, or of the form of cause, or of the nature of soul, or of the influence of evil, or of the essence of good. No distinction is presently made between laws and rules of inference and conventions of embodiment, or their kinds. The role of chance or of assumption, the recreative power of the skillful reader, the mastery of the sense of internal life, the forms of space and time: how much is known of these? The ontological significance of the subordinate clause, or the short stiff sentence regularly conjoined to more, or new words, or inversion—all passed over. Writers are seldom recognized as empiricists, idealists, skeptics, or stoics, though they ought—I mean, now, in terms of the principles of their constructions, for Sartre is everywhere recognized as an

[8] A number of the preceding points are developed in "Mirror, Mirror," concerning Nabokov, in "Pricksongs & Descants," concerning Coover, in "The Leading Edge of the Trash Phenomenon," concerning Barthelme, and in "Imaginary Borges and His Books."
[9] Others are discussed in "Even if, by All the Oxen in the World" and "The Artist and Society."

existentialist leaning left, but few have noticed that the construction of his novels is utterly bourgeois. No search is made for first principles, none for rules, and in fact all capacity for thought in the face of fiction is so regularly abandoned as to reduce it to another form of passive and mechanical amusement. The novelist has, by this ineptitude, been driven out of healthy contact with his audience, and the supreme values of fiction sentimentalized. The art of the novel is now a mature art, as constantly the source of that gratification found in the purest and profoundest contemplation as any art has ever been, and the prospect of a comprehensive esthetic that will provide for its understanding and its judgment is promising and grand. The novel is owed this. It has come, in darkness, far. But it will not stir farther until the appreciation of it has become *properly* philosophical.

THE MEDIUM OF FICTION

I t seems a country-headed
thing to say: that literature is language, that stories and the
places and the people in them[1] are merely made of words as
chairs are made of smoothed sticks and sometimes of cloth or
metal tubes. Still, we cannot be too simple at the start, since
the obvious is often the unobserved. Occasionally we should
allow the trite to tease us into thought, for such old friends,
the clichés in our life, are the only strangers we can know.
It seems incredible, the ease with which we sink through
books quite out of sight,[2] pass clamorous pages into sound-
less dreams. That novels should be made of words, and
merely words, is shocking, really. It's as though you had discovered that your wife were made of rubber: the bliss of all
those years, the fears . . . from sponge.

Like the mathematician, like the philosopher, the novelist

---

[1] For the people, see "The Concept of Character in Fiction."
[2] This, as well as the comparison with mathematics, is returned to
in "In Terms of the Toenail: Fiction and the Figures of Life."

makes things out of concepts. Concepts, consequently, must be his critical concern: not the defects of his person, the crimes on his conscience, other men's morals, or their kindness or cruelty. The painter squeezes space through his pigments. Paint stains his fingers. How can he forget the color he has loaded on his brush or that blank canvas audience before him? Yet the novelist frequently behaves as if his work were all heart, character, and story; he professes to hate abstraction, mathematics, and the pure works of mind. Of course, unlike poetry, and despite its distinguished figures, for a long time now the novel has been an amateur's affair, an open field for anybody's running, and it has drawn the idle, sick, and gossipaceous, the vaguely artistic—prophets, teachers, muckrakers—all the fanatical explainers, those dreamily scientific, and those anally pedantic.

Paint stains the fingers; the sculptor's hair is white with dust; but concepts have no physical properties; they do not permit smell or reflect light; they do not fill space or contain it; they do not age. "Five" is no wider, older, or fatter than "four"; "apple" isn't sweeter than "quince," rounder than "pear," smoother than "peach." To say, then, that literature is language is to say that literature is made of meanings, concepts, ideas, forms (please yourself with the term), and that these are so static and eternal as to shame the stars.

Like the mathematician. For the novelist to be at all, in any way, like a mathematician is shocking. It's worse than discovering your privates are plastic. Because there's no narration among numbers. It is logically impossible. Time's lacking.

When David Hilbert, the great logician, heard that a student had given up mathematics to write novels, he is supposed to have said: "It was just as well; he did not have enough imagination to become a first-rate mathematician."

The yammer of thought, the constant one-after-another of sounds, the shapes of words, the terrible specter of spelling, are each due to this fact that meanings are heavenly bodies which, to our senses, must somehow announce themselves. A word is a concept made flesh, if you like—the eternal presented as noise. When I spell, then, let's say, "avoirdupois," I am forming our name for that meaning, but it might, just as well, be written down "dozzo," or still more at length, with the same lack of logic, "typary," "snoddle," or "willmullynull." "Avoirdupois." An unreasonable body. Nonetheless lovely. "Avoirdupois."

There is a fundamental contradiction in our medium.[3] We work with a marble of flaws. My mind is utterly unlike my body,[4] and unless you're an angel, so, I am certain, is yours. Poor Descartes really wrote on the problems of poets: word sense and word sound, math and mechanics, the mind and its body, can they touch? And how, pray God, can they resemble? In the act of love, as in all the arts, the soul should be felt by the tongue and the fingers, felt in the skin. So should our sounds come to color up the surface of our stories like a blush. This adventitious music is the only sensory quality our books can have. As Frost observed, even the empty sentence has a sound, or rather—I should say—*is* a series of nervous tensions and resolves. No artist dares neglect his own world's body, for *nothing else,* nothing else about his book is physical.

In the hollow of a jaw, the ear, upon the page, concepts now begin to move: they appear, accelerate, they race, they hesitate a moment, slow, turn, break, join, modify, and it be-

[3] See "Gertrude Stein: Her Escape from Protective Language."
[4] The contrast which is meant here is not that often alleged to exist between thought and feeling, but that between consciousness and things.

comes reasonable to speak of the problems of narration for the first time. Truly (that is to say, technically), narration is that part of the art of fiction concerned with the coming on and passing off of words—not the familiar arrangement of words in dry strings like so many shriveled worms, but their formal direction and rapidity. But this is not what's usually meant.

For most people, fiction is history; fiction is history without tables, graphs, dates, imports, edicts, evidence, laws; history without hiatus—intelligible, simple, smooth. Fiction is sociology freed of statistics, politics with no real party in the opposition; it's a world where play money buys you cardboard squares of colored country; a world where everyone is obediently psychological, economic, ethnic, geographical—framed in a keyhole and always nude, each figure fashioned from the latest thing in cello-see-through, so we may observe our hero's guts, too, if we choose: ah, they're blue, and squirming like a tickled river. For truth without effort, thought without rigor, feeling without form, existence without commitment: what will you give? for a wind-up world, a toy life? . . . six bits? for a book with a thicker skin? . . . six bucks? I am a man, myself, intemperately mild, and though it seems to me as much deserved as it's desired, I have no wish to steeple quires of paper passion up so many sad unelevating rears.

Nay, not *seems*, it *is* a stubborn, country-headed thing to say: that there are no events but words in fiction. Words mean things. Thus we use them every day: make love, buy bread, and blow up bridges. But the use of language in fiction only mimics its use in life. A sign like GENTS, for instance, tells me where to pee. It conveys information; it produces feelings of glad relief. I use the sign, but I dare not dawdle under it. It might have read MEN or borne a moustache. This kind of sign passes out of consciousness, is extinguished by its use. In literature, however, the sign remains; it sings; and we return to it again and again.

In contrast, the composer's medium is pure; that is, the tones he uses exist for music, and are made by instruments especially designed. Imagine his feelings, then, if he were forced to employ the meaningful noises of every day: bird calls, sirens, screams, alarm bells, whistles, ticks, and human chatter. He could plead all he liked that his music was pure, but we would know that he'd written down sounds from a play unseen, and we would insist that it told a story. Critics would describe the characters (one wears a goatee) and quarrel over their motives, marriages, or mothers, all their dark genes. Although no one wonders, of a painted peach, whether the tree it grew on was watered properly, we are happily witness, week after week, to further examination of Hamlet or Madame Bovary, quite as if they were real. And they are so serious, so learned, so certain—so laughable—these ladies and gentlemen. Ah well, it's merely energy which might otherwise elucidate the Trinity.

So the novelist makes his book from boards which say LADIES and GENTS. Every scrap has been worn, every item handled; most of the pieces are dented or split. The writer may choose to be heroic—poets often are—he may strive to purify his diction and achieve an exclusively literary language. He may pretend that every syllable he speaks hasn't been spit, sometimes, in someone else's mouth. Such poets scrub, they clean, they smooth, they polish, until we can scarcely recognize their words on the page. "A star glide, a single frantic sullenness, a single financial grass greediness," wrote Gertrude Stein. "*Toute Pensée émet un Coup de Dés,*" wrote Mallarmé. Most novelists, however (it is one of the things that make them one), try to turn the tattering to account—incorporate it cleverly—as the painter does when he pastes up a collage of newspaper, tin foil, and postage stamps. He will recognize, for example, that stories are wonderful devices for controlling the speed of the mind, for resting it after hard climbs; they give a reassuring light to a dark place, and help the reader hold, like handsome handles, heavy luggage on long trips.

A dedicated storyteller, though—a true lie-minded man —will serve his history best, and guarantee its popularity, not by imitating nature, since nature's no source of verisimilitude, but by following as closely as he can our simplest, most direct and unaffected forms of daily talk, for we report real things, things which intrigue and worry us, and such resembling gossip in a book allows us to believe in figures and events we cannot see, shall never touch, with an assurance of safety which sets our passions free. He will avoid recording consciousness since consciousness is private—we do not normally "take it down"—and because no one really believes in any other feelings than his own. However, the moment our writer concentrates on sound, the moment he formalizes his sentences, the moment he puts in a figure of speech or turns a phrase, shifts a tense or alters tone, the moment he carries description, or any account, beyond need, he begins to turn his reader's interest away from the world which lies among his words like a beautiful woman among her slaves, and directs him toward the slaves themselves. This illustrates a basic principle: if I describe my peach too perfectly, it's the poem which will make my mouth water . . . while the real peach spoils.

Sculptures take up space and gather dust. Concepts do not. They take up us. They invade us as we read, and they achieve, as our resistance and their forces vary, every conceivable degree of occupation. Imagine a worry or a pain, an obsessive thought, a jealousy or hate so strong it renders you insensible to all else. Then while it lasts, you are that fear, that ache, for consciousness is always smaller than its opportunities, and can contract around a kernel like a shell. A piece of music can drive you out and take your place. The purpose of a literary work is the capture of consciousness, and the consequent creation, in you, of an imagined sensibility, so that while you read you are that patient pool or cataract of concepts which the author has constructed; and though at first it might seem as if the richness of life had been replaced by something less so—senseless noises, abstract meanings, mere shadows of worldly employment—yet the new self with which fine fiction and good poetry should provide you is as wide as the mind is, and musicked deep with feeling. While listening to such symbols sounding, the blind perceive; thought seems to grow a body; and the will is at rest amid that moving like a gull asleep on the sea. Perhaps we'll be forgiven, then, if we fret about our words and continue country-headed. It is not a refusal to please. There's no willfulness, disdain, exile . . . no anger. Because a consciousness electrified by beauty—is that not the aim and emblem and the ending of all finely made love?

Are you afraid?

THE CONCEPT OF CHARACTER
IN FICTION

I have never found a hand-
book on the art of fiction or the stage, nor can I imagine
finding one, that did not contain a chapter on the creation
of character, a skill whose mastery, the author of each man-
ual insists, secures for one the inner secrets of these arts:
not, mind you, an easy thing: rather as difficult as the whole
art itself, since, in a way, it *is* the whole art: to fasten in the
memory of the reader, like a living presence, some bright
human image. All well and good to paint a landscape, evoke
a feeling, set a tempest loose, but not quite good enough to
nail an author to his immortality if scheming Clarence, fat,
foul-trousered Harry, or sweetly terraced Priss do not
emerge from the land they huff and rage and eat in fully
furnished out by Being; enough alive, indeed, to eat and huff
in ours—dear God, more alive than that!—sufficiently enlarged by genius that they threaten to eat up and huff down
everything in sight.

Talk about literature, when it is truly talk about something going on in the pages, if it is not about ideas, is gen-

erally about the people in it, and ranges from those cries of wonder, horror, pleasure, or surprise, so readily drawn from the innocently minded, to the annotated stammers of the most erudite and nervous critics. But it is all the same. Great character is the most obvious single mark of great literature. The rude, the vulgar, may see in Alyosha nothing more than the image of a modest, God-loving youth; the scholar may perceive through this demeanor a symbolic form; but the Alyosha of the untutored is somehow more real and present to him than the youth on his street whom he's known since childhood, loving of his God and modest too, equally tried, fully as patient; for in some way Alyosha's visionary figure will take lodging in him, make a model for him, so to reach, without the scholar's inflationary gifts, general form and universal height; whereas the neighbor may merely move away, take cold, and forget to write. Even the most careful student will admit that fiction's fruit survives its handling and continues growing off the tree. A great character has an endless interest; its fascination never wanes. Indeed it is a commonplace to say so. Hamlet. Ahab. Julien Sorel. Madame Bovary. There is no end to their tragedy. Great literature is great because its characters are great, and characters are great when they are memorable. A simple formula. The Danish ghost cries to remember him, and obediently—for we are gullible and superstitious clots—we do.

It hasn't always been a commonplace. Aristotle regarded character as a servant of dramatic action, and there have been an endless succession of opinions about the value and function of characters since—all dreary—but the important thing to be noted about nearly every one of them is that whatever else profound and wonderful these theories have to say about the world and its personalities, characters are clearly conceived as living outside language. Just as the movie star deserts herself to put on some press agent's more alluring fictional persona, the hero of a story sets out from his own landscape for the same land of romance the star reached by stepping there from life. These people—Huckleberry Finn, the Snopeses, Prince Myshkin, Pickwick, Molly Bloom—seem to have come to the words of their novels like a visitor to town . . . and later they leave on the arm of the reader, bound, I suspect, for a shabbier hotel, and dubious entertainments.

However, Aristotle's remark was a recommendation. Characters ought to exist for the sake of the action, he thought, though he knew they often did not, and those who nowadays say that given a sufficiently powerful and significant plot the characters will be dominated by it are simply answered by asking them to imagine the plot of *Moby Dick* in the hands of Henry James, or that of *Sanctuary* done into Austen. And if you can persuade them to try (you will have no success), you may then ask how the heroes and the heroines come out. The same disastrous exercise can be given those who believe that traits make character like definitions do a dictionary. Take any set of traits you like and let Balzac or Joyce, Stendhal or Beckett, loose in a single paragraph to use them. Give your fictional creatures qualities, psychologies, actions, manners, moods; present them from without or from within; let economics matter, breeding, custom, history; let spirit wet them like a hose: all methods work, and none do. The nature of the novel will not be understood at all until this is: *from any given body of fictional text, nothing necessarily follows, and anything plausibly may*. Authors are gods—a little tinny sometimes but omnipotent no matter what, and plausible on top of that, if they can manage it.[1]

---

[1] This has already been discussed in "Philosophy and the Form of Fiction." In "Mirror, Mirror," I complain that Nabokov's omnipotence is too intrusive.

The Concept of Character in Fiction

Though the handbooks try to tell us how to create characters, they carefully never tell us we are making images, illusions, imitations. Gatsby is not an imitation, for there is nothing he imitates. Actually, if he were a copy, an illusion, sort of shade or shadow, he would not be called a character at all. He must be unique, entirely himself, as if he had a self to be. He is required, in fact, to act *in character*, like a cat in a sack. No, theories of character are not absurd in the way representational theories are; they are absurd in a grander way, for the belief in Hamlet (which audiences often seem to have) is like the belief in God—incomprehensible to reason—and one is inclined to seek a motive: some deep fear or emotional need.

There are too many motives. We pay heed so easily. We are so pathetically eager for this other life, for the sounds of distant cities and the sea; we long, apparently, to pit ourselves against some trying wind, to follow the fortunes of a ship hard beset, to face up to murder and fornication, and the somber results of anger and love; oh, yes, to face up—*in books*—when on our own we scarcely breathe. The tragic view of life, for instance, in Shakespeare or in Schopenhauer, Unamuno, Sartre, or Sophocles, is not one jot as pure and penetratingly tragic as a pillow stuffed with Jewish hair, and if we want to touch life where it burns, though life is what we are even now awash with—futilely, stupidly drawing in—we ought not to back off from these other artifacts (wars, pogroms, poverty: men make them, too). But of course we do, and queue up patiently instead to see Prince Hamlet moon, watch him thrust his sword through a curtain, fold it once again into Polonius, that foolish old garrulous proper noun. The so-called life one finds in novels, the worst and best of them, is nothing like actual life at all, and cannot be; it is not more real, or thrilling, or authentic; it is not truer, more complex, or pure, and its people have less spontaneity, are less intricate, less free, less full.[2]

It is not a single cowardice that drives us into fiction's fantasies. We often fear that literature is a game we can't afford to play—the product of idleness and immoral ease. In the grip of that feeling it isn't life we pursue, but the point and purpose of life—its facility, its use. So Sorel is either a man it is amusing to gossip about, to see in our friends, to puppet around in our dreams, to serve as our more able and more interesting surrogate in further fanciful adventures; or Sorel is a theoretical type, scientifically profound, representing a deep human strain, and the writing of *The Red and the Black* constitutes an advance in the science of—what would you like? sociology?

Before reciting a few helpless arguments, let me suggest, in concluding this polemical section, just how absurd these views are which think of fiction as a mirror or a window onto life—as actually creative of living creatures—for really one's only weapon against Tertullians is ridicule.

There is a painting by Picasso which depicts a pitcher, candle, blue enamel pot. They are sitting, unadorned, upon the barest table. Would we wonder what was cooking in that pot? Is it beans, perhaps, or carrots, a marmite? The orange of the carrot is a perfect complement to the blue of the pot, and the genius of Picasso, neglecting nothing, has surely placed, behind that blue, invisible disks of dusky orange, which, in addition, subtly enrich the table's velvet brown. Doesn't that seem reasonable? Now I see that it must be beans, for above the pot—you can barely see them—are

---

[2] I treat the relation of fiction to life in more detail in "In Terms of the Toenail: Fiction and the Figures of Life." The problem is handled in other ways in "The Artist and Society," "Even if, by All the Oxen in the World," and "The Imagination of an Insurrection."

quaking lines of steam, just the lines we associate with boiling beans . . . or is it blanching pods? Scholarly research, supported by a great foundation, will discover that exactly such a pot was used to cook cassoulet in the kitchens of Charles the Fat . . . or was it Charles the Bald? There's a dissertation in that. And this explains the dripping candle standing by the pot. (Is it dripping? no? a pity. Let's go on.) For isn't Charles the Fat himself that candle? Oh no, some say, he's not! Blows are struck. Reputations made and ruined. Someone will see eventually that the pot is standing on a table, not a stove. But the pot has just come from the stove, it will be pointed out. Has not Picasso caught that vital moment of transition? The pot is too hot. The brown is burning. Oh, not *this* table, which has been coated with resistant plastic. Singular genius—blessed man—he thinks of everything.

Here you have half the history of our criticism in the novel. Entire books have been written about the characters in Dickens, Trollope, Tolstoi, Faulkner. But why not? Entire books have been written about God, his cohorts, and the fallen angels.

2

Descartes, examining a piece of beeswax fresh from the hive, brought it near a flame and observed all of its sensible qualities change. He wondered why he should believe that wax remained. His sensations lent him nothing he could fasten his judgment firmly to. Couldn't he give that puddle in his hand another name? He might have added that the sleights of the mountebanks did not bewilder him. Somehow he knew milady's hanky didn't disappear in a fist to emerge

39

as a rose. It occurred to Descartes then that perhaps his imagination was the unifying faculty. But the wax was capable of an infinite number of spills, reaching every stage of relaxation, and he was unable, he writes in what is now a brilliant phrase, "to compass this infinity by imagination." How then? Some higher, finer capacity was required. His knowledge of the wax, soft or hard, sweet or flat, became an intuition of the mind.

Like so many philosophical arguments, this one was erected upside down, and consequently is a bit unsteady on its head. How, I'd rather ask, from the idea of wax, can we predict and picture just this sticky mess? What do we see when we peer through a glass of words?

If we ask this question of Hume, he will give us, as usual, a brilliantly reasonable, and entirely wrong answer—out of the habit empiricists have, I suppose, of never inspecting their experience. Nothing is more free than the imagination of man, he says; "it can feign a train of events with all the appearance of reality . . ." *With all the appearance of reality* . . . Then we might suppose that it's my imagination which allows me to descend from a writer's words, like a god through the clouds, and basket down on sweet Belinda's belly at the moment of her maximum response (or less excitingly, to picture upon the palm in my mind a slowly sprawling blob of molten wax).

To imagine so vividly is either to be drunk, asleep, or mad. Such images are out of our control and often terrifying. If we could feign with *every* appearance of reality, we would not wish to feign *Nostromo*, or even *Pride and Prejudice*. Of course, the imagination cannot give us every appearance of reality, and just as well, but perhaps it can give us every appearance of a *faded* reality: the shadow of Belinda's body on the bed (so far has this theory fallen through the space of a sentence!), an image seen the way I see this print and paper now, though with the mind's disocular eye. Or, as Gilbert Ryle writes:

> Sometimes, when someone mentions a blacksmith's forge, I find myself instantaneously back in my childhood, visiting a local smithy. I can vividly "see" the glowing red horseshoe on the anvil, fairly vividly "hear" the hammer ringing on the shoe and less vividly "smell" the singed hoof. How should we describe this "smelling in the mind's nose"?[3]

Certainly not by explaining that there is a smell in me, a shadow of a smell, a picture of a smell, an image, and putting to my noseless spirit the task of smelling it. Not as a bruise to its blow, as Ryle says, are our imaginings related to our experience. Yet Hume sometimes supposes that imagination works like madness. If it can give to fiction all the appearance of reality, how is one to know what to believe when an author's words, stirring in us like life, managing our minds with the efficiency of reality, throw Anna Karenina under the train's wheels before our eyes?

Here is the whole thing in a single passage:

> The imagination has the command over all its ideas and can join and mix and vary them in all the ways possible. It may conceive fictitious objects with all the circumstances of place and time. It may set them in a manner before our eyes, in their true colors, just as they might have existed. But as it is impossible that this faculty of imagination can ever, of itself, reach belief, it is evident that belief consists not in the peculiar nature or order of ideas, but

[3] In *The Concept of Mind* (New York: Barnes & Noble, 1950).

in the manner of their conception and in their feeling to the mind.[4]

The name of this feeling is belief, and I am given it by the
greater intensity and steadiness with which actual impressions occupy me—a narrow difference, one only of degree.
Don't mystery stories make us lock our doors?

But I should suppose that "seeing things" through novels
did not involve succumbing to a drunken frenzy, finding
animals in walls or naked ladies draped on desert rocks like
some long celibate Saint Anthony.

We do visualize, I suppose. Where did I leave my gloves?
And then I ransack a room in my mind until I find them.
But the room I ransack is abstract—a simple schema. I leave
out the drapes and the carpet, and I think of the room as a
set of likely glove locations. The proportion of words which
we can visualize is small, but quite apart from that, another
barrier to the belief that vivid imagining is the secret of a
character's power is the fact that when we watch the pictures which a writer's words have directed us to make, we
miss their meaning, for the point is *never* the picture. It also
takes concentration, visualization does—takes slowing down;
and this alone is enough to rule it out of novels, which are
never waiting, always flowing on.

> Instantly Hugh's shack began to take form in her
> mind. But it was not a shack—it was a home! It
> stood, on wide-girthed strong legs of pine, between
> the forest of pine and high, high waving alders and
> tall slim birches, and the sea. There was the narrow
> path that wound down through the forest from the

4 Hume, *An Enquiry Concerning Human Understanding* (New
York: Oxford University Press). There is reason to suppose that
Hume thinks the imagination plays with ideas only after they have
lost all vivifying power. Then, however, their arrangement could
satisfy only our conceptions of things, not our perceptions of them.

shore, with salmonberries and thimbleberries and wild blackberry bushes that on bright winter nights of frost reflected a million moons; behind the house was a dogwood tree that bloomed twice in the year with white stars. Daffodils and snowdrops grew in the little garden.[5]

And so forth. Do you have all that? the salmonberries and the thimbleberries? I'm afraid you'll be all day about it. One reason is that our imaginings are mostly imprecise. They are vague and general. Even when colored, they're gray.

A hare vaguely perceived is nevertheless a specific hare. But a hare which is the object of a vague image is a vague hare.[6]

Consequently, writing which carefully defines its object, however visual its terms, sets the visual successfully aside. It does, that is, if what we see inside us are misty visual schema. But

Suppose that I have an image of a head that is non-specific about baldness, is this not rather queer? For presumably this head must be neither bald nor not bald nor even a half-way house with just a few hairs.[7]

Enter Mr. Cashmore, who is a character in *The Awkward Age*.

Mr. Cashmore, who would have been very red-headed if he had not been very bald, showed a single eyeglass and a long upper lip; he was large and jaunty, with little petulant movements and intense ejaculations that were not in the line of his type.

[5] Malcolm Lowry, *Under the Volcano* (New York: Reynal and Hitchcock, 1947).
[6] Sartre, *Psychology of Imagination* (New York: Citadel, 1961).
[7] J. M. Shorter, "Imagination," in *Mind*, LXI.

We can imagine any number of other sentences about Mr. Cashmore added to this one. Now the question is: what is Mr. Cashmore? Here is the answer I shall give: Mr. Cashmore is (1) a noise, (2) a proper name, (3) a complex system of ideas, (4) a controlling conception, (5) an instrument of verbal organization, (6) a pretended mode of referring, and (7) a source of verbal energy.[8] But Mr. Cashmore is not a person. He is not an object of perception, and nothing whatever that is appropriate to persons can be correctly said of him. There is no path from idea to sense (this is Descartes' argument in reverse), and no amount of careful elaboration of Mr. Cashmore's single eyeglass, his upper lip or jauntiness is going to enable us to *see* him. How many little petulant movements are there? Certainly as many as the shapes which may be taken by soft wax. If we follow Hume, we think we picture things through language because we substitute, on cue, particular visual memories of our own, and the more precisely language defines its object, the less likely we are to find a snapshot in our book to fit it. Our visualizations interfere with Mr. Cashmore's development, for if we think of him as someone we have met, we must give him qualities his author hasn't yet, and we may stubbornly, or through simple lack of attention, retain these later, though they've been explicitly debarred. "On your imaginary forces work," *Henry V*'s

---

[8] (1) He is always a "mister," and his name functions musically much of the time. "He was an odd compound, Mr. Cashmore, and the air of personal good health, the untarnished bloom which sometimes lent a monstrous serenity to his mention of the barely mentionable, was on occasion balanced or matched by his playful application of extravagant terms to matters of much less moment." What a large mouthful, that sentence. His name (2) locates him, but since he exists nowhere but on the page (6), it simply serves to draw other words toward him (3), or actualize others, as in conversation (7), when they seem to proceed from him, or remind us of all that he is an emblem of (4), and richly interact with other, similarly formed and similarly functioning verbal centers (5).

Prologuer begs. "Piece out our imperfections with your thoughts . . . Think, when we talk of horses, that you see them / Printing their proud hoofs i' th' receiving earth," and then the audience (and the similarly situated novel reader) is praised for having done so; but this is worse than the self-congratulating pap which periodically flows from the bosom of the "creative" critic, because these generous additions destroy the work as certainly as "touching up" and "painting over." The unspoken word is often eloquent.

> *Well, I finally met Mr. Mulholland.*
> *Oh, what's he like?*
> *He has large thumbs.*

Characters in fiction are mostly empty canvas. I have known many who have passed through their stories without noses, or heads to hold them; others have lacked bodies altogether, exercised no natural functions, possessed some thoughts, a few emotions, but no psychologies, and apparently made love without the necessary organs. The true principle is direct enough: Mr. Cashmore has what he's been given; he also *has* what he *hasn't*, just as strongly. Mr. Cashmore, in fact, has been cruelly scalped.

Now, is there a nose to this Mr. Cashmore? Let's suppose it—but then, of what sort? We're not told. He is an eyeglass without eyes, he has no neck or chin, his ears are unexplored. "Large"—how indefinite a word. But would it have been better to have written "sixteen stone"? Not at all, nor do we know how this weight is disposed. If it is impossible to picture Mr. Cashmore, however carefully we draw him, will it be easier to limn his soul? Or perhaps we may imagine that this sentence describes not Mr. Cashmore, out or in, but his impression—what sort of dent he makes in his surroundings. He gives the impression of a man who would have been redheaded if he hadn't been bald. Very well. What impression, exactly, is that? Will it do to think of Mr. Cashmore as a man with red eyebrows and a red fringe above his ears, but otherwise without hair? That would rephrase Mr. Cashmore, and rephrase him badly. The description of Mr. Cashmore stands as James wrote it, even if Mr. Cashmore hasn't a hair on his body. As a set of sensations Mr. Cashmore is simply impossible; as an idea he is admirably pungent and precise.

Similarly, it is not at all correct to infer that because Mr. Mulholland has thumbs, he has hands, arms, torso, self. That inference destroys the metaphor (a pure synecdoche), since his thumbs are all he seems to be. Mr. Mulholland is monumentally clumsy, but if you fill him in behind his thumbs, clumsiness will not ensue.

So sometimes, then, we are required to take away what we've been given, as in the case of Mr. Cashmore's red hair; sometimes it's important to hold fast to what we've got and resist any inclination we may have to elaborate, as in the case of Mr. Mulholland, who I said had thumbs; and sometimes we must put our minds to the stretch, bridging the distances between concepts with other concepts, as in the two examples which follow; or we may be called upon to do all these things at once, as in what I promise will be my final misuse of poor Mulholland.[9]

> *Well, I finally met Mr. Mulholland.*
> *Oh, what's he like?*
> *A silver thimble.*

[9] The entire matter is far more complicated than I have indicated. Not only is there a linear order of apprehension (the reader is first told Mr. Mulholland has been seen, then that he was walking his thumbs), but also an order, in depth, of implications. Analysis, in searching out these implications, frequently upsets this order, bringing the bottom to the top. Meanings, uncovered, must be put back as they were found. It is a delicate operation.

The Concept of Character in Fiction

I saw Mr. Mulholland today.
Oh, what was he doing?
Walking his thumbs.

Mr. Mulholland's face had
a watchful look. Although
its features had not yet arrived,
they were momentarily expected.

To summarize, so far:

1. Only a few of the words which a writer normally uses to create a character can be "imaged" in any sense.

2. To the extent these images are faded sensations which we've once had, they fill in, particularize, and falsify the author's account.

3. To the degree these images are as vivid and lively as reality is, they will very often be unpleasant, and certainly can't be "feigned." Then words would act like a mind-expanding drug.

4. To the degree these images are general schema, indistinct and vague, the great reality characters are supposed to have becomes less plausible, and precise writing (so often admired) will interfere with their formation.

5. Constructing images of any kind takes time, slows the flow of the work; nor can imagining keep up, in complexity, with the incredibly intricate conceptual systems which may be spun like a spiderweb in a single sentence.

6. We tend to pay attention to our pictures, and lose sight of the meaning. The novelist's words are not notes which he is begging the reader to play, as if his novel needed something more done to it in order to leap into existence.

Words in daily life are signposts, handles, keys. They express, instruct, command, inform, exhort—in short, they serve; and it is difficult to think of our servants as kings.[10] But among real things words win the gold medals for Being. Ortega y Gasset asks us to imagine we are looking through a window at a garden.

> The clearer the glass is, the less (of the glass) we will see. But then making an effort we may withdraw attention from the garden; and by retracting the ocular ray, we may fixate it upon the glass. Then the garden will disappear in our eyes and we will see instead only some confused masses of color which seem to stick to the glass. Consequently to see the garden and to see the glass in the windowpane are two incompatible operations. . . . Likewise he who in the work of art aims to be moved by the fate of John and Mary, or of Tristan and Iseult, and readjusts to them his spiritual perception will not be able to see the work of art. . . . Now the majority of people are unable to adjust their attention to the glass and the transparency which is the work of art; instead they penetrate through it to passionately wallow in the human reality which the work of art refers to. If they are invited to let loose their prey and fix their attention upon the work of art itself, they will say they see nothing in it, because, indeed, they see no human realities there, but only artistic transparencies, pure essences.[11]

Ortega seems to believe, however, that words are windows through which something can be seen, and I have argued that words are opaque, as opaque as my garden gloves and trowel, objects which, nevertheless, may vividly remind me

[10] See "Gertrude Stein: Her Escape from Protective Language," and "The Medium of Fiction."

[11] Ortega y Gasset, *The Dehumanization of Art* (New York: Anchor Books, 1956).

of spring, earth, and roses. Or Uncle Harry, Africa, the tsetse fly, and lovesick elephants.

On the other side of a novel lies the void. Think, for instance, of a striding statue; imagine the purposeful inclination of the torso, the alert and penetrating gaze of the head and its eyes, the outstretched arm and pointing finger; everything would appear to direct us toward some goal in front of it. Yet our eye travels only to the finger's end, and not beyond. Though pointing, the finger bids us stay instead, and we journey slowly back along the tension of the arm. In our hearts we know what actually surrounds the statue. The same surrounds every other work of art: empty space and silence.[12]

3

A character, first of all, is the noise of his name, and all the sounds and rhythms that proceed from him. We pass most things in novels as we pass things on a train. The words flow by like the scenery. All is change.[13] But there are some points in a narrative which remain relatively fixed; we may depart from them, but soon we return, as music returns to its theme. Characters are those primary substances to which everything else is attached. Hotels, dresses, conversations, sausage, feelings, gestures, snowy evenings, faces—each may fade as fast as we read of them. Yet the language of the novel will eddy about a certain incident or name, as Melville's always circles back to Ahab and his wedding with

---

[12] The way in which both the reader and the world are drawn into the novel is discussed in "In Terms of the Toenail: Fiction and the Figures of Life."

[13] Of course nothing prevents a person from feeling that life is like this. See "A Spirit in Search of Itself."

the white whale. Mountains are characters in Malcolm Lowry's *Under the Volcano,* so is a ravine, a movie, mescal, or a boxing poster. A symbol like the cross can be a character. An idea or a situation (the anarchist in *The Secret Agent,* bomb ready in his pocket), or a particular event, an obsessive thought, a decision (Zeno's, for instance, to quit smoking), a passion, a memory, the weather, Gogol's overcoat—anything, indeed, which serves as a fixed point, like a stone in a stream or that soap in Bloom's pocket, functions as a character. Character, in this sense, is a matter of degree, for the language of the novel may loop back seldom, often, or incessantly. But the idea that characters are like primary substances has to be taken in a double way, because if any thing becomes a character simply to the degree the words of the novel qualify it, it also loses some of its substance, some of its primacy, to the extent that it, in turn, qualifies something else. In a perfectly organized novel, every word would ultimately qualify one thing, like the God of the metaphysician, at once the subject and the body of the whole.[14] Normally, characters are fictional human beings, and thus are given proper names. In such cases, to create a character is to give meaning to an unknown X; it is *absolutely* to *define;* and since nothing in life corresponds to these Xs, their reality is borne by their name. They *are,* where it *is.*

Most of the words the novelist uses have their meanings already formed. Proper names do not, except in a tangential way. It's true that Mr. Mulholland could not be Mr. Mull, and Mr. Cashmore must bear, as best he can, the curse of his wealth forever, along with his desire for gain. Character has

[14] There is no reason why every novel should be organized in this way. This method constructs a world according to the principles of Absolute Idealism. See "Philosophy and the Form of Fiction."

a special excitement for a writer (apart from its organizing value) because it offers him a chance to give fresh meaning to new words. A proper name begins as a blank, like a wall or a canvas, upon which one might paint a meaning, perhaps as turbulent and mysterious, as treacherous and vast, as Moby Dick's, perhaps as delicate, scrupulous, and sensitive as that of Fleda Vetch.

I cannot pause here over the subject of rhythm and sound, though they are the heartbeat of writing, of prose no less than poetry.

> Their friend, Mr. Grant-Jackson, a highly pre-ponderant pushing person, great in discussion and arrangement, abrupt in overture, unexpected, if not perverse, in attitude, and almost equally ac-claimed and objected to in the wide midland region to which he had taught, as the phrase was, the size of his foot—their friend had launched his bolt quite out of the blue and had thereby so shaken them as to make them fear almost more than hope.[15]

Mr. Grant-Jackson is a preponderant pushing person be-cause he's been made by *p*'s, and the rhythm and phrasing of James's writing here prepares and perfectly presents him to us. Certainly we cannot think of Molly Bloom apart from her music, or the gay and rapid Anna Livia apart from hers.

If one examines the texture of a fiction carefully, one will soon see that some words appear to gravitate toward their subject like flies settle on sugar, while others seem to emerge from it. In many works this logical movement is easily dis-cernible and very strong. When a character speaks, the words seem to issue from him and to be acts of his. Description first forms a *nature*, then allows that nature to *perform*. We must be careful, however, not to judge by externals. Barkis says

[15] Henry James, "The Birthplace."

that Barkis is willing, but the expression *functions* descriptively to qualify Barkis, and it is Dickens' habit to treat speech as if it were an attribute of character, like tallness or honesty, and not an act. On the other hand, qualities, in the right context, can be transformed into verbs. Later in the book don't we perceive the whiteness of the whale as a design, an intention of Moby Dick's, like a twist of his flukes or the smashing of a small boat?

Whether Mr. Cashmore was once real and sat by James at someone's dinner table, or was instead the fabrication of James's imagination,[16] as long as he came into being from the world's direction he once existed outside language. The task of getting him in I shall call the problem of rendering. But it must be stressed (it cannot be stressed too severely) that Mr. Cashmore may never have had a model, and may never have been imagined either, but may have come to be in order to serve some high conception (a Mr. Moneybags) and represent a type, not just himself, in which case he is not a reality *rendered*, but a universal *embodied*.[17] Again, Mr. Cashmore might have had still other parents. Meanings in the stream of words before his appearance might have suggested him, dramatic requirements may have called him forth, or he may have been the spawn of music, taking his substance from rhythm and alliteration. Perhaps it was all of these. In well-regulated fictions, most things are *overdetermined*.

So far I have been talking about the function of a character in the direct stream of language, but there are these two other dimensions, the rendered and the embodied, and I should like to discuss each briefly.

[16] Some aspects of this imagination are dealt with in "The High Brutality of Good Intentions," and "In the Cage."
[17] See "Philosophy and the Form of Fiction."

If we observe one of J. F. Powers' worldly priests sharpening his eye for the pin by putting through his clerical collar, the humor, with all *its* sharpness, lives in the situation, and quite incidentally in the words.[18] One can indeed imagine Powers thinking it up independently of any verbal formula. Once Powers had decided that it would be funny to show a priest playing honeymoon bridge with his housekeeper, then his problem becomes the technical one of how best to accomplish it. What the writer must do, of course, is not only render the scene, but render the scene inseparable from its language, so that if the idea (the chaste priest caught in the clichés of marriage) is taken from the situation, like a heart from its body, both die. Far easier to render a real cornfield in front of you, because once that rendering has reached its page, the cornfield will no longer exist for literary purposes, no one will be able to see it by peering through your language, and consequently there will be nothing to abstract from your description. But with a "thought up" scene or situation, this is not the case. It comes under the curse of story. The notion, however amusing, is not literary, for it might be painted, filmed, or played. If we inquire further and ask why Powers wanted such a scene in the first place, we should find, I think, that he wanted it in order to embody a controlling "idea"—at one level of abstraction, the worldliness of the church, for instance. If he had nuns around a kitchen table counting the Sunday take and listening to the Cubs, *that* would do it. Father Burner beautifully embodies just such a controlling idea in Powers' celebrated story "The Prince of Darkness." Both rendering and embodying involve great risks because they require working into a scientific order of words what

18 I enlarge on this aspect of Powers' work in "The Bingo Game at the Foot of the Cross."

was not originally there. Any painter knows that a contour may only more or less enclose his model, while a free line simply and completely is. Many of the model's contours may be esthetically irrelevant, so it would be unwise to follow them. The free line is subject to no such temptations. Its relevance can be total. As Valéry wrote: There are no details in execution.

Often novelists mimic our ordinary use of language. We report upon ourselves; we gossip. Normally we are not lying; and our language, built to refer, actually does. When these selfsame words appear in fiction, and when they follow the forms of daily use, they create, quite readily, that dangerous feeling that a real Tietjens, a real Nickleby, lives just beyond the page; that through that thin partition we can hear a world at love.[19] But the writer must not let the reader out; the sculptor must not let the eye fall from the end of his statue's finger; the musician must not let the listener dream. Of course, he will; but let the blame be on himself. High tricks are possible: to run the eye rapidly along that outstretched arm to the fingertip, only to draw it up before it falls away in space; to carry the reader to the very edge of every word so that it seems he must be compelled to react as though to truth as told in life, and then to return him, like a philosopher liberated from the cave, to the clear and brilliant world of concept, to the realm of order, proportion, and dazzling construction . . . to fiction, where characters, unlike ourselves, freed from existence, can shine like essence, and purely Be.

[19] See "The Medium of Fiction."

IN TERMS OF THE TOENAIL: FICTION AND THE FIGURES OF LIFE

How easy it is to enter. An open book, an open eye, and the first page lifts like fragrance toward us so we read, "Two mountain chains traverse the republic. . . ." Later we say to a friend, "I have begun Malcolm Lowry's novel *Under the Volcano*." A sentence read, a sentence spoken, both imparting information, one accurate as to Mexico, the other to our actions. The town is well south of the Tropic of Cancer, but we are buying groceries in Bayonne or teaching at Vassar. Our eye blinks, our mind wanders, the doorbell buzzes, and time between the two ranges ceases, or rather it waits, hushed, held like a lungful of air; for our hero, the Consul, will always be there, sitting in some bar or other, *perfectamente borracho*, drunk on guilt, and drinking mescal. How easy to enter. How difficult to remain. It reads like a guide, the beginning of this book. The walls of the town are high, the streets and lanes twist, the roads wind. There are four hundred swimming pools— four hundred—and many fine hotels. It's a resort city with the unpronounceable Indian name—Quauhnauhuac—like the groan of a duck. The day is the Day of the Dead, the first of November, 1939. But we are in '50 or '85, and our eyes ache. Still it's like a report on ourselves, despite the differences, an account of Oil City, Pa.: dates, places, persons, conversations, parties, politicking, lies. Or it is history which hasn't happened yet but may begin to any day; and as we read we find ourselves companions to a landscape or a dog, a shattered marriage, broken street, a doctor, brother, drunkard, deep ravine—each familiar (Oil City has its own steep slopes)—and in that sense our meeting with the text can seem quite seamless, the book and cigarette we hold no different fundamentally from the glass which imprisons Geoffrey Firmin. Life here, life there—then much the same. Words here, words there—then similar as well; the sentences hauling their communications from station to station like heavily freighted trains. The Consul has a beard, fair hair, few friends . . . and two mountain chains traverse the republic.

But is *Under the Volcano* really a biography, a one-day history of a man, and is its advantage in being imaginary that it can with confidence report details biographers can rarely have? Novels are made of such details, no doubt of that. But what biographer would want them?—the Consul observing that it is only eight-thirty and taking off his glasses; the Consul tracing with the toe of one dress shoe a pattern in the porch tiles; the Consul hanging up the telephone receiver the wrong way; the Consul sweating profusely and hunting a cantina, or thinking suddenly of Don Quixote, or sucking a lemon, reading a menu, being shaved. Facts by the thousands here, in Henry James, throughout the pages of *War and Peace* or *Ulysses*—all trivialities, items which could never find their way into any serious history.

And Geoffrey Firmin is no George Washington or General Lee, even by allegation; he shapes nothing, affects few; and his body slides down a ravine. This novelist, indeed, has a passion for the unimportant: bus and railroad schedules, for example, theater marquees, boxing posters, an old volume of Elizabethan plays; but this passion is in no way extraordinary —Jane Austen liked hats and hair ribbons. What, too, of our own feelings for these obscure, superfluous, nonexistent people, and their queer creators, obscure, superfluous, and nearly nonexistent themselves, who, throughout their lives, do nothing—the man Malcolm Lowry, a drunkard too, who rounded the world as a sailor, wrote a few strange stories, was twice married, and, *perfectamente borracho,* choked to death on his own vomit?

We shall never verify this history. It rests nowhere in our world. Our world, in the first place, lacks significance; it lacks connection. If I swallow now—what of it? if I pass a cola sign—no matter; if I pet a striped cat, or tell a tiny lie, put down the tenth page of the *Times* to train my puppy —nothing's changed. And the real mountains of Mexico, those two chains which traverse the republic, exist despite us and all our feelings. But the Popocatepetl of the novel is yet another mountain, and when, in the first chapter, we are taken on a tour of the town, the facts we are given have quite a different function. Lowry is constructing a place, not describing one; he is making a Mexico for the mind where, strictly speaking, there are no menacing volcanoes, only menacing phrases, where complex chains of concepts traverse our consciousness, and where, unlike history, events take place in the moment that we read them—over and over as it may be, irregularly even, at widely separated times— whenever we restore these notes to music. Each of us, too, must encounter and enter the book alone, bring our lifetime to it, since truly it is a dark wood, this Mexico, a southern hell we're being guided through, and although simply begun, it is difficult to remain, to continue so terrible a journey. In this conceptual country there are no mere details, nothing is a simple happenstance, everything has meaning, is part of a net of essential relations. Sheer coincidence is impossible, and those critics who have complained of this quality in Lowry[1] have misunderstood the nature of the novel. They would not complain of the refrain of a song that its constant reappearance was coincidence. So the Ferris wheel of the festival—for this is the Day of the Dead, after all—will turn in our eyes as it turns in the Consul's, the burning wheel of Buddhist law, "its steel twigs caught in the emerald pathos of the trees," appearing just as often as design demands.

Nothing like history, then, *the Volcano* ties time in knots, is utterly subjective, completely contrived, as planned and patterned as a magical rug where the figure becomes the carpet. Nothing like a country or a town—no Oil City— *the Volcano* is made of a series of names which immediately become symbolic, and reverberate when struck like a hundred gongs. Even drunkenness has a different function, for the Consul does not drink so we may better understand drunkenness, and though he is ridden with guilt, his guilt is as fictional as he is. The Consul's drinking frees the language of the book, allows it to stagger and leap like verse, gives Lowry the freedom to construct freely. The Consul's stupors are the stupors of poetry, as madness was for Lear and his fool, and chivalry for Cervantes.

The Volcano is a mountain. We must climb. And it is difficult to maintain a foothold at first. Yet soon we begin

---

[1] Ford is frequently accused of it, so is Nabokov. I make this complaint about Nabokov myself, though for different reasons, in "Mirror, Mirror."

to feel the warmth at its core, and few books will finally flow over us so fully, embed us in them as the citizens of Pompeii were bedded by their mountain, the postures of their ordinary days at once their monuments, their coffins, and their graves. Of novels, few are so little like life, few are so formal and arranged; there are few whose significance is so total and internal. Nonetheless, there are scarcely any which reflect the personal concerns of their author more clearly, or incline us as steeply to a wonder and a terror of the world until we fear for our own life as the Consul feared for his, and under such pressures yield to the temptation to say what seems false and pedestrian: that this book is about each of us—in Saint Cloud, Oil City, or Bayonne, N.J.—that it is about drunkenness and Mexico, or even that it is about that poor wretch Malcolm Lowry.

A scene: the Consul and his friend, M. Laruelle, in conversation. M. Laruelle is advising the Consul to go home to bed, for God's sake. His wife has returned to him, and hasn't he been howling for just that? yet here he is drinking, carrying on in the same disagreeable manner which drove her away in the first place. But tequila, the Consul claims, is healthful—not like mescal—and clarifies, marvelously, one's thoughts and perceptions. Perhaps, sometimes, when you have calculated the amount exactly, M. Laruelle admits, you do see more clearly:

> But certainly not the things so important to us despised sober people, on which the balance of any human situation depends. It's precisely your inability to see them, Geoffrey, that turns them into the instruments of the disaster you have created yourself. Your Ben Jonson, for instance, or perhaps it was Christopher Marlowe, your Faust man, saw the Carthaginians fighting on his big toe-nail. That's like

the kind of clear seeing you indulge in. Everything seems perfectly clear, because indeed it is perfectly clear, in terms of the toe-nail.

Fiction is life in terms of the toenail, or in terms of the Ferris wheel, in terms of tequila; it is incurably figurative, and the world the novelist makes is always a metaphorical model of our own. It will be my concern, in what follows, to suggest something of the way in which metaphors function, and how such fictional models are made. But let's begin with something simpler—small enough to close our mouths and minds on, something from one of those nail-gazing Elizabethans.

2

Hamlet, Horatio, and Marcellus walk upon the castle platform awaiting midnight and Hamlet's father's ghost. Hamlet says, "The air bites shrewdly; it is very cold," and Horatio answers, "It is a nipping and an eager air." Hamlet and Horatio do not think of it as cold, simply. The dog of air's around them, shrewd and eager, running at heels. The behavior of this dog is wittily precise in their minds. It nags—shrewishly, wifelike. The air is acidulous, too, like sour wine.[2] Hamlet and Horatio, furthermore, are aware of the physical quality of their words. Horatio not only develops Hamlet's implicit figure, he concludes the exchange with the word that began it, and with sonorous sounds. The nature of the weather is conveyed to us with marvelous exactitude and ease, in remarks made by the way, far from the center of action; so that we find ourselves with knowl-

[2] This is very likely the primary meaning of "eager."

edge of it in just the offhand way we would if, bent on meeting a king's ghost, we too went through the sharp wind. Yet Hamlet's second clause is useless. "The air bites shrewdly" is the clause that tells us everything. It is cold. The wind is out. The wind is alive, malevolent with wise jaws. The two clauses have a very clear relation. The first is metaphorical, the second literal. Both are about the weather, but one is art, the other not.

If we knew the temperature was ten degrees and the wind force five, we might imagine rather well how cold the wind would feel on the cheek, how persistently it might lift the flaps of jackets and enter sleeves, and we might give expression straight away to the fact of our feeling: the wind is cold. The inference we should draw, as familiar as it is, lies dark in its own empowering, for the relation of the pure and empty structure that is mathematics to the scientifically expressed observation, and both of these again to the cold wind of experience, are not yet understood relations. Perhaps one can say that the scientist works always through a quantitatively abstract system, and that his purpose seems to be to find ways to represent the vague and informal qualitative content of experience within a rationally well-ordered formal scheme. But Hamlet's and Horatio's words rely in no obvious way upon the mathematical or scientific, and we are forced, in what is really a very complicated and very peculiar manner, to infer the same phenomenon we reached from ten degrees and force five from logical absurdities, strange comparisons, and silly riddles. The speed with which we make our inferences should not deceive us of the fact we make them. The air bites, therefore the air is alive. The air bites shrewdly, therefore the air is wise. It is eager, so it feels. These deductions, upon the information that it nips, and the immediate conclusion that it nips as dogs nip, give us the dog of the air itself. To communicate the nature of the weather, Shakespeare has introduced an altogether novel set of concepts; novel, that is, with respect to the idea of weather as such; and it is through these concepts that we understand the kind of wind and cold we're in, just as, through the mathematical, the scientist tries to understand the experienced weather too. And I think it will be obvious to anyone who fairly examines the meaning of Shakespeare's language that it renders the weather with a precision quite equal to the precision of the scientific, although the scientific precision is of a different kind.

To resort to a commonplace example: if we represent the strength and direction of any force by the length and position of an arrowed straight line, we can readily examine and resolve, by the construction of parallelograms, any forces collected about a point and expressing themselves from there. Our inferences in these cases are made possible only by the rules of representation we have permitted ourselves to make, for it is these rules which place the physical forces in the maw of Euclid's reasoning machine.[3] In a sense yet to be fully discovered, the technique of the artist is like that of the scientist. He invariably views the transactions of life through a lens of concept: through the shrew, the wife; through the wife, the dog; and through the dog, the cold and persistent wind.

From "the day is without warmth," from "the water is frozen in the well," from "it is ten below," from "it is a nipping and an eager air"—from each of these we can infer the cold; first analytically, from the definition of the state; second, from the effect, reasoning to the cause; third, by construction, from the manner of our representing tempera-

[3] See "Philosophy and the Form of Fiction."

ture within a formal system; and fourth, from the characteristic maneuvers of art and metaphor. Metaphor is a manner of inferring; a manner of setting down as directly and briefly and simply as possible whatever is necessary for the inference desired, although the conclusion may require premises that are neither brief nor plain and do not seem direct, since direction, in both art and metaphor, is often indirection elsewhere; for it is as much a matter of concern there to seek the severe straight way as it is in science and mathematics to seek the same. But metaphor is more than a process of inference; it is also a form of presentation or display.

The distinction involved is familiar enough. There are at least two ways of finding out about frogs. You can read about frogs or you can raise frogs and watch them. The Count can be described to you or introduced. Annie can say she is weary or fall all of a heap. A description can serve as a premise from which certain conclusions can be reached and this is the way ordinary argument proceeds. The connective tissues of such an argument, moreover, are linguistic. They fasten words, they do not stretch between things; and the rules that permit the movement that is the essence of every inference are rules about the uses of our language or the uses of some language; they are not laws of nature that experiment discovers. Insofar as metaphor is argumentative and inferential it can be made out to be systematic and formal—bound purely in every part by its own rules, just as art as a whole is, and concerned only with its faithfulness to them. When I say that the Count is fair and tall and frogs are jumpy and green I name their habits and their properties, but when Annie sinks wordlessly to the carpet, nothing is actively inferred; the act does not automatically fall into an abstract system.

Yet Annie has argued her weakness. She has done so directly, her material a rich and inexhaustible context that language can only peevishly pick over. The roll of her eyes, the pallor in her face, the sag of her flesh, the shadow of her bones: they testify together and by no means alone to the correctness of our conclusion. This conclusion is neither described by the event nor reached by logically ordered propositions, although logically ordered propositions could be imagined that would imitate it. It is not displayed as the sag and the pallor of the faint are, nor is it symbolically present. We are not compelled to see in her swoon a moral fall and evidence of a moral frailty, though when the Consul collapses in a steep street while guiltily hunting a cantina, we must. Still, quite apart from these things, Annie's weakness has been shown.

The word "show" is equivocal in a useful way, for it means both display and demonstration. Showing argues and showing produces acquaintance. It presents to the mind one thing in order that the mind may seem to have possession of another. The length of the Count's trousers shows his height to his tailor. The most interminable stream of words can never equal, in its production of detail, the incredible number in Annie's proof, or, in its unity, the complete simplicity of her faint. No curve comes easily of straight lines. Yet metaphor must somehow create the illusion of that context, make with its abstractions some display if it is going to possess the qualities we know it has. Metaphors argue. They endeavor also to produce acquaintance: the frog who jumps, the Count who is tall. "It is a nipping and an eager air" has qualities of both proof and meeting. It describes one very strange thing in order that we may infer and in some equally strange way feel another. It seems to present us with the cold rather than name it, and it seems to argue the cold rather than be it.

It is far from customary to think of metaphor as a kind of model making—in terms of system, presentation, and inference—or of fiction as life in terms of the toenail (more metaphors—curse their constant intrusion); it is, in fact, tactless to suggest any similarities with science, for isn't it the cold destroyer of the qualitative world, an enemy of feeling, concubine to the computer? More metaphors—and surely false ones. The scientist, after a time, finds himself with a store of observations of the natural world on the one hand, and a system of pure mathematical connections on the other. Within the mathematical system he can make inferences with great speed and accuracy. Unfortunately the system is empty; it has no content; it tells him nothing about the world. His observations tell him nothing either, for logical connections cannot be perceived; his data remain disorganized; there are no paths through it for the mind. But if he decides to represent a body by a point and motion by a line, then the system becomes concrete, at once trapping a vast number of physical things in a web of logical relations. In this way the scientist makes his model. The model is not to be confused with the world of ordinary experience, and the connections it establishes, made possible entirely by the rules of representation the scientist adopts, are not connections in any sense inherent in things. The model can be used to make predictions which mere observation is helpless to do, and in that manner its utility can be estimated. Thus the shadow made by a tree can be carried past the rather qualitative understanding of the eye into the dominion of number by representing the passage of light as a straight line. The light, the shadow, and the tree now form the sides of an

Euclidean triangle, and upon that triangle all kinds of useful operations can be performed. The system is a lens through which the world is seen . . . or rather, it furnishes a scheme through which the world is thought.

Metaphors rarely have a thoroughly formal and abstract lens, but when they do the resemblance to the scientific case is striking. If one lover says sadly to the other: "We shall always be as far apart as we are now; we meet only in illusion," the figure is drawn from geometry and the rule is: let lives travel in straight lines; while the conclusion is: since our lives are parallel, we shall never meet. And it is a commonplace that such lines seem to converge at the horizon. Donne's famous compass comparison is of the same sort.

Metaphors are used with varying degrees of figurative commitment. If Clifford is truly and completely seen as a mouse, then the character of his skin, the size and color of his eyes, the quality of his movements, the strength of his moral fiber, as well as countless other things, are known at once, and the whole system of meanings gathered under "mouse" is brought to bear upon poor Clifford—not serially, a step at a time, as in a proof, but wholly, totally, and at once. We need to know, too, how long we are to retain this commitment. Is Clifford a mouse just for the moment, in this line or paragraph, or are we to carry the mouse in our pocket through the entire book? The Consul, momentarily overcome by something more than mescal, has begun to make love to his wife, yet he is certain of failure already, he thinks of the bar he will flee to. Then:

> This image faded also: he was where he was, sweating now, glancing once—but never ceasing to play the prelude, the little one-fingered introduction to the unclassifiable composition that might still just follow. . . .

The commitment of this image is complete; these, indeed, are opening bars, and as it is morning, soon in peace and silence, the cantinas themselves will open, the Consul will enter one—they are named for their music as much as their mescal—to fashion a song from the rhythms of alcohol.

Metaphors which are deeply committed, which really mean what they say, are systematic—the whole net of relationships matters. But the moment the mind moves through the system establishing certain points of comparison and denying others, then the system is replaced by its interpretation. Each time we refer to someone as a mouse we beat the same path through the concept until at last this path is broad and movement is easy and immediate. The sense of traveling through strange lands is lost, and when we no longer have to hunt for the point of the comparison, we begin, quite justly, to wonder why Clifford wasn't called shy and frightened in the first place; for, of course, Clifford could have been a mouse for every reason, his whole life seen through that system; but this particular metaphor has slid even beyond proportion to comparison—where the metaphor says, in effect, Clifford is like a mouse because both are afraid—until it is nearly a case of catachresis, which has little or no figurative commitment, the word "mouse" being wrongly used to mean someone shy and easily frightened.

We are inclined to think that in metaphors only one term is figurative—"mouse," not "Clifford"—but this inclination should be resisted; it is frequently mistaken. When the Consul plays upon the body of his wife, it's not merely love that's seen as music making (he the performer, his wife the instrument); our understanding of music is also altered, conceived through love (in this case of an inadequate kind). The terms are inspecting one another—they interact—the figure is drawn both ways. Sometimes the metaphor's stress is heavier on one side than another (as I think it is here), but often the emphasis is nearly equal, as if we were seeing mice through Clifford. This can be determined only in context, and of course it would take quite a context to Clifford a mouse.

I should now like to suggest that the form and method of metaphor are very much like the form and method of the novel. If metaphor is a sign of genius, as Aristotle argued, it is because, by means of metaphor, the artist is able to organize whole areas of human thought and feeling, and to organize them concretely, giving to his model the quality of sensuous display. But I do not wish to suggest, by the comparisons with science that I have made, that the value of metaphor lies in its truth, or in its power to produce those brilliant flashes of dogmatic light which I believe are called "insights" among the critics who pursue literature because they prefer philosophy but will not submit to the rigorous discipline of systematic thought.

If the metaphors in a few lines of poetry can be complex —and they can intoxicate us as easily as mescal can—consider, for instance, the rather difficult question Lady Macbeth puts to her husband: "Was the hope drunk wherein you dressed yourself? Hath it slept since? And wakes it now, to look so green and pale at what it did so freely?" (try dressing yourself in drunken clothing—it isn't easy), or the great cry of Antony: "The hearts that spanieled me at heels, to whom I gave their wishes, do discandy, melt their sweets on blossoming Caesar; and this pine is barked that overtopped them all" (where he seems to envy Caesar's being presently pissed on because pissed on so sweetly)—then imagine the Oriental deviousness, the rich rearrangements, the endless complications of the novel conceived as I suggest it should be, as a monumental metaphor, a metaphor we move at length through, the construction of a mountain with its view, a different, figured history to stretch beside our own, a brand-new ordering both of the world and our understanding; for most of us do live under our lives like creatures covered by a sea or shadowed by a mountain, a volcano, its edges deepened further by ravines.

3

In Mexico, Malcolm Lowry was drunk more than once. Perhaps he tipped himself over in the air as the Consul does at the dying edges of the fair when, pursued by begging children who recognize his condition, he cages himself in the loop-o-plane and turns his dizziness topsy-turvy. The Consul has wobbled away from his conversation with M. Laruelle—a conversation, we learn, which was very likely imaginary—to confront menacing images at every step; and let us pretend that Lowry did so too, that at some festival on the Day of the Dead in Mexico he had himself held upside down, pipe, pennies, passport falling from his pockets; still, however he might have felt about it, it was not himself, not his soul's debris which now showered from him like a cloud, the cage that contained him was not a confessional, and pipe, pennies, passport were all that fell; he was not, even momentarily, absolved; yet the Consul, so suspended, has this experience, rains more than coins upon the kids below, and his overturning moment, composed with extraordinary vividness and power, takes on a brilliant glow, for by putting a piece of possibly personal experience in such language, Lowry has made a marvelous model for us, concrete in its depiction, abstract in its use, and universal in its significance.

In short, even the apparently literal language of the novel

has a figurative function, but in saying so I don't mean to
suggest that the riderless horses, the mountains, garden,
clouds, and cantinas of *Under the Volcano* are metaphors
for mountains, horses, gardens, barrancas, or cantinas in
our world, in our Oil Cities or Saint Clouds; for, although
details are used, they are escaped—pierced through—and
when the Consul falls over in the road, the concreteness of
the scene presented should keep us to the concreteness of
our own, each immediate and personal yet as shared as
breathing, so we don't dare make a mean abstraction of it,
crying out as though we were critics: ah, look, the fall of
man! oh, feel again the foolish frailties of flesh! or, dear
me, how hard life is to mount, how slow to summit! (all
such shouts are vulgar and may rouse the Consul from his
swoon before the proper words do); rather we see our
own life in the same fashion Lowry has envisioned Firmin's;
what we take away and keep is the novel's figurative form;
we reconceive our own acts in his manner; hear, in our
own ears, similar symbolic tones; and finally everything
becomes clear—clear, that is, in terms of one quite bent and
dirty toenail, since on another toe there might not be
Carthaginians in combat, but Buicks broken down, or dis-
graced angels falling into Indiana. The object of that mousy
metaphor was Clifford; the object of every novel is its
reader. And when the metaphor is meant, we look for
Clifford's tail; and when the metaphor is apt, we find it.
The novel does the same thing to us; there is no point it does
not touch. Certainly details are different. Clifford hasn't a
real tail either. Nor does Hamlet's wind bark. What would
make the metaphor if they were just the same?

Yes, our lives are safely different. Why is it then that a
novel like *the Volcano* is so easy to enter yet so difficult
to endure? No, it is not an image of the human condition.

That's far too easy. It does not first address, then mail itself to some abstraction. It does not say the wind is cold, that life is hard, that Clifford is timorous and beastie. Beckett's books do not assert that life's absurd. Does that news pain me? I'm sick already if it does. The novel does not say, it shows; it shows me my life in a figure: it compels me to stare at my toes. I live in a suburb of Cincinnati, yet the Consul's bottled Mexican journey is so skillfully constructed that its image fits me—not just a piece of it with which I may identify, such sympathies rend the fabric, but the whole fantastic dangerous country, the tale in its totality.

How does it feel to be the fore end of a metaphor, especially one so fierce and unrelenting? And how does it work, exactly—this book which takes us into hell? The philosophical explanation is complex. Here I can only suggest it. But you remember how Kant ingeniously solved his problem. Our own minds and our sensory equipment organize our world; it is we who establish these *a priori* connections which we later discover and sometimes describe, mistakenly, as natural laws. We are inveterate model makers, imposing on the pure data of sense a rigorously abstract system. The novelist makes a system for us too, although his is composed of a host of particulars, arranged to comply with esthetic conditions, and it both flatters and dismays us when we look at our own life through it because our life appears holy and beautiful always, even when tragic and ruthlessly fated. Still for us it is only "as if." Small comfort for Clifford, the metaphorical mouse.

I mentioned earlier that the terms of some metaphors interact. If a rose bleeds its petals, as much strange is happening to blood as to rose, and if the weight of Lowry's novel at one end of the seesaw lifts me, I, with my weight at the other, will in a moment lift *it*. Thus when Geoffrey Firmin, who lives upside down—standing in Mexico as though it were China—is swung right side up by the loop-o-plane; when his possessions spill from him, cleansing his pockets; when he thinks with fierce delight: let it go! let everything go!—as all these details, these whirling meanings interpret us, put into our world unique new relations (a hunchbacked Chinese sold the Consul *his* ticket), our right side upness is seen suddenly as drunken and wrong; as we are tipped like him and our cars fall from us, our house in the suburbs, our plastic wives or the hubbies whom we are indentured to; as we are put by Lowry's art beneath the volcano, in the cage of the spin plane, in a dangerous cantina; we, from our side, from our point of view, fulfill Geoffrey Firmin, round him in a way no novel by itself could ever do, and there is a perfect metaphorical interaction between us—just as blood becomes petal-like in my little example;[4] indeed, a triple transformation has occurred, for Malcolm Lowry, desperately drunk once and trapped in Cuernavaca (renamed in the novel for that duck's loud groan), more than once threatened with death by tequila, by mescal many times in a soft dark bar, has created an image for his life too, and conceived it as shaded by a shining volcano.

The novelist may fling his language from him as that First Bang blew the stars, pretend to a distance and blacken each relation; he may claim no acquaintance with garbage cans, say he has never ridden a bicycle, assert he's not once crawled through mud, companion to a gunnysack, and not once waited with a cardboard tree and empty road

---

[4] I conceive the reader's participation in the novel in this way rather than in the role of "helpful coauthor." See "The Concept of Character in Fiction."

for anyone, let alone Godot (we should accede to this; he *may* be honest); yet we can be confident that sometime it has been "as if"; that he has placed himself only at a metaphorical distance from his creation, has hidden his face while exposing his privates. On the other hand a novelist like Malcolm Lowry may wear his words next to his skin, keep them as close as underclothing, cry out loudly: this is real, true, honest—this happened to me; yet it will no longer matter, his words will never directly describe him, neither terrors nor torso, love affairs or other follies; for they shall have run away to poetry, free of their father and certain to sin. Only a figurative resemblance can be painted on a toenail.

Although *Under the Volcano* has many flaws, it is strong where most recent novels are weak: it has no fear of feeling. Even our finest contemporary work—that of Beckett and Borges and Barth, for instance—as conscious of metaphoric form as it is, with every part internally and wonderfully related; subtle sometimes as Lowry seldom is; scrupulous to maintain a figurative distance between author, work, and reader, and resisting every effort at literal interpretation; insisting, indeed, upon the artifices of the author; has achieved many morose, acid, and comic effects. Certainly the work of these writers is as challenging as any which fiction affords (I don't mean merely puzzling, but profound); yet they've been led too far toward fancy, as Coleridge called it, neglecting, somewhat, in the forming of their figures, the full responsive reach of their readers, that object (as I take it) of their labors.[5] Their books act on us. We are Clifford,

[5] It seems to me that this is also true, in the same relative and variable way, of the work of John Hawkes, Donald Barthelme ("The Leading Edge of the Trash Phenomenon"), Robert Coover ("Pricksongs & Descants"), and, of course, Vladimir Nabokov ("Mirror, Mirror").

and Clifford is a mouse. Unhappy man. But we are too much a passive term in this relation. Listening to the voice that makes up Beckett's *How It Is* saying,

> take the cord from the sack there's another object tie the neck of the sack hang it from my neck knowing I'll need both hands or else instinct it's one or the other and away right leg right arm push pull ten yards fifteen yards halt

or reading the list of Pierre Menard's visible works with which Borges intends to delight us,

> a) A Symbolist sonnet which appeared twice (with variants) in the review *La conque* (issues of March and October 1899).
> b) A monograph on the possibility of constructing a poetic vocabulary of concepts which would not be synonyms or periphrases of those which make up our everyday language, "but rather ideal objects created according to convention and essentially designed to satisfy poetic needs" (Nîmes, 1901).
> c) A monograph on "certain connections or affinities" between the thought of Descartes, Leibniz and John Wilkins (Nîmes, 1903),

and so on through

> s) A manuscript list of verses which owe their efficacy to their punctuation,

we find first our physical condition, and then our mental and creative life (have we missed those heavy allusions to Paul Valéry? not we!) rendered in a figure; yet how difficult it is for us to return that favor, to use our lives, as various as they may appear to be, to enfigure *them*. We stay those whiskered Cliffords mice have seen. Still, perhaps not entirely. Often these things are matters of a little more or a little less. We may be writers or academics with bibliographies of our own; we are certainly acquainted with lists, both shopping and laundry, lists of things to do crossed out as they are done, and it is possible to look at the works of Pierre Menard in the light of our own, reverse our positions. Still, not easy. We've been sent no invitation. In Faulkner, Lowry, and Lawrence, however, or in Bellow and Elkin, this reversal is commanded, and carefully controlled.[6]

When I peer at the web of a spider, I can choose to see there geometry; I can discover sine curves on shells or in love affairs angles of ninety degrees. On the other hand, I can also find shell shapes in my sine curves, sexual sinuosities, my geometry can seem haunted and covered with webbery. Similarly, then, do we intermeet Geoffrey Firmin; not merely on our toenail do we perceive Carthaginians fighting; among the tangles of their arms we notice the toes, feet, limbs, and eyeshines which both watch and reflect them; by means of this metaphorical mutuality, our mountains cross Mexico, our addictions become the former British Consul's.

Models, however, aren't real. And metaphorical models are even less so. Light does not travel in straight lines, we only represent it that way. Nor are all the features of our mathematics features of our data. Twice 25 is 50, but 50 Fahrenheit is not twice warmer than its half. With metaphorical models the discrepancies are even greater. Although the scientific model yields testable results (triangulation does give us the height of the steeple), our fictional conclusions, the inferences we draw there, remain forever in the expanding spaces of the novel. Clifford's eyes

---

[6] See "From Some Ashes No Bird Rises."

are bloodshot and tiny, his face pointed, he has a nose twitch, he continually scurries, then attentively stops. We know what his house looks like; we know how he eats, works, and worries; our attitudes are precisely defined. Have we reduced the image? Is he now a list of such facts? Not at all, for Clifford does not scurry like a man, he scurries like a mouse. And if one says, examining Clifford, you see, he hasn't a nose twitch, your figure is false, the proper reply should be: whoever claimed he had? he simply behaves *as if* he had one. In a metaphor that's meant, the descent to the literal can never be made. And as I've pointed out, when the terms interact, we should begin to see Clifford-like qualities among our friends who are mice.

How comparatively easy it is to capture Clifford, whistle up a sour wind, intoxicate the hopes of the Thane of Cawdor—after all, they're only imaginary, these winds, Thanes, and Cliffords; another matter if we must, with the same metaphor, render Chuck, Frank and Harry, Martha and Lou; fashion a lens to look at these lifetimes, both as lived now and as they may be lived later, in Saint Cloud, Sioux City, or Cincinnati; and achieve, when we can, the reader's ardent whole participation in what has to be a purely conceptual relation, a poetic involvement with language. No wonder the novel is long. No wonder, either, that at the edge of *the Volcano*, the danger is real though its source is a fiction, an image perceived on a drunkard's toenail, for such a book says to each of its readers more than that two mountain chains traverse the republic; it says what Rilke wrote of another work of art, the torso of an archaic Apollo:

There is no place
that does not see you. You must change your life.

PART TWO

GERTRUDE STEIN:
HER ESCAPE FROM
PROTECTIVE LANGUAGE

I
t has not proved helpful to the understanding of Gertrude Stein's creative works that she wrote so much herself to justify and explain them. It has not been helpful either that her autobiographies are rich and charming or that she took such care with the rituals of genius, finally fashioning for herself a personality as eloquent and commanding as her Roman face. Of this she never tired, and she began again and again. But in her life she knew too many foolish men and women, became too willingly a legend among them, something to be seen in Paris like the Eiffel Tower. They attacked her with their admiration and she encouraged it. She gave them manuscripts to market and they handed them around as signs of their complete release from common sense. She composed their portraits and they read these aloud and had them printed on expensive paper and dropped about like cards of visitation. Her art must have seemed an ideal medium for making known their own confusions, and I imagine it was

comforting to see how all of it proceeded from one so sure, oracular, and solid. All in all she was a gesture more decisive and more meaningful than they could ever make themselves, and when they left her it was often to wobble about the world like Mabel Dodge, enshrining foolishness. They would receive their portraits and they would write to say how pleased their friends were, how delighted. "Am I really like that, Gertrude? how very wonderful to be!"

Her stories, poems, and plays lie beside the mass of modern literature like a straight line by a maze and give no hold to the critic bent on explication. Art to be successful at nearly any time dare not be pure. It must be able to invite the dogs. It must furnish bones for the understanding. Interest then has sought the substitutes that she provided for it. There has been prolonged and largely malicious gossip about her and her circle and those famous friendships that finally faded. And there have been all those horrid little essays whose titles she might have enjoyed arranging into piles: The Notion of Time in Gertrude Stein, repeated again and again. Only a few people, and nearly all of them are writers, have done as Donald Sutherland advises in his book about her (the advice comes too late for Mr. Sutherland to have taken it):

> Forget all this talk about her work and do not prepare to have an opinion of your own to tell. Simply read her work as if that were to be all.[1]

Gertrude Stein has mostly been, therefore, an anecdote and a theory and a bundle of quotations. The advice of Mr. Sutherland is certainly simple but it seems too hard. Once admired by a few without judgment, she is now censured by many without reason, and that perplexity her work and

[1] *Gertrude Stein: A Biography of Her Work* (New Haven: Yale University Press, 1951), p. 200.

person have created, as Coleridge noted the connection, has contained sufficient fear to predispose some minds to anger.

B. L. Reid, whose book is the most recent attack,[2] makes all the customary substitutions. He describes it, with an easy presumption of its power, as "an essay in decapitation" and he genuinely believes that it destroys her reputation. On the other hand, Mr. Reid insists, Gertrude Stein has no literary reputation. She is "effectively dead as a writer" and "nobody really reads her." The critics have ignored her and all the important essays about her can be lightly ticked across the fingers of a single hand. As a result she occupies her present literary position by default. It is Mr. Reid's intention, apparently, to drag Miss Stein from the dizzy height to which ignorance, calumny, and neglect have raised her. But there has been a "sizable flurry" of books about her; Yale is unaccountably printing her previously unpublished work;[3] and while no one reads her, "everybody continues to talk knowingly and concernedly about her." Mr. Reid must have been standing on this shore of his confusion when he subtitled his book, "A Dissenting Opinion," for these words imply the presence in it of a carefully composed and calmly judicial argument, fashioned to overcome an opposition equally deliberate and well-defined, while his book is, in fact, a muddled and angry piece of journalese whose only value lies in how well it expresses the normal academic reaction and how superbly it contains and how characteristically it uses those malicious inferences fear lends so readily to anger.

[2] *Art by Subtraction: A Dissenting Opinion of Gertrude Stein* (Norman: University of Oklahoma Press, 1958). It was the most recent when, in 1958, I wrote this. Hemingway's nastiness, in *A Moveable Feast*, is mostly personal.

[3] I understand that her will left some funds for this purpose.

The first of these inferences is double-jointed. It permits Mr. Reid to malign Miss Stein's work by maligning Miss Stein, and her work, of course, is the major source of evidence against her.

He begins his book with an anthology of critical exclamations, nearly all violent, amid which he tries to find his place as an impartial judge, one who will refrain from the mindless flattery or the vulgar abuse Miss Stein customarily receives. Too many critics, he complains, disturbed by the degree of their feelings, fail to bed their conclusions safely on a text and try to make their points by shouting. But Mr. Reid's claim to objectivity and scholarship is sheer pretense, a rhetorical stance that he assumes to aim his blows, most of which follow a feint toward generosity.

> There is no point in vilifying Gertrude Stein. She is the victim of her pathology rather than her villainy. (205)

> . . . one cannot, of course, impugn her sexuality. Dark suspicions are certainly possible, but I am more inclined to attribute her literary attitude toward sex to that pathological ability to compartmentalize her mind that I have called near schizophrenic. (74)

> If Gertrude Stein is a genius, she is one in the vulgar sense of the term: perversely elevated, isolated, inhuman. (170)

As Mr. Reid proceeds, like a warrior given courage by his own noise, he enlarges his anger, showing he can make his points as loudly as anybody.

> It is finally just to say that Gertrude Stein's true position is anti-literary, anti-intellectual, and often

antihumane and antimoral. Her whole orientation
is ruthlessly egocentric. (191)

Not satisfied with this list of crimes, Mr. Reid goes on to
"document" what he repeatedly calls Miss Stein's schizo-
phrenic pathology by complaining that she once confessed
that anything in oil on a flat surface could hold her attention
("indiscriminate ingestiveness"), that she described a fire
once as "one of those nice American fires that have so
many horses and firemen to attend them" ("antihumane
and egocentric"), that she referred to war as a form of
dancing ("monumental detachment"), that she liked to
arrange buttons and hunt hazel nuts ("enormous patience
with triviality"), enjoyed Burma Shave rhymes ("unproduc-
tive catholicity"), and never learned to speak French
perfectly ("ivory tower").[4]

If in the first instance Mr. Reid replaces Miss Stein's
work with Miss Stein, in the second he substitutes her
critical writings for her creative ones. And these he system-
atically misreads. In a book that is heavily marbled with
quotation, there are only a few examples from her creative
work and even these are used for autobiographical purposes.
There is not a single analysis of any of her stories, poems,
and plays. Mr. Reid gives no concrete evidence of having
read them, and surely this is the critic's first responsibility.[5]

The critical essays show Miss Stein at her best, Mr. Reid
says, but he brings to their explication the willful literal-

[4] Strangely, Mr. Reid makes little use of Wyndham Lewis, who
attacked Miss Stein in *Time and Western Man* (Boston: Beacon
Press, 1957), and he does not seem to know Katherine Anne Porter's
essay "The Wooden Umbrella," which is one of the most rhetorically
effective personal attacks in modern literature.
[5] What should we think of someone who undertook to estimate the
achievement of Henry James by reading the prefaces and *The Middle
Years*, examining some of the letters, and studying Percy Lubbock?

83

mindedness of an investigating congressman. He is so intent upon conviction that he often misses the tone of her language,[6] fails to follow the directions in the context,[7] supplies no historical background for her remarks,[8] blurs essential distinctions,[9] and is prevented from dealing justly with some of the ideas he does understand because he regards them, having come from Miss Stein, as peculiar and mad, even though they may be (and are) characteristic of an entire movement in modern literature that begins at least as far back as Gautier's preface to *Mademoiselle de Maupin* and contains many of the most important literary figures of our time. One example of his way of reading should be enough.

In *The Geographical History of America* Miss Stein writes:

> It is only in history government, propaganda that it is of any importance if anybody is right about anything. Science well they never are right about anything not right enough so that science cannot go on enjoying itself as if it is interesting, which it is. . . . Master-pieces have always known that being right would not be anything because if they were right then it would not be as they wrote but as they thought and in a real master-piece there is no thought, if there were thought then there would be that they are right and in a master-piece you cannot be right, if you could it would be what you thought not what you do write.
> Write and right.

[6] Her remark about the nice American fires, for instance. Reid, p. 193.
[7] *Ibid.* War is dancing.
[8] As, for example, her allusions to Shelley in the discussion of God and Mammon: Reid, ch. 3.
[9] Between the artist as artist and the artist as citizen, soldier, friend, etc. See below.

Of course they have nothing to do with one another.[10]

And Mr. Reid declares that this passage makes the "full antimorality and anti-intellectualism of her position abundantly clear."[11] On a page following, Mr. Reid quotes Miss Stein again:

> . . . master-pieces exist because they came to be as something that is an end in itself and in that respect it is opposed to the business of living which is relation and necessity.[12]

This displays "the full preciosity, the distasteful hermetic quality" of her anti-intellectualism.[13] I cannot understand what is precious, distastefully hermetic, or anti-intellectual about thinking that the values of masterpieces are intrinsic, or that they constitute a system in themselves or that they are composed for their own sakes, nor is there anything about the Kantian language Miss Stein uses that gives any strength to that impression.

[10] *Geographical History*, pp. 198–99. Reid, p. 76. In other words: It is fortunate for science that its methods give only probable and fallible results, for absolutes halt inquiry. Only politicians and propagandists need absolutes. The purpose of art is not the enunciation of such Truths or their discovery, but rather that of presentation and rendering. Masterpieces do not depend upon being True but upon being faithful and exact, for if they depended upon being True, how many of them would there be?

[11] Reid, *ibid.* What is evident in this passage is the stumbling in the style, but Mr. Reid never complains about bad writing in this sense.

[12] *What Are Masterpieces*, p. 90. Reid, p. 78.

[13] Reid, *ibid.* Compare F. M. Ford: "The one thing you can not do is to propagandise, as author, for any cause. You must not, as author, utter any views: above all you must not fake any events. . . . It is obviously best if you can contrive to be without views at all: your business with the world is rendering, not alteration." *Joseph Conrad* (1924), p. 208. Ford does not mean that an author, as a private person, ought to have no opinions. He means what Stein means, that write and right have nothing to do with one another. This may be a mistake but it can scarcely be evidence of pathology.

It is clear from the opinions Mr. Reid expresses here and there that Miss Stein's work embodies principles that upset his whole notion of art, but he is so far from grasping what these principles are that he prefers to linger without, talking about her talk about it, where there is safety. And he is naturally upset that anyone should admire these mad babblings or their complacent author or that the English language should absorb any of the qualities of her absurd style. If only she hadn't written *Three Lives;* if only she hadn't insisted on the Picassos when she and Leo split the spoils;[14] if only she hadn't written all those compelling aphorisms or hadn't put together phrases that fasten themselves in the memory like great lines of verse (one wants to laugh at the pigeons on the grass, and does, but the pigeons aren't disturbed and fail to fly); if only William James had thought less highly of her or if Hugo Munsterberg hadn't called her "an ideal student";[15] if she had lost her wit and magnetism and gone strange as her writing did, and if her lectures had failed and the soldiers had been bored and if her writing had continued in its obscurity and hadn't, at the close of her life, clarified again and become strong at the end; if she hadn't been so sure of herself, so tough and so consistent; if, really, she hadn't written *Yes Is for a Very Young Man* or "The Coming of the Americans"; then it might be easier to dismiss her as a fraud or a neurotic lady with too much leisure, as a lesbian or a Jew or just another of the wild ones, or as genius, even, destroyed by ego; Mr. Reid wouldn't have felt any need to write his book. Certainly he would not have felt,

[14] Leo didn't want them. He wanted the Renoirs, as he didn't care much for Picasso. He always said that Gertrude knew nothing about painting. *The Flowers of Friendship*, ed. Donald Gallup (New York: Knopf, 1953), pp. 86, 91.

[15] *Ibid.*, p. 4.

against all the facts, so alone with his anger, in the camp of "dissent"—with most of the world on his side.

The writings of Gertrude Stein became a challenge to criticism the moment they were composed and they have remained a challenge. This challenge is of the purest and most direct kind. It is wholehearted and complete. It asks for nothing less than a study of the entire basis of our criticism, and it will not be put off. It requires us to consider again the esthetic significance of style; to examine again the ontological status of the artist's vision, his medium, and his effect.[16] None of the literary innovators who were her contemporaries attempted anything like the revolution she proposed, and because her methods were so uncompromising, her work cannot really be met except on the finest and most fundamental grounds. *Finnegans Wake*, for instance, is a work of learning. It can be penetrated by stages. It can be elucidated by degrees. It is a complex, but familiar, compound. One can hear at any distance the teeth of the dogs as they feed on its limbs. With Miss Stein, however, one is never able to wet one's wrists before cautiously trusting to the water, nor can one wade slowly in. There the deep clear bottom is at once.

In *Things As They Are*,[17] Gertrude Stein's first story, the pressures that shaped her style show plainly. The novel is a psychological analysis of the relationship among three

[16] I am always calling for such a program (see, for example, "Philosophy and the Form of Fiction"), but I never do much more than cry out.

[17] Written in 1903 and called, significantly, *Quod Erat Demonstrandum;* no effort was made to publish it until it was "discovered" among her things and sent to Louis Bromfield for his opinion in 1931. He found it "vastly interesting" but thought publication would be difficult. (*The Flowers of Friendship*, pp. 249–50.) It was retitled and published by the Banyan Press, Pawlet, Vermont, in 1951. The quotations that follow were taken purposely from the same scene.

women, one of whom, Adele, is clearly the author, and it is equally transparent that the fiction is a stratagem against the self to take its secrets, for the novel has no other subject than the strength and character of its author's sexuality and the moral price she must pay if she wishes to indulge it. Such an intimate inquiry might have been lurid, should at least have been interesting, but is remarkably dull instead. The self is revenged and keeps its secrets.

The language of *Things As They Are* is not very promising. It is abstract, monotonous, pompous, vague. Circumlocution, euphemism, pedantry bring the story to its knees. Its rhythms are held back; they go with stilted care. Even those passages in which Miss Stein permits herself to touch the air are afraid, and the mark of the graduate essay is everywhere.

> One usually knows very definitely when there is no chance of an acquaintance becoming a friendship [*sic*] but on the other hand it is impossible to tell in a given case whether there is. (15)

The characters cannot pay one another compliments without getting them up like letters of recommendation.

> Adele you seem to me capable of very genuine friendship. You are at once dispassionate in your judgments and loyal in your feelings; tell me will we be friends. (15)

The wit is weary and rhetorical.

> "You were very generous," she said "tell me how much you do care for me." "Care for you my dear" Helen answered "more than you know and less than you think." (15)

Thought is not permitted any real precision but, held off by the shame and intimacy of the subject, merely apes it. The result is protective speech. One way in writing of not coming near an object is to interpose a kind of neutralizing middle tongue, one that is neither abstractly and impersonally scientific nor directly confronting and dramatic, but one that lies in that gray limbo in between, composed of the commonest words because its objects are the objects of every day, and therefore a language that is simple and unspecialized, yet one whose effect is flat and sterilizing because its words are held to the simplest naming nouns and verbs, connectives, prepositions, articles, and pronouns, the tritest adjectives of value, a few adverbs of quantity and degree, and the automatic flourishes of social speech—good day, how do you do, so pleased.[18] This desire to gain by artifice a safety from the world—to find a way of thinking without the risks of feeling—is the source of the impulse to abstractness and simplicity in Gertrude Stein as it is in much of modern painting, where she felt immediately the similarity of aim.[19]

Protective language names, it never renders.[20] It replaces events with speech. It says two people are in love, it does not show them loving. Jeff and Melanctha talk their passion. Protective language, then, must be precise, for in a world of dangerous objects which by craft of language have been circumvented, there remains a quantity of unfastened feeling that, in lighting elsewhere, will turn a harmless trifle into symbol. Name a rose and you suggest romance, love, civil war, the maidenhead. The English language is so rich in its associations that its literature tends to be complex and carry its meanings on at many levels. Conrad, who, as Ford re-

---

[18] Another way of not coming near a sexual subject is discussed in "From Such Ashes No Bird Rises."

[19] Mr. Reid very frequently complains of the flat effect of this language and comments on its evasiveness.

[20] See "In Terms of the Toenail: Fiction and the Figures of Life."

marks, wanted to write "a prose of extreme limpidity," often bitterly complained that English words were never words; they were rather instruments for causing blurred emotions.[21] Protective speech must cut off meanings, not take them on. It must find contexts that will limit the functions of its words to that of naming. Gertrude Stein set about discovering such contexts.

Dull, flat, repetitious, thin, and cowardly—these are the more obvious qualities of this euphemistic language. To these are added, in the experimental stage where disassociation is also sought, the qualities of confusion and tedious surprise. *Things As They Are,* largely written in the simpler style, gets at nothing as it is. Many later works (large portions of *Lucy Church Amiably,* for instance), experimenting bravely, choke in the coils of their own locutions. I cannot imagine a language more thoroughly and obstinately inartistic, and Mr. Reid's objections would be fair and mild enough if her course had ended here; but she was often able to take another step, the last available to protective speech: that of giving to her words the feelings that arise from things; that of creating from her words real objects, valuable for themselves, capable of an independent existence, as physical as statuary. In *Things As They Are* one can mark the isolated moments when she struck her special note, but in *Three Lives* she plays a constant music all her own.[22]

The transfer of emotion must be made by means of every physical resource (rhythm, pattern, shape, and sound). How interminably her lovers talk, and how abstractly, yet her rhythms and repeating patterns make an auditory image of her lovers' passion.

[21] Ford, *op. cit.,* p. 214. In Reid see ch. 7.
[22] I try to say something about the whole problem in "The Stylization of Desire."

> "Well you trust me then Melanctha, and I certainly love you Melanctha, and seems like to me Melanctha, you and me had ought to be a little better than we certainly ever are doing now to be together. You certainly do think that way, too, Melanctha to me. But may be you do really love me. Tell me, please, real honest now Melanctha darling, tell me so I really always know it in me, do you really love me?" (198)[23]

The rise and fall of the name Melanctha, its marvelous quality as a sensuous pause and organizing sound, are used again and again, as here:

> "I don't see Melanctha why you should talk like you would kill yourself just because you're blue. I'd never kill myself Melanctha just 'cause I was blue. I'd maybe kill somebody else Melanctha 'cause I was blue, but I'd never kill myself. If I ever killed myself Melanctha it'd be by accident, and if I ever killed myself by accident Melanctha, I'd be awful sorry." (87)

Nor is *Three Lives* an isolated success.

> Old ones come to be dead. Any one coming to be an old enough one comes to be a dead one. Old ones come to be dead ones. Any one not coming to be a dead one before coming to be an old one comes to be an old one and comes then to be a dead one as any old one comes to be a dead one.[24]

Like most dirges, all this says is that people die. In doing so it sticks closely to its point, more scrupulous in this than

23 *Three Lives* (1909). Quotations are from the New Directions edition.
24 *The Making of Americans* (New York: Harcourt Brace, 1934), p. 419.

most. But it is not death that has the power; it has been deprived. The power is in the word.

> They stayed there and were gay there, not very gay
> there, just gay there. They were both gay there,
> they were regularly working there both of them
> cultivating their voices there, they were both gay
> there.[25]

Modern criticism has lived like a shrew upon paraphrase and explanation. Literature, it holds, is made of signs and the significance of literature, especially prose, lies in the meaning of these signs. The whole tendency of Gertrude Stein's work is to deny this. She was right to do so. Art is not a form of simple communication. It is this principle, explicit in her work, that, because he has failed to clearly grasp and understand it, has perplexed Mr. Reid.[26]

Words have sound and shape. Even the written word wears a halo of unvoiced sound while the spoken word bears the image of its written shape. But sound and shape are accidental properties of words and make up what Aristotle might have called their material cause, for signs are perfectly transparent. They possess only spirit. The logician commonly distinguishes between the physical *token*, which is any actual instance of a word, and the conceptual *type*, which is the idea of the word apart from any particular specimen of it.[27] The distinction removes the temptation to suppose that some

[25] "Miss Furr and Miss Skeene," *Geography and Plays* (Boston: Four Seas, 1922), p. 17.

[26] Sutherland discusses this problem with what seems to me a good deal of intelligence, *op. cit.*, pp. 83 ff. Although I restate this position many times (see "The Medium of Fiction," for example), Paul Valéry says it better than I ever could. See his essay "Poetry and Abstract Thought," to mention one (*The Art of Poetry* [New York: Vintage]).

[27] This is inexact, for the distinction involves many subtleties, but I think it is exact enough here for my purposes.

one written word, for instance, is that word entirely, so that if the word is erased it ceases to exist in the language. Obviously all that ceases to exist are the marks that make that instance of the word (the token), and not the word itself (the type). Every effort of language to call attention to its indispensable though semantically irrelevant body is treasonous to its function, for the function of the physical is to bear the meaning, not to be the meaning; it is to point beyond itself to the notion it represents, not to grimace and grandstand and walk fearsomely on wire.

So ordinarily language ought to be like the gray inaudible wife who services the great man: an ideal engine, utterly self-effacing, devoted without remainder to its task; but when language is used as an art it is no longer used merely to communicate. It demands to be treated as a thing, inert and voiceless. Properties that it possesses accidentally as a sign it suddenly possesses essentially. Why should it matter that "bush" begins with a *b*? That any word has the sound or shape it has: that it is long or short, formed with the tongue or lips or teeth, uttered from the throat or through the mouth or nose, pronounced with a rising or a falling note, clipped or slurred, spoken slowly, fast; that it is stressed in one way or another, habitually whispered or mumbled or roared, surrounded by questionable gestures or impeccable clothes; that it is associated with other shapes and sounds because it happens to resemble them, or for reasons even more fortuitous; that it was Latin once or came from Greek or is used only by people who stammer at ladies as an exercise in discretion; that any word has or is any of these things, although they may explain the origin of its meaning or the limits of its social use or simply the way, in the language, it is produced, is a fact about the word as fundamentally irrelevant to its purely communicative function as the flavor of food to its nutritional value or the color of a locomotive to its force.

In every art two contradictory impulses are in a state of Manichean war: the impulse to communicate and so to treat the medium of communication as a means, and the impulse to make an artifact out of the materials of the medium and so to treat the medium as an end. Calligraphy is an obvious instance. The elaboration that can be accorded the letter *r*, for example, far outruns its meaning, yet it would receive no elaboration at all if it were not a letter. One is tempted, therefore, to see in the elaboration some explication of the meaning of the letter, some search for mystic essence even, while at the same time the elaborations reduce it to a pure design whose interest lies wholly in the movement and harmony of lines in space. A sign will tend to make more and more of its physical nature intrinsic to its function by placing more and more meaning on more and more parts of itself. In this way it becomes iconic and the distinction between the sign and its object is progressively broken down. Instead of reducing the strength of the token as one might expect, this attempt to increase the generality of the sign by scooping its material into its type increases immeasurably the uniqueness of the token until it is a token of nothing but itself, for continuously one is invited to wonder if there are not more properties of the sign that can be given significance, and the sign is searched with the thoroughness of a treasure island. So words become the objects they mean while objects are given qualities proper to their names. This is, of course, the action of magic. Levels of language are destroyed. Logical types are deliberately confused. Ends are telescoped into means. Types are merged with tokens. Signs are identified with things. In a sense, the serious aim of language is ignored and even made fun of. And insofar as the literary arts use signs in this way, it is wholly misleading to describe them as forms of communication. They are devoted, quite as much, to the manufacture of intentionally useless objects. The attraction to the artist of the word made flesh, the love of the word as a resonance or a shape in space, is the least understood of all esthetic phenomena, being perhaps so purely a property of the creative consciousness and the first quality of which the insensitive are usually deprived.

> Trembling was all living, living was all loving, some one was then the other one. Certainly this one was loving this Ada then. And certainly Ada all her living then was happier in living than any one else who ever could, who was, who is, who ever will be living.[28]

In her effort to escape a purely protective language and make a vital thing of words, Gertrude Stein unsettled the whole of prose. Her abstractness enlarged the vocabulary of exciting words and made for some of the dullest, flattest, and longest literature perhaps in history. Her experiments in dis-association enlivened many dead terms and made her a master of juxtaposition.[29] They also created bewildering and un-pleasant scatterings of sound. Her success in uniting thought and feeling in the meaning and movement of speech showed that rhythm is half of prose, and gave it the power of poetry without the indecency of imitation. It also nearly made her a mystic and sent her wildly after essences and types. She studied grammar creatively, as few writers have, though little concrete seemed to come of it, and she was sometimes made to sound an utter idiot by present tense and Time.

---

[28] "Ada," *Geography and Plays*, p. 16.
[29] This can be examined best in the latter half of *A Long Gay Book*, in *Tender Buttons*, and on a larger scale in *Ida*, a late surrealistic novel rich in symbolism, a rare thing for Gertrude Stein.

She rid her works of anecdote and scene and character and drama and description and narration one by one and in both a theoretical and applied way raised the serious question of their need and function.[30] None of her contemporaries had her intellectual reach, few her persistence and devotion, though many had more industry and insistence on perfection.

In some such way, it seems to me, rather than in the way of Mr. Reid, her measure should be made. But calmly, above all, and slowly. She reads easily when an impatient mind does not hasten the eye. We habitually seek some meaning and we hurry. But each word is an object to Gertrude Stein, something in a list, like the roll call of the ships, and lists are delightful simply for the words that are on them.

> Winter and wet is on the apple, that means more
> handkerchief of any color, the size is the same when
> the pillow is little. That is the way to be conscious.
> A perfume is not neater.[31]

I think that sometimes she brings prose by its own good methods to the condition of the lyric. And everyone knows some perfectly beautiful lyrics that mean hardly anything.

> Please the spoons, the ones that are silver and have
> sugar and do not make mischief later, do not ever
> say more than listening can explain.

[30] Although her influence continues (it seems evident to me in the work of Barthelme and Beckett), many contemporary experimenters are merely, in ignorance, repeating her work, and often repeating it badly.

[31] This and the following quotation are from *A Long Gay Book* in *G.M.P. and Two Shorter Stories* (Paris: Plain Edition, 1932), p. 102.

THE LEADING EDGE OF THE
TRASH PHENOMENON

Comanches are invading the city. The hedges along the Boulevard Mark Clark have been barbed with wire. "People are trying to understand." This is "The Indian Uprising," the finest story in Donald Barthelme's new collection. There's fruit on the table, books, and long-playing records. Sylvia, do you think this is a good life? *Unspeakable Practices, Unnatural Acts* is the third and best of Barthelme's books, and each of them has seemed unnatural; certainly none speaks. A captured Comanche is tortured. The work of Gabriel Fauré is discussed. The nameless narrator sands a hollow-core door he intends as a table. He has made such a table for each of the women he's lived with. There've been five. So far. Barricades are made of window dummies, job descriptions, wine in demijohns. They are also made of blankets, pillows, cups, plates, ashtrays, flutes. The hospitals have run out of wound dusting powder. Zouaves and cabdrivers are rushed to the river.

William H. Gass

This unit was crushed in the afternoon of a day that
began with spoons and letters in hallways and under
windows where men tasted the history of the heart,
cone-shaped muscular organ that maintains *circula-
tion of the blood.*

It is impossible to overpraise such a sentence, and it is
characteristic: a dizzying series of swift, smooth modula-
tions, a harmony of discords. "With luck you will survive
until matins," Sylvia says, and then she runs down the Rue
Chester Nimitz, uttering shrill cries. Or she runs down
George C. Marshall Allée. Or . . . Miss R. is a schoolteacherish
type. She naturally appears for no reason. The only form of
discourse she likes is the litany. Accordingly, the 7th Cavalry
band plays Gabrieli, Boccherini. And . . .

In addition to the *way* he tells his stories, Barthelme
habitually deals with unnatural apathy and violence—unnatural indeed, but not abnormal; so ordinary, in fact, that
although we speak of killing by the countless, of lives indifferent, closed, and empty of any emotion, of cliché and
stereospeech, of trademarks and hypocrisy, we speak so
repetitiously, so often, so monotonously, that our discourse
is purely formal (a litany). The words we hear are travelogues of gossip; they are slogans, social come-ons, ads, and
local world announcements; phatic, filling our inner silence,
they produce an appearance of communion, the illusion of
knowledge. Counterfeit, they purchase jail.[1]

The war is not going well. We've used love, wine, cigarettes, and hobbies, in our barricades, to shore against our
ruin. Useless. The ghetto's been infiltered. There's a squabble
in Skinny Wainwright Square. The narrator drinks deeply,
and deeply feels the more-so of love. Sometimes the narrator

[1] See "Even if, by All the Oxen in the World," and "The Artist and
Society."

is examining maps; sometimes he's in bed, tracing scars on the back of his beloved; sometimes he's pointing proudly to his table; sometimes he is garroting the testicles of an Indian. Sometimes . . .

There are other names in this story: Jane, Block, Kenneth, and Miss R. Miss R., one feels, is not to be trusted. She recommends metal blinds for the windows; she arranges words in lines, in stacks. Perhaps she's in the pay of the enemy. She also speaks for the author. That's the trouble: everyone speaks for the author. "Strings of language extend in every direction to bind the world into a rushing, ribald whole." We try to keep informed, but in the end we know nothing. "You feel nothing," hectoring Miss R. says.

> You are locked in a most savage and terrible ignorance. . . . You may attend but you must not attend now, you must attend later, a day or a week or an hour, you are making me ill.

But where are the Indians by this time? "Dusky warriors padded with their forest tread into the mouth of the mayor." With helicopters, a great many are killed in the south, but they are mostly children from the north, the east. Like the narrator, we are captured by these Comanches; taken to a white and yellow room. "This is the Clemency Committee," Miss R. says, for it *is* she. "Would you remove your belt and shoelaces." Now, as ordered, we've removed our belts and shoelaces, and we've looked

> (rain shattering from a great height the prospects of silence and clear, neat rows of houses in the sub-divisions) into their savage black eyes, paint, feathers, beads.

The Indians with their forest tread, through one aperture or another, have padded into all of us.

Barthelme has managed to place himself in the center of modern consciousness. Nothing surrealist about him, his dislocations are real, his material quite actual. Radio, television, movies, newspapers, books, magazines, social talk: these supply us with our experience. Rarely do we see trees, go meadowing, or capture crickets in a box. The aim of every media, we are nothing but the little darkening hatch they trace when, narrowly, they cross. Computers begin by discriminating only when they're told to. Are they ahead that much? since that's the way we *end*. At home I rest from throwing pots according to instructions by dipping in some history of the Trojan war; the fête of Vietnam is celebrated on the telly; my daughter's radio is playing rock—perhaps it's used cars or Stravinsky; my wife is telling me she loves me, is performing sexercises with a yogi Monday, has accepted a proposal to be photoed without clothing, and now wonders if the draft will affect the teaching of freshman chemistry. Put end to end like words, my consciousness is a shitty run of category errors and non sequiturs.[2] Putting end to end and next to next is Barthelme's method, and in Barthelme, blessed method is everything.

In his novel, *Snow White*, he tells us about the manufacture of buffalo humps.

> They are "trash," and what in fact could be more useless or trashlike? It's that we want to be on the leading edge of this trash phenomenon, the everted sphere of the future, and that's why we pay particular attention, too, to those aspects of language that may seem as a model of the trash phenomenon.

Much interest is also shown in "stuffing," the words which fill the spaces between other words, and have the quality at once of being heavy or sludgy, and of seeming infinite or

[2] Our heterogeneous experience of language is basic to Borges, too. See "Imaginary Borges and His Books."

endless. Later we are told (Barthelme is always instructing the reader) that the seven dwarfs (for the novel is a retelling of the fairy story)

> . . . like books that have a lot of *dreck* in them, matter which presents itself as not wholly relevant (or indeed, at all relevant) but which, carefully attended to, can supply a kind of "sense" of what is going on. This "sense" is not to be obtained by reading between the lines (for there is nothing there, in those white spaces) but by reading the lines themselves. . . .

Dreck, trash, and stuffing: these are his principal materials. But not altogether. There is war and suffering, love and hope and cruelty. He hopes, he says in the new volume, "these souvenirs will merge into something meaningful." But first he renders everything as meaningless as it appears to be in ordinary modern life by abolishing distinctions and putting everything in the present. He constructs a single plane of truth, of relevance, of style, of value—a flatland junkyard— since anything dropped in the dreck *is* dreck, at once, as an uneaten porkchop mislaid in the garbage.

In the second story of this volume, Barthelme imagines that a balloon has been inflated at some point along Fourteenth Street and allowed to expand northward to the Park. Just as, in the novel, there are pages of dim-witted reaction to Snow White's long black hair, so also in this case:

> There was a certain amount of initial argumentation about the "meaning" of the balloon; this subsided because we have learned not to insist on meanings. . . .

Eventually people take parklike walks on it, and children jump from nearby buildings onto it, or climb its sides. The story is full of spurious facts and faked considerations typical of science fiction. When the narrator's girl returns from Bergen, the balloon is deflated and packed off to be stored in West Virginia, its inventor no longer a victim of sexual deprivation, the balloon's suggested cause.

If "The Indian Uprising" is a triumph of style, achieving with the most unlikely materials an almost lyrical grace and beauty, "The Balloon" is only charming; and a commercial bit like "Robert Kennedy Saved from Drowning" (a spoof of the English Lord and Elizabeth Taylor lady-magazine interview, and stuffed with syrupy cliché and honeyed contradiction) is simply cheap. Here Barthelme's method fails, for the idea is to *use* dreck, not write about it. Another short, properly savage piece, written in bureaucratic engineerese, is a "Report" on a recently developed secret word which, when "pronounced, produces multiple fractures in all living things in an area the size of four football fields." Another tells of the Police Band, which is designed to curb disturbances in the streets with its happy, loud arrival. The band is formed. It's readied; but of course it never musicks. Still another concerns two mysteriously military men who are buried in a bunker. They watch a console and each other; they watch for breakdown, something strange. They do not know for which city their bird is targeted. They watch, and they wait for relief. While we are reading, none comes. Barthelme is often guilty of opportunism of subject (the war, street riots, launching pads, etc.), and to be opportune is to succumb to dreck. Two stories, written in a flat, affected style resembling a nervous tic that's nonsignificant of nerves, both about cutouts named Edward and Pia, permit the reader to race to the finish ahead of the words, to anticipate effects, and consequently to appreciate a cleverness in the author almost equal to his own.

The Leading Edge of the Trash Phenomenon

It was Sunday. Edward went to the bakery and bought bread. Then he bought milk. Then he bought cheese and the Sunday newspapers, which he couldn't read. (It's a Swedish newspaper.)

But cleverness is also dreck. The cheap joke is dreck. The topical, too, is dreck. Who knows this better than Barthelme, who has the art to make a treasure out of trash, to see *out* from inside it, the world as it's faceted by colored jewelglass? A seriousness about his subject is sometimes wanting. When this obtains, the result is grim, and grimly overwhelming.

People were trying to understand. I spoke to Sylvia. "Do you think this is a good life?" The table held apples, books, long-playing records. She looked up. "No."

PRICKSONGS & DESCANTS

Before us we have several stacks of unread cards, maybe as many as a week's worth, and when in the course of the game we discover them, turning their faces toward us, they are placed in overlapping layers on the table. There these thin and definite narrative slices play us, though of course we say that we are playing them. Most of the fictions in Robert Coover's remarkable new volume are solitaires—sparkling, many-faceted. Sharply drawn and brightly painted paragraphs are arranged like pasteboards in ascending or descending scales of alternating colors to compose the story, and the impression that we might scoop them all up and reshuffle, altering not the elements but the order or the rules of play, is deliberate. We are led to feel that a single fable may have various versions: narrative time may be disrupted (the ten played before the nine), or the same space occupied by different eyes (jack of hearts or jack of diamonds), fantasy may fall on fact, lust overnumber love, cliché cover consternation. The characters are highly stylized like the face cards. We've had them in our hands before: Swede, the taciturn guide; Quenby, his island-lonely wife; Ola, their nubile daughter; Carl, the fisherman out from the city . . . and in other stories there are others equally standardized, equally traditional.

Just like the figures in old fairy tales and fables, we are constantly coming to forks in the road (always fateful), except here we take all of them, and our simultaneous journeys are simultaneous stories, yet in different genres, sometimes different styles, as if fantasy, romance and reality, nightmare and daydream, were fingers on the same hand. In "The Elevator," several types of self-serviced trips are imagined for its fourteen floors plus B, and the fact that the story is in fifteen numbered paragraphs seems as inevitable as the fourteen lines of the sonnet.

One of the most impressive pieces in the book in this regard is called "The Babysitter." She arrives at seven-forty, but how will her evening be? ordinary? the Tucker children bathed and put away like dishes, a bit of TV, then a snooze? Or will she take a tub herself, as she seems to have done the last time? Will she, rattled, throttle the baby to silence its screaming, allow it to smother in sudsy water? Perhaps her boyfriend will drop over for a spot of love? and bring a sadistic friend? Or maybe a mysterious stranger will forcibly enter and enter her? No—she will seduce the children; no— they will seduce her; no—Mr. Tucker, with the ease and suddenness of daydream, will return from the party and (a) surprise her in carnal conjunction with her boyfriend, (b) embrace her slippery body in the bath, (c) be discovered himself by (i) his wife, (ii) his friends, (iii) the police . . . or . . . All the while the TV has its own tale to tell, and eventually, perhaps, on the news, an account will be given of . . . While the baby chokes on its diaper pin? While the

sitter, still warm out of water, is taken by Mr. Tucker?
While both she and the children are murdered by Boyfriend
& Friend? No . . . But our author says yes to everything;
we've been reading a remarkable fugue—the stock fears
and wishes, desires and dangers of our time done into Bach.

Within the paragraphs, the language, which is artfully
arranged and colored for both eye and ear, reads often like a
scene set for the stage:

> Night on the lake. A low cloud cover. The boat
> bobs silently, its motor for some reason dead.

Or it has the quality of an image on the oblong screen which
is being described for us because we've been carried away
into the kitchen and yet wish to miss nothing: what's happening now, dear?

> Mark is kissing her. Jack is under the blanket,
> easing her panties down over her squirming hips.

The present tense is often salted with a sense of something
altogether over.

> I wander the island, inventing it. I make a sun for
> it, and trees—pines and birch and dogwood and
> firs—and cause the water to lap the pebbles of its
> abandoned shores.

While the collection is dominated by the paragraph as
playing card, there are short pseudo dramas and sections of
monologue, too, as well as patches of more traditional narrative, for this is a book of virtuoso exercises: alert, self-
conscious, instructional, and show-off. Look at me, look at
me, look at me now, says the Cat in the Hat. Indeed, Coover
is the one to watch—a marvelous magician—as the last piece,
"The Hat Act," suggests; a maker of miracles, a comic, a
sexual tease, befooler of the hicks and ultimately a vain re-

builder of Humpty Dumpty, murderer of his own muse, a victim of his own art . . . mastered by it, diddled, tricked, rendered powerless by the very power he possesses as an artist:

> At times, I forget that this arrangement is my own invention. I begin to think of the island as somehow real, its objects solid and intractable, its condition of ruin not so much an aesthetic design as an historical denouement. I find myself peering into blue teakettles, batting at spider-webs, and contemplating a greenish-gray growth on the side of a stone parapet. I wonder if others might wander here without my knowing it; I wonder if I might die and the teakettle remain. . . . Where does this illusion come from, this sensation of "hardness" in a blue teakettle . . . ?

A number of our finest writers—Barth, Coover, and Barthelme, for example—have begun to experiment with shorter forms, as Beckett and Borges before them,[1] and in many ways each wishes to instruct us in the art of narration, the myth-making imagination. The regions they have begun to develop are emphatically not like the decaying South, the Great Plains, or the Lower East Side; they are rather regions of the mind, aspects of a more or less mass college culture; and therefore the traditions—the experience—they expect to share with their readers is already largely "literary": Greek, often, with Barth's *Lost in the Funhouse*, though a broader spectrum of language received via TV, magazine, movie, and newspaper occupies Barthelme in *Unspeakable Practices, Unnatural Acts*, while biblical stories, fairy tales, and the

[1] See "The Leading Edge of the Trash Phenomenon," and "Imaginary Borges and His Books." Nabokov's example is also important. See "Mirror, Mirror."

myths and fables of popular culture most concern Coover
in the short pieces he's collected here, as well as in some
others which he has yet to reprint.[2]

Barthelme rewrote Snow White. Coover rewrites Little
Red Riding Hood (and who is the woodman but Beanstalk
Jack?); gives us a beautiful new Hansel and Gretel; adds to
our knowledge of Joseph and Mary (how did he take it?);
injects as much bitterness as flood into the story of Noah;
leans toward goatboy allegory in a tale titled "Morris in
Chains," etc., and at all times contrives to counter, even to
destroy, the meaning and power of the original.

Coover himself remarks, in a dedicatory preface addressed
to Cervantes and placed with predictable perverseness well
within the body of the book, that

> The novelist uses familiar mythic or historical forms
> to combat the content of those forms and to con-
> duct the reader . . . to the real, away from mystifica-
> tion to clarification, away from magic to maturity,
> away from mystery to revelation.

No wonder, then, that in the tale about the Ark, it's not the
high and dry Coover writes about, but the abandoned, the
drowned.

It is finally significant, I think, that the experimental
methods which interest Coover, and which he chooses to
exploit so skillfully, are those which have to do with the
orderly, objective depiction of scenes and events, those
which imply a world with a single public point of view, solid
and enduring things, long strings of unambiguous action

---

[2] Many of these qualities can be found in the superb work of John
Hawkes, too; and the fact that most of these writers *teach* writing is
scarcely surprising. That they are often on the circuit, *vocalizing* them,
counting sometimes on their personal presence for its effect, is in no
way surprising either.

joined by tight causal knots, even when the material itself is improbable and fantastic; and the consequence of his play with these techniques is the scrambling of everything, the dissolution of that simple legendary world we'd like to live in, in order that new values may be voiced; and, as Coover intends them, these stories become "exemplary adventures of the Poetic Imagination."

It is also characteristic of this kind of writing to give covert expression to its nature, provide its own evaluation; so that the imagined reader, dressed in red riding, bringing a basket to her wolf-enclosed granny and hesitating momentarily before the cover of the cottage, finally opens the door with the thought

> that though this was a comedy from which, once entered, you never returned, it nevertheless possessed its own astonishments and conjurings, its tower and closets, and even more pathways, more gardens, and more doors.

This reader, too, will subscribe to that.

MIRROR, MIRROR

The train stands still. The world is moving. Objects shatter into points of light, reflections are observant, shadows follow us like menacing dogs. All the visual qualities of things, and these predominate, are hard and impersonal. Everything's a mirror or an image in a mirror; depth is space upon a surface where every visual relationship is retained, though subtly inverted. A Nabokov novel is sliding by us, through our still attention, and the objects which it holds up to us are flat and disconnected: cathedral, shop sign, top hat, fish, a barber's copper basin. The people, head to foot, are faces (knees, toes, elbows: these are also faces); faces done in glossy printers' colors and stamped out on the covers of a million magazines, the copies of each kind the same, yet when found in different combinations, they are strangely altered (if left in the seat of a train or taken to a room, scissored up for scrapbooks, read in bed, or stacked in dusty attics to be saved), and they possess, in every place they occupy, an additional significance, as cards are changed in fresh hands, so that the two of spades on one occasion fills a flush, while on another proves to be superfluous, or as the white queen's puissant knave is rendered impotent, slid to a new square. Cards and chessmen, characters and words: all are hollow powers. Ruled by rules which confine their moves, they form a world of crisp, complex, abstract, and often elegant, though finally trivial, relations.

King, Queen, Knave is Nabokov's second Russian novel, but it's his twelfth in English, and if Gleb Struve's translation[1] of a passage from the Russian edition is accurate, and a standard sample, then the text has been revised, and improved, line by line. The work seems early only in the clarity of its intentions. Nabokov's esthetic was already formed, and this book's written to its program. The author's manipulations are quite obvious, even blatant, for we're supposed to see his clever hands holding the crossed sticks, managing the strings. Smoothed (one can't be sure how much), youthful gaucheries perhaps removed, mistakes erased: its date is now much later than it was. Each verb and noun, as though in search of something sweet, fly to their modifications, and this is because the modifications manifest the master: reveal *him*, praise *him*—glorify. The result is sometimes fussily decorative, like insistent blossoms on a swatch of chintz.

> The man was leafing through the magazine, and the combination of his face with its enticing cover was intolerably grotesque. The ruddy egg woman sat next to the monster, her sleepy shoulder touching him. The youth's rucksack rubbed against his slick sticker-mottled black valise. And worst of all, the old ladies ignoring their foul neighbor munched their sandwiches and sucked on fuzzy sections of orange, wrapping the peels in scraps of paper and

[1] In his essay on Nabokov as a Russian writer in *Nabokov: The Man and His Work*, edited by L. S. Dembo (Madison, Wisc.: University of Wisconsin Press, 1968).

popping them daintily under the seat. But when the man put down his magazine and, without taking off his gloves, himself began eating a bun with cheese, glancing around provokingly, Franz could stand it no longer. He rose quickly, he lifted like a martyr his pale face, shook loose and pulled down his humble suitcase, collected his raincoat and hat and, banging his suitcase awkwardly against the doorjamb, fled into the corridor.

It's Franz (our poltroon, knave, the dull point of our triangle) whom the images are passing. He's riding third class, as befits his station; but how ugly everyone around him is (that bun-eating man has no nose), and so Franz stumbles with his bag to second class and selects a compartment occupied by our story's King and Queen. Socially, they are traveling beneath them because the Queen is stingy. Thus upper and lower meet, like teeth, in the mouth's moist middle. *Pnin* begins, too, on a train. Pnin, too, worries that he's lost his wallet. Pnin, too, like Grandmaster Luzhin, like so many others, lives in a muddle. Pnin's train is taking him the wrong way, and he has no little man to help him like Sebastian Knight does. Here it's Franz, the climber, who is going wrong. King, Queen, Knave: each stares out the window, waiting—as we're waiting—to be played. Deep in the game they stand in their squares until their master moves them. The world surrounding strangely shifts. It has inexplicable ways. What can the players be up to?[2]

[2] Answers to these and other intriguing questions of the same kind concerning most of the master's major games can be found in Andrew Field's *Nabokov: His Life and Art* (Boston: Little, Brown, 1967), in Page Stegner's *Escape into Esthetics: The Art of Vladimir Nabokov* (New York: Dial Press, 1966), in Carl R. Proffer's study, *Keys to Lolita* (Bloomington, Ind.: Indiana University Press, 1968), and in the anthology edited by Dembo (the latter provides a critical checklist whereby even fainter footprints can be followed and identified).

Nabokov has taken his title, we're told,[3] from a tale by
Andersen, but it is also *Madame Bovary*, slightly rearranged;
it is the story of the shepherd, Gyges, whose Aladdin-like
ring renders him, at will, invisible, enabling him to seduce
a queen and contrive her husband's death to seize the crown.
Franz does not know this middle-aged and tawny moustached
man's his uncle who, obscurely petitioned by the youth's own
worried mother, has promised Franz a job in town. Uncle?
Would this weak Franz, within a web of high connections
such a low relation, play so poor a prank upon Freud's
Hamlet as to wish his uncle dead and he, himself, instead, the
kingly penis in the queen's bed? Think not on't.

In Nabokov's sardonic version, the traditional romance is
burlesqued. Franz sleeps with his lady, all right, though he's
a booby in the boudoir to begin with, that is, until she
seizes his initiative; and the pair plot the death of their king,
too, quite according to custom (shall it be by shooting,
strangling, stabbing? no? by means of a subtle poison? no—
and they research the matter thoroughly, consulting en-
cyclopedias and other catalogues of magic; but the cards
say death by water finally, although events play *in*, not *from*,
their hands). At the seaside, on vacation, rowing on the
ocean, the lovers plan to empty husband from the boat, and
because he cannot swim, Nature, it's presumed, will hold him
under. Husband, however, rowing manfully, reveals a business deal he's to close in the city that's likely to net him a
tidy. Why murder a man at a moment so financially in-
opportune? Postponement proves comically fatal. The
Queen, never sturdy (and anyway a value lower than the
King), overwetted by the outing, is finessed by pneumonia
from the game. The Knave (still another count inferior) is

[3] By Field.

released from a slavery that's been sweet but also terrifying to him (the worm in the apple's no innocent either), and as the cover closes, we hear him laughing a little too merrily.

Back aboard the train, Uncle Dreyer hasn't bought Martha any strawberries (there is a reason, but never mind it), and his wife is annoyed with him. He also insists on reading poetry, and this annoys her too, because only a magazine is appropriate for journeying. (Dreyer is really reading these poems now because reference will be made to them later, though not by me.) Martha yawns, and Franz

> glimpsed the smell of her tense tongue in the red
> penumbra of her mouth and the flash of her teeth
> before her hand shot up to her mouth to stop her
> soul from escaping.

Yes. You're right. To Franz this yawn resembles "somehow those luscious lascivious autumn strawberries for which his hometown was famous." But you're wrong if you think that Martha fears her soul is trying to escape, or that Franz is of that opinion. She has no soul, though, if she had, a yawn is what it would flee through. This carriage has another passenger. Franz shall eat of these strawberries, taste this mouth often, the deity shall see to that, for all these details trolley through the book as this train does, making countless local stops:

> Presently the bed stirred into motion. It glided off
> on its journey creaking discreetly as does a sleeping
> car when the express pulls out of a dreamy station.

All the characters are invisible to one another. The world for Dreyer is a dog he plays with: here, Franz, fetch the ball. It never occurs to him that doggie's sleeping with his wife. And when he gives the young man a job in his store, he puts

him in sporting goods, where chewy balls for dogs are sold,
and other rubber implements. Only occasionally does Franz
see how much mistress Martha resembles a toad; and Franz
means nothing to her, certainly; he's just a symbol of those
dissatisfactions which she's decided suit her situation: in her
life adultery is overdue.

We must remember that mirrors reflect us quite indif-
ferently: they accept anything, and if these characters are
followed by puddles, polished steel, and shadowing walls, the
characters themselves are mirrors. They contain images, they
do not see. Two pure mirrors, facing one another, draw a
blank. Furthermore, the mirror someone sees his shape in,
which doubles him for observation, performs a task no different than the mind does in reflection, since in Nabokov
reflection is a metaphor for thought—his own. These figures
wait like mirrors, too; their movement is illusory; they blur if
they're flawed or cracked or improperly silvered. Franz
smashes his glasses and the world becomes a painting by
Monet. (How many of Nabokov's kings, queens, or knaves
have broken or mislaid their glasses; how many are myopic,
or are led by madness, strokes, or fevers into a world of
dreams?[4] Freed of natural color and the world's unshapely
forms and corners, the language rises; within the stream of
the eye, Nabokov is always lyrical and moving.[5])

[4] Answers to these and other intriguing questions of the same kind
can be found . . . etc. For more on mirrors see "Imaginary Borges and
His Books," and "Even if, by All the Oxen in the World."

[5] Novelists, today, employ all sorts of similar strategies to justify the
release of language. They return to myth or fable as Coover does
("Pricksongs & Descants"); they resort to a mock epic style (Barth's
"Menelaiad" for example); they make drunk or mad the consciousness
they are concerned with ("In Terms of the Toenail: Fiction and the
Figures of Life"); they indulge in fantasy, create grotesques, play at
dreaming and propose conundrums (like *Pale Fire;* see also "Imaginary
Borges and His Books"), seek some freedom in parody and pastiche
or in other, otherwise imprisoning historical forms such as the pica-

His characters are his clowns. They blunder comically about. Clubbed by coincidence, they trip when most passionate. With rouge on their pates and wigs on their features, their fundaments honk and trousers tear. Brought eagerly, naïvely near, beauty in a boutonniere pees on their faces. Like the other clowns, how we laugh at that. Pieces in the play, they live, unaware, in the world of Descartes' evil demon,[6] that relentless deceiver whose deceptions do not qualify, but constitute, his nature. For Descartes, perhaps, the demon was merely a philosophical fear, an academic danger and a happy thought, but not for Nabokov's creatures or his readers; for if it's not we who remain in our squares to be moved, it's ourselves the moves are made against: we are the other player. Most of Nabokov's novels (*King, Queen, Knave* is no exception) are attacks upon their readers, though not like Genêt's and much modern theater; not like Baudelaire's, who called his *lecteur* a hypocrite, because he also called him his double, his *frère*. Yet what can this mighty magician do, this godlike contriver, when forced to perform for his life like a servant, but pick the pockets of the yokels whom he entertains? No brother, then. Opponent to be beaten.

Carl Proffer's *Keys to Lolita* is an explanation, move by

---

resque or allegorical tale, and only after establishing hyperbolic conditions allow a rhetorical rise, as Elkin does with such conspicuous success in *A Bad Man;* they often find themselves experimenting without knowing quite why, lecturing the reader on the nature of technique—the art of fiction—and insisting on their almost magical skills while bamboozling their audience and defeating its every expectation. Comedy is the customary consequence—a comedy frequently filled with hostility. In every case, realism with respect to dialogue is the last to go. Even Faulkner's rhetoric does not normally reach as far as the speech of his characters. The writer's consciousness of what is possible is, at this point, severely and seriously limited.

[6] See "The Evil Demiurge."

move, of one of the great man's greater games. Here he's discussing the use of poor Annabel Lee (for only too obvious reasons):

> If Lolita-Annabel is Humbert's girl "as Vee was Poe's," it seems reasonable for the reader to expect Lolita's death. . . . The trail of deception goes something like this: At first we are led, by allusion, to suspect Lolita will be his victim. . . . Then when Charlotte Haze enters the picture . . . it seems certain Humbert will murder her. . . . Then Humbert smilingly dismisses the possibility. . . . In spite of this slap in the face, the reader still has to keep Charlotte in mind as a . . .

I wouldn't want to spoil for you the sequence of the other ploys, though reading this book and Dembo's collection is a little like cheating at crosswords. Certainly these essays wear airs of solution, as spies do suspicion. Readers of *KQKn* won't be entirely fooled. They know all threats of death by drowning are a joke. While unwrapping the Poe allusions, Proffer wonders: "Is this just another cryptrogrammatic paper chase . . . ?" He decides not, because of the deceptions they practice on us. That is, they function. Yet might not the clues in a paper chase do the same? In any case, " 'Annabel Lee' is a very serious and beautiful poem. So," he adds, "is *Lolita.*"

The funny, the comical, side-splitting Nabokovian thing is that Nabokov's novels are frequently formless, or when form presides it's mechanical, lacking instinct, desire, feeling, life (nostalgia is the honest bloodstream of his books, their skin his witty and wonderful eye); and when the form is so ruthlessly imposed from the outside, seldom allowed to grow from within, rather bearing its bones on its hide as some insects do, then not only the end, but beginning and middle as well, are directed *deus ex machina*. We perceive this at once when the critics, clothed in butcher's aprons, carving come, for they clearly regard their discussions of construction as interpretations, and as they go about their operations, we hear not a squeak from the beast. What our author possesses in plenty is technique. *Pale Fire, Lolita,* and *Sebastian Knight* are built of devices: these bones make the meat. (That deal of Dreyer's which saves him from a final tipping-out concerns the sale, for display windows, of moving manikins he's had made. It figures, but it doesn't add.)

Even the characters on occasion, as if they'd begun to doubt like Descartes, employ—to manage their world and to murder like Hermann does in *Despair*—precisely the demon's deceptive wiles and much of his disdain and malice . . . in self-defense. These elaborate shapes fail to function as form, as a mollusk might cleverly exude a shell in Gothic style it didn't use but sold, instead, in shops. Not only do the novels seem cold (though *Pnin* is not, and *The Defense* is a loving exception to everything; every move is emotional, even the last one, when Luzhin flies like a Pegasus from life to death and board to board), there is a striking contrast between their rich contrivance and the thin interest they have for the entirely engaged mind. Even a sentence which fails the demands of the body, which calls upon only the deductive faculty, which does not fuse the total self in a single act of sense and thought and feeling, is artistically incomplete, for when the great dancer leaps, he leaves nothing of himself behind, he leaps *with,* and *into,* all he is, and never merely climbs the air with his feet. Nabokov's novels often, especially as described by Proffer and by Dembo's dozen, seem like those Renaissance designs of flying machines —dreams enclosed in finely drawn lines—which are intended to intrigue, to dazzle, but not to fly.

Form makes a body of a book, puts all its parts in a system of internal relations so severe, uncompromising, and complete that changes in them anywhere alter everything; it also unties the work from its author and the world, establishing, with them, only external relations, and never borrowing its being from things outside itself. A still umbilicaled book is no more formed than a fetus.

Close to conclusion, at that resort by the sea where the drowning's planned, Nabokov puts his name to *KQKn*:

> The foreign girl in the blue dress danced with a remarkably handsome man in an old-fashioned dinner jacket. Franz had long since noticed this couple; they had appeared to him in fleeting glimpses, like a recurrent dream image or a subtle leitmotiv—now at the beach, now in a café, now on the promenade. Some times the man carried a butterfly net. The girl had a delicately painted mouth and tender gray-blue eyes, and her fiancé or husband, slender, elegantly balding, contemptuous of everything on earth but her, was looking at her with pride. . . .

King, Queen, Knave is supposed to be a game of cards, but the purpose of the playing was and is, both at the first and now, to hold the mirror up to Nabokov. One puzzle of Nabokov's long imperial career is why he's never signed his books with a large and simple *N*. It was good enough for Napoleon; and after all, Nabokov's novels *are* empires, and more than that, they're *his*.

IMAGINARY BORGES
AND HIS BOOKS

Among Paul Valéry's jottings, André Maurois observes the following: "Idea for a frightening story: it is discovered that the only remedy for cancer is living human flesh. Consequences."

One humid Sunday afternoon during the summer of 1969, in a slither of magazines on a library table, I light like a weary fly upon this, reported by Pierre Schneider: "One of Jean-Paul Riopelle's stories is about a village librarian who was too poor to buy new books; to complete his library he would, whenever he came across a favorable review in a learned journal, write the book himself, on the basis of its title."

Both of these stories are by Borges; we recognize the author at once; and their conjunction here is by Borges, too: a diverse collection of names and sources, crossing like ignorant roads: Valéry, Maurois, Riopelle, Schneider—who could have foreseen this meeting of names in *The New York Review?*

Imaginary Borges and His Books

Shaken out of sleep on a swift train at night we may un-blind our compartment window to discover a dim sign making some strange allegation; and you, reader, may unfist this paper any moment and pick up a book on raising herbs instead, a travel folder, letter from a lover, novel by Colette; the eye, mind, memory which encounters them as vague about the distance traversed as any passenger, and hardly startled anymore by the abrupt change in climate or terrain you've undergone.[1] How calm we are about it; we pass from a kiss to a verb and never tremble; and having performed that bound, we frolic or we moon among our symbols, those we've assigned to Henry Adams or those we say are by Heraclitus, as if there were nothing to it. Like the hours we spent mastering speech, we forget everything; nor do our logicians, our philosophers of language, though they may coax us like cats do their fish, very often restore what we once might have had—a sense of wonder at the mental coun-try we inhabit, lost till we wander lost into Borges, a man born as if between syllables in Argentina where even he for many years believed he had been raised in a suburb of Buenos Aires, a suburb of adventurous streets and visible sunsets, when what was certain was that he was raised in a garden, behind a wrought-iron gate, and in a limitless library of English books.[2]

[1] Unless the changes are forcibly called to our attention. See "The Leading Edge of the Trash Phenomenon."

[2] Or so he asserts in the prologue to *Evaristo Carriego*, according to Ronald J. Christ (*The Narrow Act: Borges' Art of Allusion* [New York: New York University Press, 1969]), although errors are con-stantly creeping in—his, Christ's, mine—errors, modifications, corrup-tions, which, nevertheless, may take us nearer the truth. In his little note on Carriego, does he not warn us that Carriego is a creation of Carriego? and in the parable "Borges and I" does he not say, "I am quite aware of his perverse custom of falsifying and magnifying things"? does he not award all the mischievous translations of *A Thousand and One Nights* higher marks than the pure and exact one

William H. Gass

Just as Carriego, from the moment he recognized himself as a poet, became the author of verses which only later he was permitted to invent, Borges thought of himself as a writer before he ever composed a volume. A nearsighted child, he lived where he could see—in books and illustrations (Borges says "shortsighted," which will not do); he read English authors, read and read; in clumsy English wrote about the Golden Fleece and Hercules (and inevitably, the Labyrinth), publishing, by nine, a translation of *The Happy Prince* which a local teacher adopted as a text under the impression it was the father's doing, not the son's. In Switzerland, where his family settled for a time, he completed his secondary education, becoming more and more multitongued (acquiring German), yet seeing no better, reading on. He then traveled extensively in Spain, as if to meet other authors, further books, to enlarge the literary landscape he was already living in—deepening, one imagines daily, his acquaintance with the conceptual country he would eventually devote his life to. Back in Argentina, he issued his first book of poems. He was twenty. They sang of Buenos Aires and its streets, but the few lines Christ quotes give the future away:

> Perhaps that unique hour
> increased the prestige of the street,
> giving it privileges of tenderness,
> making it as real as legend or verse.

---

of Enna Littmann? and in his conversations with Richard Burgin (*Conversations with Jorge Luis Borges* [New York: Holt, Rinehart & Winston, 1969]) does he not represent memory as a stack of coins, each coin a recollection of the one below it, and in each repetition a tiny distortion? Still we can imagine, over time, the distortions correcting themselves, and returning to the truth through a circle like a stroller and his dog.

Thus he was very soon to pass, as he says himself, from "the mythologies of the suburbs to the games with time and infinity" which finally made him famous—made him that imaginary being, the Borges of his books.

Becoming Borges, Borges becomes a librarian, first a minor municipal one like our poor French village author, and then later, with the fall of Perón, after having been removed for political reasons from that lesser post, the director of the National Library itself.

Idea for a frightening story: the books written by the unknown provincial librarian ultimately replace their originals, which are declared to be frauds. Consequences.

Inside the library, inside the books, within their words: the world. Even if we feel it no longer, we can remember from our childhood the intenser reality which opened toward us when like a casket lid a cover rose and we were kings on clipper ships, cabin boys on camel back, Columbuses crossing swimming holes to sack the Alps and set free Lilliput, her golden hair climbing like a knight up the wall of some crimson battle tent . . . things, men, and moments more than merely lived but added to ourselves like the flesh of a fruit. In Borges' case, for instance, these included the lamp of Aladdin, the traitor invented by H. G. Wells who abandoned his friend to the moonmen, and a scene which I shall never forget either, Blind Pew tapping toward the horses which will run him down. Señor Borges confides to Burgin's tape that

> I think of reading a book as no less an experience than traveling or falling in love. I think that reading Berkeley or Shaw or Emerson, those are quite as real experiences to me as seeing London. . . . Many people are apt to think of real life on the one side, that means toothache, headache, traveling and

so on, and then on the other side, you have imaginary life and fancy and that means the arts. But I don't think that distinction holds water. I think that everything is a part of life.

Emerson? Many of Borges' other enthusiasms are equally dismaying, like the Russians' for Jack London, or the symbolist poets' for Poe; on the whole they tend to be directed toward obscure or marginal figures, to stand for somewhat cranky, wayward, even decadent choices: works at once immature or exotic, thin though mannered, clever rather than profound, neat instead of daring, too often the products of learning, fancy, and contrivance to make us comfortable; they exhibit a taste that is still in its teens, one becalmed in backwater, and a mind that is seriously intrigued by certain dubious or jejune forms, forms which have to be overcome, not simply exploited: fantastic tales and wild romances, science fiction, detective stories, and other similar modes which, with a terrible theological energy and zeal, impose upon implausible premises a rigorous gamelike reasoning; thus for this minutely careful essayist and poet it's not Aristotle, but Zeno, it's not Kant, but Schopenhauer; it's not even Hobbes, but Berkeley, not Mill or Bradley, but —may philosophy forgive him—Spencer; it's Dunne, Beckford, Blöy, the Cabbalists; it's Stevenson, Chesterton, Kipling, Wells and William Morris, Browne and De Quincey Borges turns and returns to, while admitting no such similar debt to James, Melville, Joyce, and so on, about whom, indeed, in these *Conversations*, he passes a few mildly unflattering remarks.[3]

Yet in the country of the word, Borges is well traveled,

[3] I am of course not suggesting that Borges regards Wells, say, as a better writer than Joyce, or that he pays no heed or tribute to major figures. Christ's treatment of this problem is fair and thorough. He tells us, incidentally, that in an introductory course on English literature, Borges' own interests led him to stress the importance of William

and has some of the habits of a seasoned, if not jaded, journeyer. What? see Mont Saint Michel again? that tourist trap? far better to sip a local wine in a small café, watch a vineyard comb its hillside. There are a thousand overlooked delights in every language, similarities and parallels to be remarked, and even the mightiest monuments have their neglected beauties, their unexplored crannies; then, too, it has been frequently observed that our childhood haunts, though possibly less spectacular, less perfect, than other, better advertised, places, can be the source of a fuller pleasure for us because our familiarity with them is deep and early and complete, because the place is ours; while for other regions we simply have a strange affinity—they do not threaten, like Dante or the Alps, to overwhelm us—and we somehow find our interests, our designs, reflected in them. Or is it we who function as the silvered glass? Idea for a frightening story.

Thus, reading Borges, we must think of literature as a landscape, present all at once like space, and we must remember that literary events, unlike ordinary ones—drinking our coffee or shooting our chancellor—repeat themselves, although with variations, in every mind the text fills. Books don't plop into time like stones in a pond, rippling the surface for a while with steadily diminishing waves. There is only one Paris, we suppose, and one Flaubert, one *Madame Bovary*, but the novel has more than a million occurrences, often in different languages, too. Flaubert may have ridden a whore with his hat on, as has been reported, but such

---

Morris. Though Borges himself appears in most ways a modest man, such preferences are nevertheless personal and somewhat vain. Just as Borges becomes important by becoming Borges, Morris becomes important by becoming Borges, too. "An author may suffer from absurd prejudices," he tells us in his fine and suggestive lecture on Hawthorne, "but it will be impossible for his work to be absurd if it is genuine, if it responds to a genuine vision." As for Spencer, it might be worth noting that this philosopher tended to think of art as a form of *play*.

high jinks soon spend their effects (so, comparatively, does the murder of any Caesar, although its initial capital is greater), whereas one sentence, divinely composed, goes on and on like the biblical proverbs, the couplets of Pope, or the witticisms of Wilde.

We may indeed suspect that the real power of historical events lies in their descriptions; only by virtue of their passage into language can they continue to occur, and once recorded (even if no more than as gossip), they become peculiarly atemporal, residing in that shelved-up present which passes for time in a library, and subject to a special kind of choice, since I can choose now to read about the war on the Peloponnesus or the invasion of Normandy; change my climate more easily than my clothes; rearrange the map; while on one day I may have traveled through Jonson to reach Goldsmith, they are not villages, and can be easily switched, so that on the next I may arrive directly from De Quincey, Goethe, or Thomas Aquinas. New locations are constantly being created, like new islands rising from the sea, yet when I land, I find them never so new as all that, and having appeared, it is as if they had always been.[4]

It is a suggestion, I think, of Schopenhauer[5] (to whom Borges turns as often as he does to Berkeley), that what we remember of our own past depends very largely on what of it we've put our tongue to telling and retelling. It's our

[4] That all our messages are in the present tense, as I have tried to suggest, is fundamental to Barthelme's method of composition. See "The Leading Edge of the Trash Phenomenon."

[5] Borges' good friend and collaborator, Bioy Casares, once attributed to a heresiarch of Uqbar the remark that both mirrors and copulation were abominable because they increased the number of men. Borges momentarily wondered, then, whether this undocumented country and its anonymous heresiarch weren't a fiction devised by Bioy's modesty to justify a statement, and perhaps it's the same here. It should be perfectly clear, in any case, that Schopenhauer has read Borges and reflects him, just as Borges reflects both Bioy and Borges, since the remark about mirrors and copulation appears more than once.

words, roughly, we remember; oblivion claims the rest—forgetfulness. Historians make more history than the men they write about, and because we render our experience in universals, experience becomes repetitious (for if events do not repeat, accounts do), and time doubles back in confusion like a hound which has lost the scent.

Troy, many times, was buried in its own body, one city standing on the shoulders of another, and students of linguistic geography have observed a similar phenomenon. Not only are there many accounts, both factual and fictional, of Napoleon's invasion of Russia (so that the event becomes multiplied in the libraries), there are, of course, commentaries and critiques of these, and then again examinations of those, which lead, in turn, to reflections upon them, and so on, until it sometimes happens that the originals are quite buried, overcome (idea for a frightening story), and though there may be a definite logical distance between each level, there is no other; they sit side by side on our shelves. We may read the critics first, or exclusively; and is it not, in fact, true that our knowledge of most books is at least second hand, as our knowledge of nearly everything else is?

Borges knows of the treacheries of our histories (treachery is one of his principal subjects)[6]—they are filled with toothache—and in his little essay called "The Modesty of History" suggests that most of its really vital dates are secret —for instance, the introduction, by Aeschylus, of the second actor.[7] Still, this is but one more example of how, by prac-

---

[6] He published his *Universal History of Infamy* in 1935, a work which is very carefully not a universal history of infamy. See Paul de Man, "A Modern Master," *New York Review*, Nov. 19, 1964.

[7] Professor Celerent has complained bitterly that there is scarcely a history of Western Europe which troubles itself to mention Aristotle's invention of the syllogism—one of that continent's most formative events. "Suppose," he says, "that small matter had been put off, as it was in India, to the 16th century?"

ticing a resolute forgetfulness, we select, we construct, we compose our pasts, and hence make fictional characters of ourselves, as it seems we must to remain sane (Funes the Memorious remembers everything, while the Borges who receives a zahir in his drink change following a funeral one day finds the scarred coin literally unforgettable; both suffer).

It isn't always easy to distinguish *ficciones* from *inquisiciones,* even for Borges (of the famous Pierre Menard, he says: "... it's not wholly a story ... it's a kind of essay ..."), though the latter are perhaps more unfeignedly interrogations. It is his habit to infect these brief, playful, devious, solemn, *outré* notes, which, like his fictions, are often accounts of treacheries of one sort or other, with small treacheries of his own, treasons against language and its logic, betrayals of all those distinctions between fact and fancy, real life and dreaming, memory and imagination, myth and history, word and thing, fiction and essay, which we're so fond of, and find so necessary, even though keeping them straight is a perpetual difficulty.

If, as Wittgenstein thought, "philosophy is a battle against the bewitchment of our intelligence by means of language," then Borges' prose, at least, performs a precisely similar function, for there is scarcely a story which is not built upon a sophistry, a sophistry so fanatically embraced, so pedantically developed, so soberly defended, it becomes the principal truth in the world his parables create (puzzles, paradoxes, equivocations, and obscure and idle symmetries which appear as menacing laws); and we are compelled to wonder again whether we are awake or asleep, whether we are a dreamer or ourselves a dream, whether art imitates nature or nature mirrors art instead; once more we are required to consider whether things exist only while they are being perceived, whether change can occur, whether time is linear and straight or manifold and curved, whether history repeats, whether space is a place of simple locations, whether words aren't more real than their referents— whether letters and syllables aren't magical and full of cabbalistic contents—whether it is universals or particulars which fundamentally exist, whether destiny isn't in the driver's seat, what the determinate, orderly consequences of pure chance come to, whether we are the serious playthings of the gods or the amusing commercial enterprises of the devil.

It is not the subject of these compulsions, however, but the manner in which they are produced that matters, and makes Borges an ally of Wittgenstein. It is not hard to feel that Borges' creatures are mostly mad. This is, in many ways, a comforting conclusion. The causes, on the other hand, remain disturbing; they resemble far too literally those worlds theologians and metaphysicians have already made for us and in which we have so often found ourselves netted and wriggling. When Schopenhauer argues that the body in all its aspects is a manifestation of the will, he is composing poetry; he is giving us an idea for a frightening story, one which derives its plausibility from facts we are quite unpoetically aware of (teeth are for biting), but the suggestion that the will grew its body as a man might make some tool to do his bidding is a fiction which, if we responded to the cry for consequences implicit in it, would advertise its absurdity with the mad metaphysical fantasy which would grow from its trunk like a second head.

Thus the effect of Borges' work is suspicion and skepticism. Clarity, scholarship, and reason: they are all here, yet each is employed to enlarge upon a muddle without disturbing it, to canonize a confusion. Ideas become plots (how beautifully ambiguous, for Borges, that word is), whereupon those knotty tangles the philosopher has been so patiently picking at can be happily reseen as triumphs of esthetic design.[8] In the right sun suspicion can fall far enough to shadow every ideology; the political schemes of men can seem no more than myths through which they move like imaginary creatures, like fabulous animals in landscapes of pure wish; the metaphors upon which they ride toward utopia now are seldom seen (such is the price one pays for an ignorance of history) to be the same overfat or scrawny nags the old political romancers, puffing, rode at windmills in their time, and always futilely. "The illusions of patriotism are limitless." Hitler tries to turn the world into a book; he suffered from unreality, Borges claims, and collaborated in his own destruction. Under the right sun one may observe little that is novel. The world of words spins merrily around, the same painted horses rising and falling to the same tunes, and our guide delights in pointing out each reappearance. We have seen this before: in Persepolis, and also in Peking . . . in Pascal, in Plato, in Parmenides. The tone, throughout, is that of a skeptical conservative (this shows up very clearly, too, in his conversations with Burgin). Least government is best, and all are bad. They rest on myth. "Perhaps universal his-

[8] Borges has made this point repeatedly himself (in the Epilogue to *Other Inquisitions*, for example); yet his commentators persist in trying to pin on him beliefs which, for Borges, are merely materials. They want him more imaginary than he already is. Perhaps this accounts for the statement, written we can imagine with a smile, which Borges includes in each of the little prefaces he has written to imprimatur the books about him: in Barrenechea, in Burgin (he "has helped me to know myself"), in Christ ("Some unsuspected things, many secret links and affinities, have been revealed to me by this book"), though he does not refrain, in the latter instance, from adding: ". . . I have no message. I am neither a thinker nor a moralist, but simply a man of letters who turns his own perplexities and that respected system of perplexities we call philosophy into the forms of literature."

tory is the history of a few metaphors." And we have had them all already, had them all.

As a young poet Borges pledged himself to Ultraism, a Spanish literary movement resembling Imagism in many ways, whose principles he carried back to Argentina in his luggage. It demanded condensation, the suppression of ornament, modifiers, all terms of transition; it opposed exhortation and vagueness—flourish; it praised impersonality, and regarded poetry as made of metaphors in close, suggestive combinations. It was primarily a poetry of *mention*, as Borges' prose is now, and Christ has no difficulty in showing how these early slogans, like the literary enthusiasms of his childhood, continue to affect the later work. Any metaphor which is taken with literal seriousness requires us to imagine a world in which it can be true; it contains or suggests a metaphorical principle that in turn gives form to a fable. And when the *whole* is an image, local images can be removed.

Borges makes much of the independence of the new worlds implied by his fiction; they are "contiguous realities"; the poet annexes new provinces to Being; but they remain mirror worlds for all that; it is our own world, *misthought*, reflected there. And soon we find in Wittgenstein, himself, this ancient idea for a frightening story: "Logic is not a body of doctrine, but a mirror-image of the world."

Mirrors are abominable. A photographer points her camera at Borges like a revolver. In his childhood he feared mirrors—mahogany—being repeated . . . and thus becoming increasingly imaginary? In the beautiful bestiary *(The Book of Imaginary Beings)* which has just been translated for us,[9]

[9] *The Book of Imaginary Beings* by Jorge Luis Borges with Margarita Guerrero, trans. by Norman Thomas di Giovanni in collaboration with the author (New York: Dutton, 1969).

it is suggested that one day the imprisoned creatures in our looking glasses will cease to imitate us; fish will stir in the panes as though in clear water; and "we will hear from the depths of mirrors the clatter of weapons." How many times, already, have we been overcome by imaginary beings?

This bouquet which Borges has gathered in his travels for us consists largely of rather harmless animals from stories, myths, and legends, alphabetically arranged here in the texts which first reported them or in descriptions charmingly re-built by Borges. Most of these beasts are mechanically made —insufficiently imaginary to be real, insufficiently original to be wonderful or menacing. There are the jumbles, created by collage: centaurs, griffins, hydras, and so on; the mathemat-icals, fashioned by multiplication or division: one-eyed, half-mouthed monsters or those who are many-headed, sixteen-toed, and triple-tongued; there are those of inflated or deflated size: elves, dwarfs, brownies, leviathans, and fastitocalon; and finally those who have no special shape of their own—the proteans—and who counterfeit the forms of others. A few, more interesting, are made of metal, and one, my favorite, the A Bao A Qu, is almost wholly metaphysical, and very Borges.

There's no longer a world left for these creatures to in-habit—even our own world has expelled them—so that they seem like pieces from a game we've forgotten how to play. They are objects now of curiosity or amusement, and even the prospect of one's being alive and abroad, like the Loch Ness serpent or abominable snowman (neither of whom is registered here), does not deeply stir us. Borges' invented library of Babel is a far more compelling monster, with its mirrored hallways and hexagonal galleries, its closets where one may sleep standing up, its soaring and spiral stairways. Even those lady-faced vultures the harpies cannot frighten us, and hippogriffs are tame. It is that library we live in; it is that library we dream; our confusions alter not the parts of animals anymore, they lead on our understanding toward a culmination in illusion like a slut.

And which is Borges, which his double? which is the photograph? the face perverted by a mirror? image in the polish of a writing table? There is the Borges who compiles *A Personal Anthology*,[10] and says he wishes to be remembered by it, and there is the Borges who admits to Burgin that he did not put all of his best things in it; there is the Borges who plays with the notion that all our works are products of the same universal Will so that one author impersonally authors everything (thus the labors of that provincial librarian are not vain), and the Borges whose particular mark is both idiosyncratic and indelible. The political skeptic and the fierce opponent of Perón: are they one man? Can the author of *The Aleph* admire Chesterton? Wells? Croce? Kipling? And what about those stories which snap together at the end like a cheap lock? with a gun shot? Is this impish dilettante the same man who leaves us so often uneasily amazed? Perhaps he is, as Borges wrote so wonderfully of Valéry,

> A man whose admirable texts do not exhaust, or even define, his all-embracing possibilities. A man who, in a century that adores the chaotic idols of blood, earth, and passion, always preferred the lucid pleasures of thought and the secret adventures of order.

Yet can this be a figure that same age salutes? Consequences.

[10] *A Personal Anthology*, ed. Anthony Kerrigan (New York: Grove, 1967).

THE BINGO GAME AT THE
FOOT OF THE CROSS

F rom the start, nearly twenty years ago now, when his writing began to excite the admiration of the readers of *Accent*, it was evident that the stories of J. F. Powers had a very special quality, a rare richness of theme and perception; and, for all their liberal zeal and satirical intent, often an even rarer gentleness of tone. His style seemed equal to all its occasions. Direct and colloquial without being finicky, it was tilted pleasantly toward the conversational, and made its effect with undemonstrative simplicity and ease. By the time his first collection, *The Prince of Darkness*, had appeared, it was evident, too, that he was a master of the short story in at least one of its forms. Moreover, Powers seemed almost immediately to have found, in the vocation of the priest, the subject which was eventually to possess him and draw forth his best; just as he was, with equal readiness, to discover the ideal line to take with it, one that gave him his characteristic fictional "situation."

The Bingo Game at the Foot of the Cross

The trouble with Powers' second volume, for which he kept us waiting nine years, was that his best stories were still in the first one; but this was a petty complaint then, since the collection was very fine, and the title story, "The Presence of Grace," superb. Now, six years later, we have *Morte D'Urban*, Powers' third book, first novel. All told, they've been years of care, of conscious artistry—the repeated exercise of correct choice, harsh scrutiny, and continuous revision. Thus I imagine it, for nothing else can account for *Morte D'Urban*'s special excellence. The time must have been spent gathering, with a delight comparable to that which Flaubert derived from the gaffs of the bourgeois, those manifestations of our spiritual corruption from which his stories and this novel are principally composed.

Theme, subject, situation, tone—for Powers, they have not changed much as he moves from short fiction to the novel. As he himself described the new book in a recent interview in *The Critic*:

> [It] is about Father Urban being sent to this foundation of the Order in Minnesota. He had been a big-time speaker, a poor man's Fulton Sheen. He was suddenly sent up here to this white elephant, not as the rector, but as one of the boys, one of the three priests. That's my story, what he did there, how he tried to put the place on its feet, how he worked as a common workman—because that was the rector's idea about everything, saving string; the pound-foolish, penny-wise kind of man. He's what used to be called the Pullman type, now the type with the attaché case, doing lots of good and instilling a feeling in the young men in the novitiate. Father Urban was trying to develop something special for the Clementines. What it was, he was not sure—a kind of opportunism, I would say.

Powers' theme remains truly haunting; it is one that might be framed as a question: how can the spirit express itself in nature without compromise, without debasement, since one is so distant from the other, and each is obedient to different laws? Again: can a mind manipulate its body without becoming its body first? Or: is it possible for the church to do its work in the world without becoming worldly itself? And there are a hundred other ways to put it. In "Lions, Harts, Leaping Does," Powers' most beautiful story, the Franciscan priest, Didymus, is finally able to feel the truth he has so long bowed his head to, that "in trivial attachments, in love of things, was death, no matter the appearance of life. In the highest attachment only, no matter the appearance of death, was life." But as Didymus approaches the condition of the saint, wanting "nothing in the world for himself at last," he finds he is still "beset by the grossest distractions. They were to be expected, he knew, as indelible in the order of things: the bingo game going on under the Cross for the seamless garment of the Son of Man: everywhere the sign of the contradiction, and always. When would he cease to be surprised by it?" The mystic, for example, forgets his fellows in his flight toward the divine. There seems to be an obligation laid upon those who follow the Ideal to yield themselves to practice.

Thus the dilemma. There is a perfectly reasonable solution to this paradox in Aristotle, but Catholic writers are seldom long on doctrine, and the most arresting thing about Powers' priests is that they never talk theological shop. A layman will occasionally raise a question; it is always embarrassing. But whatever the doctrine—the appearance remains. The ladies leave their lipstick on the crucifix they kiss. One could regard these smears as testimony of continuing love, but

Powers does not choose to and, of course, the evidence is mostly on his side.

Yet if Powers' fundamental theme escapes the parochial residence he has given to it, his "situation" is, by contrast, quite definitely fixed and narrowly predictable: we shall see the priest, easy emblem of the fairway, hook heavily into the rough and nearly lose his ball—a new Angelflite, one of a dozen like the original disciples, given anonymously at Christmas in a box of paper grass, balls he's had to fly south, in the anonymous donor's private plane, to strike. Well? What harm? Can't priests, like presidents, play golf?

The position of the priest has always struck many people (mostly Protestants, I suppose) as curious, and Powers mentions this fact in the novel. The priest wears a uniform of spiritual dedication and physical denial, is celibate as though to celebrate it, moves through the mysteries of ritual as if he knew his way there, incanting an ancient tongue—a figure altogether strange to this world. Yet he is permitted to smoke cigars, prefer martinis, improve his game, accept personal gifts, and drive about in large cars. If the Catholic Church is to survive and grow and do its work, it must attract wealth, acquire political power, advertise itself, build, train bright ambitious men for the priesthood and put them in effective places; it must, in our competitive world, energetically compete, and to compete it must be heard, it must be chic, it must seem glamorous to the crowd, right up to date. Surely Father Urban would agree, for that is the meaning of his name. Only reasonable. The Protestants are building bowling alleys.

Powers has found the formula for his fiction in all this. He regularly sees the priest in a worldly role. The necessity of this role makes Powers' satire kind. The contradiction implied makes his irony deep. Nevertheless, it is a formula, for we can feel the force of it before we read, and in great part predict its course before that course has well begun.[1]

A few examples. In one story the relation between curate and pastor is likened to that between landlord and tenant, the particular problem being how the tenant can wrangle a writing table for his furnished room from the store gathering dust in his landlord's basement. In another, Father holds patriarchal sway over a household of women. We are treated to the irony of nuns counting collection money, while Mother nerves herself to ask Father to buy a new stove. ("The stove's all right, Sister. It won't draw properly, is all.") In perhaps the best-known of these pieces, "The Valiant Woman," what would otherwise be a dreary cliché of married life becomes deliciously comic when the participants are housekeeper and priest. They even play honeymoon bridge.

Not only does the formula, the particular "situation," give these stories their form, it supplies the details, too, and Powers is immensely gifted at filling every corner of his picture with ironies. Father Ernest Burner, the fat prince of "The Prince of Darkness," to my mind the finest of the stories of this kind, is cast as a time server in a large corporation hoping for a transfer that will mean a promotion. A victim, principally, of sloth (though all the notable sins are his in one small way or another), he receives a demotion instead. Burner golfs, of course, and in his room he practices putting through his clerical collar. (Father Urban is constantly mislaying his.) As he drives to his flying lessons (he is, we must remember, the fallen angel), Father Burner's trousers

[1] The problem of the "linguistically detachable formula" and its embodiment in language is discussed briefly, with reference to Powers, in "The Concept of Character in Fiction."

feel uncomfortably tight. He tugs "viciously at both knees, loosening the seat." So in every line: the apt symbolism, the rich irony, the identical implications. Each time, too, the shock of the contradiction is freshly felt, for instance in the easy vulgarity of the priests' thought and speech, a frequent device of the novel. "Your ass is out, Father," Monsignor Renton says.

But the formula which has served Powers' shorter fiction so well does not lend itself as readily to the longer form. His situations tend to close upon themselves, making the novel a trifle episodic. The writing is astonishingly deft, continuously comic, but Powers is too afraid of being a bore. His formula permits him repeated illustrations of the same theme, yet obstructs any deeper exploration. There's no more here than in "Lions, Harts . . ." or "The Prince of Darkness," where the material is held under greater pressure. It is perhaps the final irony, but I cannot imagine a book in which religious feeling would be more conspicuously absent, or even out of place (though I may mistake the emotion), or one whose artistry would make its compromises with the world with better grace.

THE SHUT-IN

I. B. Singer's work is re-markable for a number of reasons. Critics have called it "modern." It is not. Most of his stories take place in the past, certainly; but Gide composing *Le Roi Candaule*, or Camus his *Caligula*, writes in an unmistakably modern way. Singer's stories turn so remote a corner in the history of human consciousness, they may give the impression of com-ing from the future when they are really returning from a circumnavigation of infinity . . . and by the back way. He writes in Yiddish, but he thinks in Hebrew; or if you like, in awfully early Greek. The characters Singer creates (like the world he makes), whether he puts them down in Poland or New York, whether they live in the sixteenth century or presently, are as distant from us as the aborigines. It isn't their funny beards or costumes; it isn't because they live by law in a book that's dead as dumbbells, or engage in quaint inter-Jewish squabbles; it isn't because their lives are so compressed by custom, so driven on by superstition, that we simply feel our age superior in light and air at least; it isn't even because goose-footed devils are as real as geese there, or that from time to time evil steals from one or other body-pox its part as plague-in-chief. I have already called Singer a shut-in: this, again, not because he writes in a fossil language, risking, yet escaping, the fate of Eugène Marais; or because the world is as much a magical volume of words for him as it is for any glossing cabbalist (since he is clearly a scholar, studies up, arranges, and collects); but only because of the primitive materiality of his approach; thus what Singer's shut inside of is a metaphysics—honored, ancient—a metaphysics of that Word which once worked itself up into World, a philosophy of acts and not intentions, of prayers and rites, not states of soul, a universe in which nothing's real but *things*. There's no soul silliness in the old Old Testament, and the pneumatic psyche of the early Greek was blood, breath, shadow, water, fire, air . . . each quite substantial. So was insanity substantial; uncommon lust or rage; even eloquence belonged to property and might be stolen like one's money or one's wife. Dreams were other countries, relations attributes, and numbers round, triangular, oblong, or square. Sin was a contaminating miasma. To level the waves the Greeks would have thrown Jonah overboard too. Beliefs were commanded actions, and one's history was often just a thread between the shears. Who knew what the gods might do?[1]

The name of Descartes, Leibniz, or Maimonides may be mentioned, but it never functions structurally. (Dr. Fischelson studies Spinoza as though the *Ethics* were the Torah.) Singer frequently chooses a subject which might be called

[1] The theoretical basis for my interpretation of Singer here can be found in "Philosophy and the Form of Fiction," the opening essay of this book.

"the coming of modern consciousness," but the form of his fiction denies it ever came. The most important fact about a novelist is the kind of creation he commands, for he's the true god there—brooding, in the beginning, above a blank and dismal page. His book's in this sense sacred. He must be taken at His Word. Construction counts. It forms the world in the work we see. In the better novels, construction counts for everything, since everything is construction, and there are no "details." It's not merely the words the author puts down, then, which matter, but their type or kind, and the characteristic patterns they form, the facts (in this way) they comprise, and the manner of knowing that is therefore implied. Nor must we be bamboozled by small mimes or minor traits or little tics into supposing that our author's "modern." (There are few cozy asides to the reader, for example, no loud labels of value, or manifestos of artistic intention.) Robbe-Grillet's pathetic "scientific" recital of acts and objects reveals an almost total subjectivity. It's not the waves but the power which moves them we must measure. It is, however, true that, like Flaubert, Singer hides the arm which holds his hand. This is because, in this writer's world, everything is possible. It matters very little what is true. If something's not true now, it once was, or it will be; if it didn't happen here, it happened somewhere else. Look about. What is important is not what we may believe, but the way we choose to believe it—our fidelity, our heat. Men are moved by falsehoods just as fiercely as by truths. (This is the position, by the way, of Gimpel the fool.) Then too, times change. Opinions change. One view is nearly as bad as another . . . or as good. Evaluation— fevered praise or blame—how does it serve us? Our philosophies are partial, partisan; that is, they're human, and they will pass away. Only God, through every change, remains, though he stays hidden from us, dwells beyond us (just as Singer does), behind the blinding rays of heaven, out of sight. A sobering thought for the critic, bending over one of Singer's books, patiently construing.

The whole of Singer's fiction possesses this magnificent ontological equality (fables, fantasies, and fairy tales are therefore never out of place); it has exactly the material solidity it claims for everything, since everything is open, and in space. The sensational, the extreme and extraordinary, the violent, saintly, severe and the cruel, the divine, the human, the diabolical: all are mastered by his method, placed in a line on the same plane; ritual acts and uncontrollable savagery, marriage and murder, prayers and pogroms; for they are all acts, acts like tangible objects resting in the world. After all, the flower and the phallus both exist, so do stones in a wall, or passions in a person. This gives Singer an important freedom. If, on the one hand, facts are everything, on the other, everything can be factual. No mind and body problem here, no links to be forged between percept and object, or bridges to be built between nature and the unnatural, thought, dream, and thing. Whatever is, is matter in ritual motion. An intense sense of reality in the reader is the initial advantage. No one quite believes in any inner spirit but his own.

We have no acquaintance with another consciousness. Shut in, all we can *perceive* is a world of objects; all we can *feel* is ourselves. Pain in the person beside us is a cry and a grimace, a message sent from the inside, or so we read it, connecting our former hurts to this present crying, attributing our subjectivity to the friend we have injured, or the cat we've kicked. If we meet ourselves as strangers, "one hand asks the other by the pulse," as Donne avers, "and our eye asks our urine, how we do." But what of indemonstrable agonies, silent debates, terrors and dangers repressed for a secret reason, at enormous spiritual expense: those internal stresses hidden from the eye like weakening steel in faltering bridges? Furthermore, one weeping can disguise a thousand griefs, each different. The tears do not distinguish. They rise in joy as well as sorrow. Emotion, by behavior, is only indicated, never uniquely differentiated. Acts have particularity, too, but only part of their nature is internally determined; the feelings exercise a limited control over their manifestations, for the world makes its demands as well; it imposes on the aims of actions all kinds of means and conditions; it requires material expression be given to the soul. When there seems to be a match, when the inner state receives complete expression, each pang in one represented by an appropriate ping in the other, as with an oversubtle actor, we find the gestures hard to read, the feeling difficult to define, for it's precisely *not* our own; from behavior so subjectively determined there's no path back unless we are prepared to imitate it, and to imitate it in the same external situation, in order to discover *what it does to us*. This world, so full, is that way empty; we therefore fill it with our feeling. However strange the acts, the age, the characters have no other souls than those the readers give them. Identification, on such grounds, is inevitable and easy.[2]

We accompany a character as he leaves his house to enter a street. Hoofs ring on the cobbles, carts creak, vendors cry their wares. In Singer these sounds are never sounds *in* anyone. They are objects which we come upon impersonally; they are therefore as much ours as the character we are

---

[2] Thus we infer feelings in characters as we infer them in our friends, and the more we perceive them from the outside (like our friends), the easier this is to do. The illusion of "life" produced is not always desirable. See "The Concept of Character in Fiction."

following. Water puddles, shadows gather, snow falls: these details are not selected in deference to a consciousness. Thoughts are given words, devils materialize psychology, or we read journals, letters, and diaries which do. Decay within, like the portrait of Dorian Gray, manifests itself conveniently in drooping eyes and sallowness, wrinkles, weight, complexion, posture, loss of hair. The ritual bath is neglected; a man fouls his mouth with less than purely kosher food, or buys new shoes and shaves his beard. Singer empties out the mind the way small boys turn out their pockets.

Here's the Warden, undertaken by Trollope:

> Mr. Harding is a small man, now verging on sixty years, but bearing few of the signs of age; his hair is rather grizzled, though not grey; his eye is very mild, but clear and bright, though the double glasses which are held swinging from his hand, unless when fixed upon his nose, show that time has told upon his sight; his hands are delicately white, and both hands and feet are small; he always wears a black frock coat, black knee-breeches, and black gaiters, and somewhat scandalises some of his more hyperclerical brethren by a black neck-handkerchief.

Notice how vague and diffident this description is. Mr. Harding is *verging* on sixty years; his hair is *rather* grizzled; he *somewhat* scandalizes *some* of his hyperclerical brethren. Despite their purposiveness, "black" and "small" are repeated wearily. Almost nothing gets said that isn't nervously retracted: "though" and "but" are frequent. Trollope composes in precisely similar breaths; "and" (that empty conjunction) often serves him; "is" and "are" (the simplest and most passive of connectives) everywhere prevail; and the whole paragraph, in consequence, is slow. Slack writing and amphibolous construction reinforce these impressions in an undesirable way. Trollope characteristically works with externals, yet we can ask why this passage lacks any vigorous externality.

Normally we see things swiftly, in a single act of vision; we see grizzled Mr. Harding, we don't see Harding, then his hair, and finally that same hair's grizzled ratherness. Nor do we see a somewhat, unless there's fog. On camera, hands aren't delicately white, then small; they're small, white, delicate—at once. *Noticing*, however, is another matter. We may notice, first, the whiteness of the hands, and then in a moment also realize they're small; but noticing is a subjective act, and requires the selective operations of a mind. Mr. Harding is given his properties very sedately indeed, as though in thought, not observation. Really, the Warden isn't here, standing like a Christmas tree about to be hung with baubles. He's off in Barchester somewhere, doubtless, fulfilling his moral resolves. Presently, he is being *remembered*. We are not permitted to infer, either, that age has affected Mr. Harding's sight; we are told. We're also informed of something we might not have inferred: that his black neckhandkerchief has scandalized some of his brethren. This fact carries, in addition, the implication that the scandalized are hyperclerical. Obviously, the mind which Mr. Harding's dimly filtering through is Trollope's.

Now let Singer introduce Rabbi Benish:

> Rabbi Benish was in his sixties, but his skin was still smooth, he had lost none of his white hair, and his teeth had not fallen out. When he crossed the threshold of the prayer house for the first time after many years—tall, big-boned, with a full, round, curly beard, his satin coat reaching to the ground, the sable hat pulled down over his neck—all those

sitting there rose and pronounced the blessing in thanks to Him who revives the dead. For there had been reports that Rabbi Benish had perished in Lublin during the massacres on the eve of the Festival of Tabernacles in the year 1655. The fringes of the vest that Rabbi Benish wore between his shirt and coat tumbled around his ankles. He wore short white trousers, white stockings, and half-shoes. Rabbi Benish grasped between his index finger and thumb the thick eyebrow that hung over his right eye, lifted it the better to see, cast a glance at the darkened, peeling walls of the prayer house and its empty book chests, and loudly declared: "Enough! . . . It is the will of our blessed God that we begin anew."[3]

The Rabbi is soon in motion, and the passive verbs of linking are soon replaced with far more active ones, or they're eliminated in favor of direct qualification. The Rabbi is busy: he crosses a threshold, he grasps, he lifts, he glances, he declares. His qualities also behave; they act or suffer action. His satin coat reaches, his hat's pulled down, the fringes of his vest tumble, even his eyebrows hang. His unmoving teeth and hair are said *not* to have fallen out. The scene is clear, animated, and nowhere darkened by the presence of mind.

Now for something else. Gradgrind has just informed us that what he wants is facts.

The scene was a plain, bare, monotonous vault of a schoolroom, and the speaker's square forefinger emphasized his observations by underscoring every sentence with a line on the schoolmaster's sleeve.

[3] Of course my comments on this passage, as well as my remarks about Singer throughout, are based upon the appearance of his books *in English*. Of their nature in another language I have nothing to say.

The emphasis was helped by the speaker's square wall of a forehead, which had his eyebrows for its base, while his eyes found commodious cellarage in two dark caves, overshadowed by the wall. The emphasis was helped by the speaker's mouth, which was wide, thin, and hard set. The emphasis was helped by the speaker's voice, which was inflexible, dry, and dictatorial. The emphasis was helped by the speaker's hair, which bristled on the skirts of his bald head, a plantation of firs to keep the wind from its shining surface, all covered with knobs, like the crust of a plum pie, as if the head had scarcely warehouse-room for the hard facts stored inside. The speaker's obstinate carriage, square coat, square legs, square shoulders—nay, his very neckcloth, trained to take him by the throat with an unaccommodating grasp, like a stubborn fact, as it was—all helped the emphasis.

Trollope's description has no shape; Singer's hasn't either. On his Dickens has imposed a rhetorical scheme which, conforming so perfectly to its content, has reshaped the "facts" (so hard for Gradgrind, so soft for Dickens) to give them feeling. Gradgrind takes his qualities from the air; sound itself has greatly helped to create him, especially the hissing *s*, and this has fastened him firmly in his medium—language—where he belongs. Metaphors play over Gradgrind like psychedelic lights. In short, where Singer has seen and Trollope remembered, Dickens has imagined; for it is the imagination which has made this masterful paragraph.

When Dickens' creatures speak, subjectivity flows as from a tap into the world: personal, poetic, unique; their talk is testimony, and a pure quality of soul. For Singer, speech is an act like tugging at one's beard. Announcement, it's something solely to be heard. "Gold, gold, gold," cries a seller of oranges. "Brothers, we are lost. Let us blaspheme God," says a horse dealer. "What is there to forgive? You have been a good and faithful wife," declares Gimpel the fool. The characters think, of course, but their thought is only reported to us; we don't see the process; we are handed careful sums. They lust; they fear; they wonder: all of which means that in very specified ways, they behave.

In a world where everything has a proper name and address in objective space, one might suppose a radical particularity was possible—not only possible, but necessary. Not quite. First of all, by simple mortals, such a world cannot be *seen*. We can only pretend it's there. We can only pretend to perceive like machines. Our observations do particularize, but they do so because we bring to them ourselves, our minds, our personal concerns. A God who has complete detachment might be able to do it. Gods, then—or machines. Yet language is a scarcely kettled stew of universals and universal connectives. The unique is not very easily rendered in its terms. And faithful to his method, Singer does not particularize, he *names;* the names form lists: lists of properties, of acts and objects.

> [An imp is hiding in a mirror] . . . my little charmer suspected nothing. She stroked her left breast, and then her right. She looked at her belly, examined her thighs, scrutinized her toes. Would she read her book? trim her nails? comb her hair?

It's these collections which are unique, not the things in them.

> [The imp wonders.] Should I seduce a rabbi's daughter? deprive a bridegroom of his manhood? plug up the synagogue chimney? turn the Sabbath wine into vinegar? give an elflock to a virgin?

enter a ram's horn on Rosh Hashana? make a cantor
hoarse?

Our sense of the uniqueness of any act or object described
depends entirely on our sense of the uniqueness of the
sentences comprising the description—i.e., their form. They
cannot be merely unique in the story, they must be unique
in the language. To say that someone—Ginger—went in
and out of her house as though in a dream does not particularize her action very much. To say that Ginger's house
went in and out of *her* does, and not only because such
things don't happen very often. Coats regularly reach, but
how often has a neckcloth been trained to take its wearer
by the throat? Dickens has made Gradgrind real, in this
sense, within a page. Another writer may need an outlined
life, a book. But we shall still feel strangely distant from him
in that case, because his *distinct* presence has never, at any
point, been felt. Singer's fiction is weak in this respect, and
necessarily so, for his world does not permit the easy exercise
of the relevant techniques: he cannot interiorize, he dare not
distort or pattern too much (the public world remains
anonymous), he leans heavily on impersonal, though significant, rituals, on items equally objective for everyone, and
so he must use striking lists, rely on imps and devils of all
kinds. We've seen many beards, but not so many cloven
hoofs. Indeed, the moment the minions of Satan stir, the style
rises with new heat to meet them.

You simply can't have everything. One method may de-
prive you of another. Joyce could never accomplish, though
he uses up a city of details, Singer's fine solidity. James's
characters are singularly vaporous, remarkable balloons
whose skins are weightless and invisible.

Many of Singer's short stories are told in the first person.

The Shut-In

We know that the speaker is Jewish, but the voice is customarily noncommittal, the voice of the chronicler, the voice of tradition, a chorus for the community. It allows itself from time to time a conventional sentiment, a little awe or wonder, worried warding-off. ("God forbid it should happen to any of us.") Only the demons are permitted a personality. They are always up to mischief, of course, and consequently they never see with the machine's divine neutrality. They are selfish, partial, and they tell us more plainly than anyone else how they feel. They are, in fact, entirely human. Subjectivity, perhaps, is the devil's true property. The last demon, in the story of that name, has a character distinctly his own, and Dickens might have made him. Almost. An important exception is Gimpel, God's fool. He speaks with an imp's cheery tone though he's not as wise. Always, imps *know*. He is devoted to his wife although she's whorish and cheats on him continually. For her he steals "macaroons, raisins, almonds, cakes." For us, he makes lists to prove his feelings:

> I loved the child madly, and he loved me too.
> As soon as he saw me he'd wave his little hands
> and want me to pick him up, and when he was
> colicky I was the only one who could pacify him.
> I bought him a little bone teething ring and a little
> gilded cap.

Gimpel does not differ a bit from the demon in this need to establish behavioral proof: "I eat dust. I sleep on a feather duster. I keep on reading gibberish."

Gimpel is God's fool because he still believes in devils, dreams, and fairies. He can be tempted by one to put a stream of his pee in the bread dough, but he can be persuaded by another to bury what he's baked. The rabbi whom the last demon fails to lure toward sin does not wrestle with his conscience and then win; he asks instead to see his tempter's feet. The coming world is one where demons will not ply their trade because the people there, having taken evil *in*, can sin very well without them. "Satan has cooked up a new dish of kasha." It's called enlightenment:

> The Jews have now developed writers. Yiddish ones, Hebrew ones, and they have taken over our trade. We grow hoarse talking to every adolescent, but they print their kitsch by the thousands and distribute it to Jews everywhere. They know all our tricks—mockery, piety. They have a hundred reasons why a rat must be kosher. All that they want to do is redeem the world.

In the role of Messiah. In a world without God all is fallen; there is no one—nothing—to seduce. No, subjectivity is not the devil's bailiwick, after all. And in a brilliant and bitter passage, put in the mouth of the final demon, Singer tells us why he prefers to remain shut in the old ways like leaves closed between the covers of a holy book:

> There are no more Jews, no more demons. The women don't pour out water any longer on the night of the winter solstice. They don't avoid giving things in even numbers. They no longer knock at dawn at the antechamber of the syna-gogue. They don't warn us before emptying the slops. . . . The *Book of Creation* has been returned to the Creator. Gentiles wash themselves in the ritual bath. . . . There is no longer an Angel of Good nor an Angel of Evil. No more sins, no more temptations! The generation is already guilty seven times over, but Messiah does not come. To whom should he come? Messiah did not come for

the Jews, so the Jews went to Messiah. There is
no further need for demons. . . . I am the last, a
refugee. I can go anywhere I please, but where
should a demon go? To the murderers?

This demon lives at last only on a Yiddish book. He swallows the letters. The book itself is written in the manner of the moderns. "The moral of the book is: neither judge nor judgment." But the letters are still old-fashioned—some nourishment in them. And when the demon has sucked the substance from them, what then? will that be the end of him? will he die of uselessness and hunger, driven from his function the way the motored carriage drove the horse? He seems to think so, but we who've read his author know his outlook better. There's a new life waiting for him in these novels and these stories. However, he will have to make some slight adjustments. He will have to consent to live forever in a fiction. As for the rest of us, we readers, fallen Jew or faithless gentile: well, Isaac Bashevis Singer can be rabbi, if he wishes, for us all.

PART THREE

A SPIRIT IN SEARCH OF ITSELF

He spent half his life in carriages, buttoned into boats and trains. Days passed like railway windows. "Every state of the soul was a landscape," his friend Flournoy said. Thus he changed—by drifting his location. Awareness was a river. Ideas, feelings had no edges, wore themselves away in one another, not unlike a married couple. Indeed, reality might be a sea, and from time to time a high wave lift a spirit like a nonplussed fish into the part we were a simple cup of. Nonetheless, consciousness was merely action on its way to action; an American traveler on a purchased tour, moving to move, having *been* in order —farther and farther—to *be*. But William James switched his images as he switched his means of transportation. First experiences blazed trails, he insisted. Trails were attractive and tended to be trod. Habits were such neural paths, and we should be especially mindful of our young, and carefully choose their first impressions. One cannot say that William's first impressions were not chosen. His father was never "unmindful," never, alas, unconcerned. He was, instead, a soft tyrannical improver, the sort who pats the pillow next to him in the sun and firmly says: I think it would be better for you over *here*. But thought was far too stimulating for him, turned his head, and the family's path, in those earlier years, resembled a whimsical ricochet. Purposefully, Henry senior shook the tree, and the fruit fell at random.

Do not allow your children to "be torn up by the roots every little while as we were," Alice wrote her brother later, when he contemplated carting them abroad. "Of all things don't make the mistake which brought about our rootless and accidental childhood." She spoke with some feeling, for their father had removed them from their home, school, locality, and even country of residence as readily and as often as he had replaced their nurse or governess or tutor (until each child was only, as William said of Henry, a "native of the James family"), and since William was right about first impressions, at least as far as they concerned himself, he could not follow his sister's advice. What had begun as a purely geographical zigzag had, by then, become a troublesome vacillation of will and a powerful restlessness of spirit.

All the Jameses bore the marks of movement, in some ways William most. "Experience" was a holy verb, his books its conjugation, and few men have been more willing than he was to entertain the new, the fresh, outrageous—and among ideas, the lonely. His "sensuous education," as his father put it, was remarkably complete at an early age. Except for the dark area of sexuality, he was overexposed. His spirit complained by tormenting its body. He suffered from backaches, eye trouble, stomach upsets, seasickness, fevers, melancholia, neurotic indecisions and debilities, insomnia, mania, and a sort of pacing, zooish irritability. For some of these ills even advancing age, an enlarged liberty, successful work and marriage, appreciation—fame—brought no re-mission. He was a James. His father had permitted every-thing but childhood. Though the boys argued brilliantly at table and Father was charmingly, if destructively, eccentric, an amateur at everything—spiritual, severe, and analytic—his wife ruled a household described by a Cabot as stiff, stupid, poky, and banal.

The older children's backs ached because of the load they bore. William knew his soul was sick. He wanted desperately an ardent heart, a healthy mind. It would require an enor-mous effort, but an effort not impossible. "I may not study, make, or enjoy—but I can will." After all, Will was his name. As a young man he began by expelling certain thoughts he felt were poisoning him. He began at the same time to believe in positive, useful, life-enhancing things . . . in the freedom of that will, for instance, so necessary to the whole performance. "My first act of free will shall be to believe in free will." "I will go a step further with my will, not only act with it, but believe as well; believe in my indi-vidual reality and creative power." James was not, though sometimes he seems, the sweaty director of a YMCA. It is easy to trivialize him. He was, it must be said, despite his scientific training, his respect for experience, his resolute facing-up to life, wondrously innocent, enormously naïve. In a way he was a great man because of the innocence and naïveté he retained, since it enabled him to act, to be gen-erous and kind, to will and continue willing a better world despite all the evidence of its unredeemable evil (which he saw and to a degree understood and accepted). Just as he had tried to fashion a finer climate for his soul from the very winds and lightning of its storms. There is something foolish in that, and something sublime . . . something miraculous, too—for he succeeded.

Professor Gay Wilson Allen, whose biography of Walt

Whitman, another democratic pluralist and professional naïf, was quite properly admired when it appeared about ten years ago, has certainly done as well again with *William James*. He does not so obviously dote upon his subject; he does not struggle to convince; he does not heap his man with praise. Nor does he endeavor to give extended accounts of the philosopher's ideas. These discretions, I believe, were wise. Wisest of all, perhaps, was his decision (I think of it as that) to write his history in the tongue of James. There is no more sensitive, resonant, or lively language. Father, the older boys, and Alice (then later William's wife, an Alice, too) wrote and spoke and spoke and wrote—spoke of their writing and wrote of their speaking—with an energy which would weary the rest of us merely to measure. Each voice has its own sound, and each has an enviable range and honesty of feeling. Each hand is as equal to fact as to phrase, and the family style raises over everything it touches that whole heaven of wit and nearly palpable reflection which is the plainest mark of the family's genius.

Mr. Allen's own conjectures are modest. He hides himself in his arrangements. Thus this history of a James is not so redolent with reference nor so warm with suggestion (Henry might have said) as it might have been, but it is more appropriate to its man for that restraint, and Mr. Allen's careful splicing of quotations into his own considerable account to form one rich and smoothly flowing narrative must be admired by all who have ever attempted the same. Especially, it seems to me, he succeeds in rendering that particular American condition in his subject which Henry called his brother's "Williamacy of mind."

William's career is instructive. He begins as a student of painting. However, apart from his mediocre talent, he was psychologically unsuited to it. Paintings sit still in their frames, colors persevere in their contours. He tries chemistry but that is insufficiently human. Anatomy, physiology, and medicine follow. At last he seems to settle in the country of the mind . . . there to establish Williamacy. In his great work on psychology, he turns out our heads as you'd turn out your pockets—loose change, door keys, cigarettes, a torn-up ticket, trouser lint—but if there's a contraceptive down there disguised as a coin, your fingers aren't going to fish for it. An unfair description. Still, in the two bulky volumes of *The Principles of Psychology* there is one small portion devoted to the sexual, and this is headed, demurely, LOVE. After a curious essay of a few pages on that instinct (we shrink from sex as much as we pursue it), James confesses: "These details are a little unpleasant to discuss." His interest in faith healers, mediums, and the spirit world later brought him to the brink of Freud, but inwardness was illness, and William, not about to peek over, backtracked quickly for a brisk workout in the gym.

Williamacy suggests the sovereign and the social. His brother's mind was not the same. It was downward, curly, Henryesque. "He and I are so utterly different in all our observances and springs of action, that we can't rightly judge each other," William said.[1] Perhaps it was a case of Shem the Penman, Shaun the Post. They did share an unremitting, almost puritanical, moral concern; a profound distrust of abstraction. Both placed an ultimate value on consciousness, and in consciousness had a preference for feeling. So they were blooms on the same plant, but otherwise their differences were many, important, and emblematic. Like diverging coordinates, they map our national space, and by finding our qualities on them, we fix our place.

[1] I discuss these differences again in "The High Brutality of Good Intentions" and "In the Cage."

William displays his inward life more readily than Henry, who was secretive and stoical. William weighted will and action, Henry sensibility and contemplation. William saw small point in custom, ritual, and history; he was democratic with people and opinions. Henry's books and body became the very books and body of tradition: stately, formal, courtly, and aristocratic. William perceived the value of quantity; he liked openness and health, *Gemütlichkeit* and hiking; life on the stretch. Henry valued contraction and focus; *his* tree grew its leaves on its roots. But William reached his peak in the *Psychology*, and afterward he could only broaden his experience, visit ideas, give expression to his kindness, his tolerance, his human concerns; for the illness which drew him to the medicine of the mind in the first place, one suspects, would tolerate no underlooking; the habits of his life permitted seeing far and wide, not seeing deep.

After a life lived uneasily among his nerves, William receives a real wound. He strains his heart. Mr. Allen's story of those final years, last days, is extremely moving. William's wife, Alice, is eloquent and brave. William remains restless; is given to suicidal hiking in hills, physically hunting an unphysical cure. A cure. In *The Varieties of Religious Experience* he also sought a cure. And his description of these spiritual conditions is no way short of beautiful. But he never finds what he wants: a mental medicine for mental discomfort, an idea which will work like a drug, beliefs you can swallow with the will. He thought that spirits, if there were any—those striking intruders—lived like the Lapps in lands just beside us, so if we boarded a boat, or merely rounded the right corner, we might bump into them. His sister Alice growled to her diary: "I suppose the thing 'medium' has done more to degrade the spiritual conception than the grossest forms of materialism or idolatry: was there ever anything transmitted but the pettiest, meanest, coarsest facts and details: anything rising above the squalid intestines of human affairs?"

In Rye, Henry and William fall ill together, and William's wife mothers both selflessly. Nevertheless, everyone travels, in transit to the end. The group returns to America, where William dies. "No pain at the last and no consciousness," Alice writes. "Poor Henry, poor children." No consciousness. No change. A cure at last.

IN THE CAGE

From Rye, where he has taken up residence in Lamb House, Henry James wires to London: "Are you utterly absent or can you dine with me Friday at seven to go afterwards with three others to the theatre?" James has passed his pale bescribbled paper across the counter toward the visible half of the clerk; he has paid, and paid by the word (a fact which could not fail to impress an author, since it was so perfectly the reverse of his own manner of making a living); he has pondered, as he had more than once before, the exposure of his message to a stranger, and wondered at the clerk's opportunities to observe and construe these brief pieces of privacy.

The clerks, it seemed to him, were quite closed in, enmeshed; they worked in every way in narrow quarters, inconveniently cornered in some conveniently local grocery; their relation to the public was wholly disinterested and practical; and yet they were in possession of so many bits of the public's personal property, bits usually of the better off who lived in a wider, freer world, presumably, than these servants who handled their telegrams did, that the novelist could not help but inquire of himself just what they made of these messages; or rather, what, if the right consciousness were caught in such a cage, it might compose from the words slid over the counter, the sounds sent out on the wire.

No doubt it is important to consider why Henry James was so predisposed to see his small scene in this way rather than in some other, but the reasons are not difficult to find. The arts of conversation which his circle cultivated were, in great part, the gossipaceous arts: that of making much out of little, of displaying your wit and inventive facility, your ability to amuse, without boring your listeners with too many ideas, or unpleasantly stretching their minds on the rack of an "issue." It was a world which took an intense but mainly anecdotal interest in people, and which was therefore also on its guard against just the same exposure of itself which it so assiduously sought to gain against others.

Telegrams often had that quality of being cryptic and secret, and certainly, from the clerk's station, had to seem like the shards from vessels which in their wholeness could never be observed. Henry James could not fail to see here another instance of a parallel he had drawn several times already, and was to draw again, to draw out even to infinity in *The Sacred Fount*: the ultimate worthlessness of the social exchanges he regularly participated in, the weak and unreal interest of people in one another, the guarded, protective nature of their social speech, and the greed of the novelist for the same material—the need in that role to reach through and beyond all tea talk to the selves it hid, to whatever real life moved like the mole was believed to somewhere beneath the softly raised and silently shoveled foothills of its passage.

Almost the first thing that strikes us about this professional

William H. Gass

London stroller, country-house visitor, and dinner guest, this
diligent cyclist, tourist, and correspondent, is his passion
for epistemology, his habitual self-conscious sense of standpoint: both his moral and esthetic sensibilities are dependent
on it, and his style, his rich metaphorical manner of seeing,
continually reflects it.[1] Rootless from the beginning, in his
world but never of it (the whole James family suffered
from motion sickness),[2] he lives in London as one lives on
a ledge . . . where it is always dangerous to be unaware. To
reach out, belong to, touch—how important this is to him;
but he must be satisfied to confer embraces on his friends
as though he were granting degrees, to buss both cheeks in
the continental manner, to command his friend Fullerton,
"Hold me then . . . with any squeeze; grip me with any
grip; press me with any pressure; trust me with any trust,"
to wire his friends to visit him at Lamb House, or to cry,
"lean on me as on a brother and a lover," in his letters to
the young sculptor Andersen.

> The port from which I set out was, I think, that
> of the *essential loneliness of my life*. . . . This
> loneliness . . . what is it still but the deepest thing
> about one? Deeper, about *me*, at any rate, than
> anything else; deeper than my "genius," deeper
> than my "discipline," deeper than my pride, deeper,
> above all, than the deep counterminings of art.

So he interrogates sailors; he cycles, strolls, takes tea; he
moves his eyes in search of images, and what he must overcome, in his elaboration of them, is their own inherent as-
ifness, of which he is deeply suspicious. "You see too much,"
Mrs. Briss tells the narrator of *The Sacred Fount*. "You talk

---

[1] This relationship and its expression in James's style is the subject of
"The High Brutality of Good Intentions."
[2] See the piece on William: "A Spirit in Search of Itself."

too much. . . . You're abused by a fine fancy. . . . You build up houses of cards." Any part of life which can't be directly rendered must be inferred, and when all that is seen are mated pairs of boots and shoes in "promiscuous hotel doorways" (as James remarked when writing of D'Annunzio), one is very much tempted, defensively, to say:

> Detached and unassociated these clusters of objects present, however obtruded, no importance. What the participants do with their agitation, in short, or even what it does to them, *that* is the stuff of poetry, and it is never really interesting save when something finely contributive in themselves makes it so.

Participants? agitations? Mr Edel thinks this statement very wise, but I think it's evasive bunk, and I think James, in the depths of his loneliness, knew it. The exact sensuous feel of things was something, on occasion, he expressed a clear desire and even a preference for:

> He wanted the hour of the day at which this and that had happened, and the temperature and the weather and the sound, and yet more the stillness, from the street, and the exact look-out, with the corresponding look-in, through the window and the slant on the walls of the light of afternoons that had been.

Participants? agitations? Clever, social, down-the-nose words. These agitations frequently affect the spirit precisely because they are so often so simple and complete in themselves, because they possess so much intrinsic interest, so much forgetfulness of self, because they are so remorselessly *physical*. Spiritual signs are very fine but boots are better evidence. Nor can we reason from effect to cause, as Hume observed, except on the basis of constant conjunction. This look-out, with its corresponding look-in, James seems never to have sufficiently had, and there is more of mystery and evil than eagerness and glee in the inferences he draws. The shoes may be real but ghosts roll on the bed. *The Awkward Age? What Maisie Knew? The Sacred Fount? The Turn of the Screw?* Throughout this volume, too,[3] "The grey years gather; the arid spaces lengthen, damn them!" Art, pride, discipline, genius . . . *In the Cage* . . .

Where Mr. Edel is now, receiving the many messages of Henry James. They are hardly telegrams; on the other hand, they are hardly revelations either—cryptic in their very completeness, deviously shaped. More than a million words hem him in: novels, stories, notebooks, letters, plays, critical essays and travelogues, reminiscences by both the subject and his friends—countless testimonies of all kinds—the debris of a wholly literary life; yet he must imagine more than he can see, feel further than he has felt, deduce the kernel from the shell: clarify, interpret, rearrange. Mr. Edel cannot close his ears, as James did, when the anecdote becomes long; he must employ "the common lens of history," for his subject is finally inert, famously dead, a choice piece of the past. The novelist is henceforth (and how he would be horrified to hear it) fair game; where once one might have thought to "hunt him up" in London or at Rye, now he must, it seems, be "hunted down" in five volumes of a life which bears his name as a monument might . . . as, for example, Grant's Tomb or the Lincoln Tunnel.

Mr. Edel tells us that *In the Cage*, which was the first story Henry James wrote after he moved to Rye, was created "out of immediate emotion." Immediate emotion is a condition Mr. Edel is all too eager to believe in, and it leads him

---

[3] *Henry James: The Treacherous Years 1895–1901*, by Leon Edel (New York: Lippincott, 1969).

to suggest that the tale reflects its author's sense of "isolation from his clubs and the murmurs of London society." The trouble is that it reflects the opposite if anything. The distance in this story is an economic one. James, for a change, is on the other side of the wire, handing messages *in*, and although his heroine is customarily full of conjecture, the weight of this small novel falls elsewhere.

> What could still remain fresh in her daily grind was the immense disparity, the difference and the contrast, from class to class, of every instant and every motion. . . . What twisted the knife in her vitals was the way the profligate rich scattered about them, in extravagant pleasures and sins, an amount of money that would have held the stricken household of her frightened childhood . . . together for a lifetime.

James may be missing the pleasures of London—certainly he is telegraphing, issuing invitations—but his sense of himself and the price of his pleasures is far from comfortable. In fact, one of the more important customers is called Lord Rye.

Of course, Mr. Edel does not miss the economic motif, but as a biographer he does not wag James's tale this way; his method is so narrowly "psychological" that the actual psychology of his subject frequently escapes him, and he is often so intent on fastening James's feelings and behavior to the distant past, interpreting any story to which his history has risen in terms of ground floor and basement (as if the clearest explanation of the French Revolution could be found in the character of Charlemagne), that he skips every floor in between—an omission which seems all the stranger when he has troubled, before, to give a lengthy description of each of them.

But these numerous details of day to day seem for the

most part not to count; instead, to a frame formed in childhood, life is seen to administer a few powerful and wrench-
ing shocks: the Miss Woolson affair, for instance (described
in the preceding volume), or the disasters of *Guy Domville*,
the upsetting heartsickness of his brother, William, or an
uncommonly warm and physical feeling for a sculptor half
his age; and certainly it would be wrong not to measure
such shocks, to graph the depth and duration of their shake,
but what we tend to lose with such a stress on traumas is
any feel for the weight of the ordinary, any sense of the
accretions or the erosions of every day, the impact on the
camel of each added straw, or the strength of the back each
threatens to break. Sibling rivalries, castration complexes,
homosexual tendencies, oedipal longings: these are common,
we may suppose, to many men, none of whom possesses the
style and the mind of this master; they tell us too little, and
even in one life make our explanations increasingly monotonous and empty; since what is any life, from this point of
view, but a repeating pattern of family relations, one where
every war is the first war refought? so that the answers to
our whys have a persistent dull sameness: basement, basement, basement.

Should James have had a biographer at all (especially one
so impressive as Mr. Edel, who must be measured against the
best) if he had not written novels? James captured no
castles, laid waste no countrysides (though in the next volume he will motor through them—we must wait for that);
his audience was always modest, often bewildered, soft and
mannerly with its applause. Thus he made no fortune, sailed
no steam yacht à la Arnold Bennett, nor authored an important column for the papers; he never fought with strenu-
ous men, fish, or climates, nor escaped dramatically from
wrecked trains; he had no lurid love affairs which sent him

with a quip to sickness, jail, and death like Oscar Wilde; he altered public policies not a jot, had no famous enemies, engaged in no vulgar quarrels, and avoided Shaw's smart-aleck image altogether; he invented no new gadgets, made known no unknown territories, proposed no new philosophy, uncovered no new truths nor spoke with shocking candor about old ones, and could not bring himself to catch VD or take up drugs or die with panache—suicidally. He merely wrote his novels like the useless man he was, and what is striking about these if not their quality, their extraordinary refinement, their personality, their style? for they shimmer and stink of idleness and isolation, detachment and removal. In one sense he was simply a spy, his novels guessing games. And when he thought to venture into life he threw his pen at the stage. Periodically he would endeavor to be *base*, but he could not hear American spoken without pain, and he would persistently correct young ladies on their speech. What did he do, one wonders, to punish his erections? And he wrote, in effect, in his notebooks, that his study—not his bedroom, parlor, or garden—was the proper enclosure for his life. Here he prayed to his genius as one might to a muse, and the lines he put upon paper were the lines he chose for his face. The history of such a man must somehow contrive to be the history of his imagination—what feeds it, what it does with what it gains, how it embodies itself in its work—since his words were those servants who did his living for him; and consequently every sign of significant change in the nature of that imagination will mark an important moment in the life of its owner.

In the particular period covered by this volume (from the collapse, amid catcalls, of his play *Guy Domville* to the bodiless mysteries of *The Sacred Fount*, the leading edge of his later phase) two such changes occur, and one of these

Mr. Edel treats with wonderful understanding and completeness. James responds to every rebuff by becoming more artful and indirect, more difficult, circumspect, and delicate. To challenge his "manner" was to force him to choose it— to reaffirm all by redoubling everything; so that after his failure to be cheap and theatrical (while Wilde—well, it was hardly bearable—while Wilde and Pinero *scored*), he returns to his fiction determined to demonstrate his abilities as a dramatist in his own way.

Henceforth he will take charge of everything. Are directors uninstructable, actors hammy, settings vulgar, critics and audience dense? He replaces them all, including theater and curtain, with his own words, and makes of *The Awkward Age*, for instance, a novelized play—one perfectly performed and perfectly perceived . . . since performed and perceived *by him*. Much in life defeated Henry James, but because he was an artist of rare stubbornness and courage, he would not allow himself a loss on his chosen field.

In the middle of *Maisie*, so it is claimed, James began dictating to a typist, and the new method of materializing his thought at once altered his style. The event, however, is not of much importance to Mr. Edel, a page or two will do for it, and he is satisfied to repeat this customary glib explanation of James's later manner, possibly because he simply thinks it is correct, or because style (as a dominating feature of Henry James) interests him rather little. Yet it is inconceivable that an artist so careful even his extravagances were calculated could allow the machine he now dictated to to dictate to him. Once his hand was free of the pen, his mind simply flew in even more characteristic circles; his imagination was able, more directly, to manifest itself, and he began to brood upon his subjects as few writers have brooded, before or since. "I can be trusted, artless youth,"

James replied to Morton Fullerton, who had wondered about the effect of the typewriter, "not to be simplified by any shortcut or falsified by any facility." The imagination which now spoke out loud for itself was fully formed (it would not have spoken this way twenty years before), and could be relied on; the changes dictation might incline James toward were already being *willed*.

Themes, plots, subjects, givens—*those* Mr. Edel treats at length (indeed, he won't let them alone) because he believes, quite properly, I suppose, that they are significant psychologically; but they are also significant in other ways, and these get scant weight. James is distressed by the Wilde case for a number of reasons, as he is by the Dreyfus affair, but Mr. Edel is preparing us for James's strangely flavored letters to Andersen (on the principle, perhaps, of at least one "ah-ha!" per volume), so that we are never permitted to infer much more than that on most public questions James was admirably humane.

Although there is little religious feeling in him, there is much moral passion, and if James is puritanical, he is puritanical in a typically Henryesque fashion (what shocks him about Symonds is not the man's homosexuality, but his public proclamation of it); if his language is consistently condescending (Ford Madox Ford's friends used to excuse Ford by saying he would condescend to God if given the opportunity); if it is often prissily fastidious and circumloquacious, moving in a panic of discretion toward its subject with cautious little rushes and retreats like a squirrel approaching peanuts in an unfamiliarly scented hand; even if it tends to make everything over, give to everything the saving salt of Henry James; nevertheless, however deeply the outside is drawn in, the "great world" remains in essence as it is. The very words which often made his cage allowed him to escape from it, for his thoughts followed not their own bent but the convolutions of their object; he overcame his standpoint by recognizing so many of them, discovering such a multitude of sides and shades and variations, seeing (as he hoped and often bragged) "all round," that we are inclined to find him, in his faithfulness to people, situations, and human arrangements—in his habit of putting everything in an assayer's balance—overly mental; we find him, in short, as Mr. Edel frequently shows him to us: as driven by demons, personal chagrins, as taking and rendering mainly the landscape of his spirit, when in fact a good part of his best self is simply composed of the outside, "the other," the precisely observed; and his moral anger is directed at all those who infringe human freedom, who make pawns of people, who feast on the poor, the naïve, or the powerless, who use love to *use* (though these ethical matters Mr. Edel rarely mentions); and in those sentences which mark the movement of his mind, his steady shift of position and deepening of view, we ourselves can complain of being caught—caged—victimized. His sentences have such complex insides, they amaze, and we wonder if they have either end or purpose; if we shall ever emerge. The object we sought to have explained seems obscured by the explanation; it is no longer a scene we see, it is a sentence we experience.

Still this, after all, is art, and in James the art is urged upon us; it puts itself forward aggressively, as one nursing merit who has been so far insufficiently recognized. However, so is patience urged on us, and soundings—clear enunciation. Always vocal, a speaker's art from the first (one reason he may have been misled to the stage), his writing became frankly music of a slow and resonant sort; not merely baroquely decorated, but full of pauses—breaths—pauses for savoring, silences for listening and learning in, not simply hastening duncedly on. *In short, in fine,* he would say, before suspending himself like a spider from another length. Yet these lines, so full of after- and before-thought we wonder if the first thought's there, are absolutely necessary, for the first thought is often sentimental, operatic, as dreamy about life as the girl in the cage who cadged her romances from yellow-frocked novels. Undress his plots and what you'll find is naked melodrama, the raw material of a thousand "female" fictions, soft shapes for the lady books.

It is all the more a triumph over self, then, that his sentences should be, in the harshest contemporary sense, subversive: they undermine our eyes, they speak of values in the act of perishing; but, perhaps, since Mr. Edel's portrait on this point is faithful to the customary one, I am wrong to think of James in any social sense as a revolutionary. Perhaps he was simply gouty from rich foods and wine, a leisured parasite whose pen defended his person, who clicked his tongue at Symonds and the fate of poor Wilde, groaned nicely about Dreyfus although suffering the anti-Semitism of Bourget (in detesting anti-Semites, one should never exceed the polite), toured Italy to revive old "impressions," sold stories to pay for his house and servants, and shaved his beard one gay spring day to reappear young.

Because James's life had so little excitement, Mr. Edel appears to feel he should add some, arranging his work in short, easily swallowed chapters, beginning each dramatically, and striking a portentous note at the end. The devices are without exception cheap; they come straight from bad novels; and they tell us more about Mr. Edel's attitude toward his subject than anything else, for they invariably falsify for the sake of a small effect, a tiny *frisson*. There are also innumerable variations on "little did he know then that . . . " or "having endured X, he was now ready to write Y," and so on.

The prefatory remarks Mr. Edel makes about his method seem both inconsistent in themselves and inconsistently followed in practice. Stressing the importance of Freud, Mr. Edel nevertheless says: "The physical habits of the creative personality, his 'sex life' or his bowel movements, belong to the 'functioning' being and do not reliably distinguish him from his fellow-humans." Why, if he wishes in any way to follow Freud, does he want to slight these "agitations"; why, if they are as slight as he claims, does he then drop broad hints about some of them on every other page; and why, if these things do not reliably distinguish James from his fellow-humans, does he expect other general unconscious patterns to do so? He complains that "Biography has for too long occupied itself with the irrelevancies of daily life . . ." yet his own account seems full of them. Mr. Edel wants to explain James's genius, to find the secret sources of his imagination, and about James he certainly explains a good deal; but the creature in Mr. Edel's cage is not, it seems to me, the golden singing bird. James says that the narrator of *The Sense of the Past*

> wanted the unimaginable accidents, the little notes of truth for which the common lens of history, however the scowling muse might bury her nose, was not sufficiently fine. He wanted evidence of a sort for which there had never been documents enough, or for which documents mainly, however multiplied, would never *be* enough.

Mr. Edel wants, that, too.

THE HIGH BRUTALITY OF
GOOD INTENTIONS

The great question as to a poet or a novelist is, How does he feel about life? what, in the last analysis, is his philosophy?

HENRY JAMES

Art, Yeats wrote in his essay on "The Thinking of the Body," "bids us touch and taste and hear and see the world, and shrinks from what Blake calls mathematic form, from every abstract thing, from all that is of the brain only, from all that is not a fountain jetting from the entire hopes, memories, and sensations of the body." Yet the world that we are permitted to touch and taste and hear and see in art, in Yeats's art as much as in any other, is not a world of pure Becoming, with the abstractions removed to a place safe only for philosophers; it is a world invested out of the ordinary with formal natures, with types and typicals, by abstractions and purest principles; invested to a degree which, in comparison with the real, renders it at times grotesque and always abnormal. It is charged with Being. Touching it provides a shock.

The advantage the creator of fiction has over the moral philosopher is that the writer is concerned with the exhibition of objects, thoughts, feelings, and actions where they are free from the puzzling disorders of the real and the need to come to conclusions about them. He is subject only to those calculated disorders which are the result of his refusal, in the face of the actual complexities of any well-chosen "case," to take a stand. The moral philosopher is expected to take a stand. He is expected to pronounce upon the principles of value.[1] The writer of fiction, insofar as he is interested in morals, rather than, for instance, metaphysics, can satisfy himself and the requirements of his art by the exposure of moral principle in the act, an exposure more telling than life because it is, although concrete, concrete in no real way—stripped of the irrelevant, the accidental, the incomplete—every bit of paste and hair and string part of the intrinsic nature of the article. However the moral philosopher comes by his conclusions, he does not generally suppose (unless he is also a theologian) that the world is ordered by them or that the coming together of feelings and intents or the issuance of acts or the flow of consequences, which constitute the moral facts, was designed simply in order to display them.[2]

It is the particular achievement of Henry James that he was able to transform the moral color of his personal vision into the hues of his famous figure in the carpet; that he found a form for his awareness of moral issues, an awareness that was so pervasive it invaded furniture and walls and ornamental gardens and perched upon the shoulders of his people a dove for spirit, beating its wings with the violence of all Protestant history; so that of this feeling, of the moving wing itself, he could make a *style*. This endeavor was both aided and hindered by the fact that, for James, art and

[1] Many contemporary philosophers feel that his function is to analyze meanings, not to discover or defend values. Some common defenses are discussed in "The Case of the Obliging Stranger."

[2] See "Philosophy and the Form of Fiction."

morality were so closely twined, and by the fact that no theory of either art or morality has footing unless, previous to it, the terrible difficulties of vision and knowledge, of personal construction and actual fact, of, in short, the relation of reality to appearance had been thoroughly overcome.[3] James's style is a result of his effort to master, at the level of his craft, these difficulties, and his effort, quite apart from any measure of its actual success with these things, brought to the form of the novel in English an order of art never even, before him, envisioned by it.

Both Henry James and his brother were consumed by a form of The Moral Passion. Both struggled to find in the plural world of practice a vantage for spirit. But William was fatally enmeshed in the commercial. How well he speaks for the best in his age. He pursues the saint; he probes the spiritual disorders of the soul; he commiserates with the world-weary and encourages the strong; he investigates the nature of God, His relation to the world, His code; he defends the possible immortality of the soul and the right to believe: and does all so skillfully, with a nature so sensitive, temperate and generous, that it is deeply disappointing to discover, as one soon must, that the lenses of his mind are monetary, his open hand is open for the coin, and that the more he struggles to understand, appreciate, and rise, the more instead he misses, debases, and destroys.[4]

> In the religion of the once-born the world is a sort of rectilinear or one-storied affair, whose accounts are kept in one denomination, whose parts have just the values which naturally they appear to have, and of which a simple algebraic sum of pluses and minuses will give the total worth. Happiness and

---

[3] See "In the Cage."
[4] See "A Spirit in Search of Itself" for more on William's character and his differences with Henry.

religious peace consist in living on the plus side of the account. In the religion of the twice-born, on the other hand, the world is a double-storied mystery. Peace cannot be reached by the simple addition of pluses and elimination of minuses from life. Natural good is not simply insufficient in amount and transient, there lurks a falsity in its very being. Cancelled as it all is by death if not by earlier enemies, it gives no final balance, and can never be the thing intended for our lasting worship.[5]

Even when William, in a passage not obviously composed with the bookkeeper's pen, makes a literary allusion, as here:

Like the single drops which sparkle in the sun as they are flung far ahead of the advancing edge of a wave-crest or a flood, they show the way and are forerunners. The world is not yet with them, so they often seem in the midst of the world's affairs to be preposterous . . .[6]

it turns out to be a covert reference to "getting and spending."

Henry James was certainly aware that one is always on the market, but as he grew as an artist he grew as a moralist and his use of the commercial matrix of analogy[7] became

[5] *The Varieties of Religious Experience* (New York: Modern Library), p. 163. God does a wholesale not a retail business, p. 484. The world is a banking house, p. 120. Catholic confession is a method of periodically auditing and squaring accounts, p. 126. Examples could be multiplied endlessly, not only in *The Varieties* but in all his work. In *The Varieties* alone consult pages: 28, 38, 39, 133, 134, 135, 138, 330, 331, 333, 340, 347, 429 n., 481, 482.

[6] *Ibid.*, p. 450.

[7] Mark Schorer's expression: "Fiction and the Matrix of Analogy," *The Kenyon Review*, XI, No. 4 (1949). The commercial metaphor pervades James's work and has been remarked so frequently that it scarcely requires documentation.

markedly satirical or ironic and his investigation of the human trade more self-conscious and profound until in nearly all the works of his maturity his theme is the evil of human manipulation, a theme best summarized by the second formulation of Kant's categorical imperative:

> So act as to treat humanity, whether in thine own person or in that of any other, in every case as an end withal, never as a means only.

Nothing further from pragmatism can be imagined, and if we first entertain the aphorism that though William was the superior thinker, Henry had the superior thought, we may be led to consider the final effect of their rivalry,[8] for the novels and stories of Henry James constitute the most searching criticism available of the pragmatic ideal of the proper treatment and ultimate worth of man. That this criticism was embodied in Henry James's style, William James was one of the first to recognize. "Your methods and my ideals seem the reverse, the one of the other," he wrote to Henry in a letter complaining about the "interminable elaboration" of *The Golden Bowl*. Couldn't we have, he asks, a "book with no twilight or mustiness in the plot, with great vigour and decisiveness in the action, no fencing in the dialogue, no psychological commentaries, and absolute straightness in the style?"[9] Henry would rather have gone, he replies, to a dishonored grave.

The Portrait of a Lady is James's first fully exposed case of human manipulation; his first full-dress investigation, at the level of what Plato called "right opinion," of what it

---

[8] Leon Edel develops this theme in the first volume of his biography: *Henry James: The Untried Years, 1834–1870* (Philadelphia: Lippincott, 1953).

[9] Quoted by R. B. Perry, *The Thought and Character of William James*, 2 vols. (Boston, 1935), I, 424.

means to be a consumer of persons, and of what it means to be a person consumed. The population of James's fictional society is composed, as populations commonly are, of purchasers and their purchases, of the handlers and the handled, of the users and the used. Sometimes actual objects, like Mrs. Gareth's spoils, are involved in the transaction, but their involvement is symbolic of a buying and a being sold which is on the level of human worth (where the quality of the product is measured in terms of its responsiveness to the purchaser's "finest feelings," and its ability to sound the buyer's taste discreetly aloud), and it is for this reason that James never chooses to center his interest upon objects which can, by use, be visibly consumed. In nearly all of the later novels and stories, it is a human being, not an object—it is first Isabel Archer, then Pansy—who is the spoil, and it is by no means true that only the "villains" fall upon her and try to carry her off; nor is it easy to discover just who the villains really are.

Kant's imperative governs by its absence—as the hollow center. It is not that some characters, the "good" people, are busy being the moral legislators of mankind and that the others, the "bad" people, are committed to a crass and shallow pragmatism or a trifling estheticism; for were that the case, *The Portrait* would be just another skillful novel of manners and James would be distinctly visible, outside the work, nodding or shaking his head at the behavior of the animals in his moral fable. He would have managed no advance in the art of English fiction. James's examination of the methods of human consumption goes too deep. He is concerned with all of the ways in which men may be reduced to the status of objects, and because James pursues his subject so diligently, satisfying himself only when he has unraveled every thread, and because he is so intent on avoiding in himself what he has revealed as evil in his characters and exemplifying rather what he praises in Hawthorne, who, he says, "never intermeddled,"[10] the moral problem of *The Portrait* becomes an esthetic problem, a problem of form, the scope and course of the action, the nature of the characters, the content of dialogue, the shape and dress of setting, the points-of-view, the figures of speech, the very turn and tumble of the sentences themselves directed by the problem's looked-for solution, and there is consequently no suggestion that one should choose up sides or take to heart his criticism of a certain society nor any invitation to discuss the moral motivations of his characters *as if* they were surrogates for the real.[11]

The moral problem, moreover, merges with the esthetic. It is possible to be an artist, James sees, in more than paint and language, and in *The Portrait*, as it is so often in his other work, Isabel Archer becomes the unworked medium through which, like benevolent Svengali, the shapers and admirers of beautifully brought out persons express their artistry and themselves. The result is very often lovely, but it is invariably sad. James has the feeling, furthermore, and it is a distinctly magical feeling, that the novelist takes possession of his subject through his words; that the artist is a puppeteer; his works are the works of a god. He constantly endeavors to shift the obligation and the blame, if there be any, to another: his reflector, his reverberator, his sensitive gong. In *The Portrait* James begins his movement toward the theory of the point-of-view. The phrase itself occurs incessantly. Its acceptance as a canon of method means the loss of a single, universally objective reality. He is com-

---

10 "Nathaniel Hawthorne," *The American Essays of Henry James,* ed. Leon Edel (New York: Vintage, 1956), p. 23.
11 See "The Concept of Character in Fiction."

mitted, henceforth, to a standpoint philosophy, and it would seem, then, that the best world would be that observed from the most sensitive, catholic, yet discriminating standpoint. In this way, the esthetic problem reaches out to the metaphysical. This marvelous observer: what is it he observes? Does he see the world as it really is, palpitating with delicious signs of the internal, or does he merely fling out the self-capturing net? James struggles with this question most obviously in *The Sacred Fount* but it is always before him. So many of his characters are "perceptive." They understand the value of the unmolded clay. They feel they know, as artists, what will be best for their human medium. They will *take up* the young lady (for so it usually is). They will *bring* her *out*. They will *do for* her; *make something of* her. She will be *beautiful* and *fine*, in short, she will inspire *interest*, *amusement*, and *wonder*. And their pursuit of the ideally refractive medium parallels perfectly Henry James's own, except he is aware that his selected lens dare not be perfect else he will have embodied a god again, and far more obnoxious must this god seem in the body of a character than he did in the nib of the author's pen; but more than this, James knows, as his creations so often do not, that this manipulation is the essence, the ultimate germ, of the evil the whole of his work condemns, and it is nowhere more brutal than when fronted by the kindest regard and backed by a benevolent will.

The Portrait of a Lady, for one who is familiar with James, opens on rich sounds. None of his major motifs is missing. The talk at tea provides us with five, the composition of the company constitutes a sixth, and his treatment of the setting satisfies the full and holy seven. The talk moves in a desultory fashion ("desultory" is a repetitive word) and in joking tones ("That's a sort of joke" is the repetitive phrase) from health and illness, and the ambiguity of its value, to boredom, considered as a kind of sickness, and the ambiguity of its production.[12] Wealth is suggested as a cause of boredom, then marriage is proposed as a cure. The elder Touchett warns Lord Warburton not to fall in love with his niece, a young lady recently captured by his wife to be exhibited abroad. The questions about her are: has she money? is she interesting? The jokes are: is she marriageable? is she engaged? Isabel is the fifth thing, then—the young, spirited material. Lord Warburton is English, of course, while the Touchetts are Americans. Isabel's coming will sharpen the contrast, dramatize the confrontation. Lastly, James dwells lovingly on the ancient red brick house, emphasizing its esthetic appeal, its traditions, its status as a work of art. In describing the grounds he indicates, too, what an American man of money may do: fall in love with a history not his own and allow it, slowly, to civilize him, draw him into Europe. Lord Warburton is said to be bored. It is suggested that he is trying to fall in love. Ralph is described as cynical, without belief, a condition ascribed to his illness by his father. "He seems to feel as if he had never had a chance." But the best of the ladies will save us, the elder Touchett says, a remark made improbable by his own lack of success.

The structure of the talk of this astonishing first chapter foreshadows everything. All jests turn earnest, and in them, as in the aimless pattern of the jesters' leisure, lies plain the essential evil, for the evil cannot be blinked even though it may not be so immediately irritating to the eye as the evil

[12] Illness, in James's novels, either signifies the beautiful thing (the Minny Temple theme) or it provides the excuse for spectatorship and withdrawal, the opportunity to develop the esthetic sense (the Henry James theme).

of Madame Merle or Gilbert Osmond. There is in Isabel herself a certain willingness to be employed, a desire to be taken up and fancied, if only because that very enslavement, on other terms, makes her more free. She refuses Warburton, not because he seeks his own salvation in her, his cure by "interest," but rather because marriage to him would not satisfy her greed for experience, her freedom to see and feel and do. Neither Warburton nor Goodwood appeals as a person to Isabel's vanity. She is a great subject. She will make a great portrait. She knows it. Nevertheless Isabel's ambitions are at first naïve and inarticulate. It is Ralph who sees the chance, in her, for the really fine thing; who sees in her his own chance, too, the chance at life denied him. It is Ralph, finally, who empowers her flight and in doing so draws the attention of the hunters.

Ralph and Osmond represent two types of the artist. Osmond regards Isabel as an opportunity to create a work which will flatter himself and be the best testimony to his taste. Her intelligence is a silver plate he will heap with fruits to decorate his table. Her talk will be for him "a sort of served dessert." He will rap her with his knuckle. She will ring. As Osmond's wife, Isabel recognizes that she is a piece of property; her mind is attached to his like a small garden plot to a deer park. But Ralph obeys the strictures *The Art of Fiction* was later to lay down. He works rather with the medium itself and respects the given. His desire is to exhibit it, make it whole, refulgent, round. He wants, in short, to make an image or to see one made—a portrait. He demands of the work only that it be "interesting." He effaces himself. The "case" is his concern. *The Portrait*'s crucial scene, in this regard, is that between Ralph and his dying father. Ralph cannot love Isabel. His illness prevents him. He feels it would be wrong. Nevertheless, he takes, he says, "a great interest" in his cousin although he has no real influence over her.

> "But I should like to do something for her. . . . I should like to put a little wind in her sails. . . . I should like to put it into her power to do some of the things she wants. She wants to see the world for instance. I should like to put money in her purse."

The language is unmistakable. It is the language of Iago. Ralph wants her rich.

> "I call people rich when they're able to meet the requirements of their imagination. Isabel has a great deal of imagination."

With money she will not have to marry for it. Money will make her free. It is a curious faith. Mr. Touchett says, "You speak as if it were for your mere amusement," and Ralph replies, "So it is, a good deal." Mr. Touchett's objections are serenely met. Isabel will be extravagant but she will come to her senses in time. And Ralph says,

> ". . . it would be very painful to me to think of her coming to the consciousness of a lot of wants she should be unable to satisfy. . . ."
> "Well, I don't know. . . . I don't think I enter into your spirit. It seems to me immoral."
> "Immoral, dear daddy?"
> "Well, I don't know that it's right to make everything so easy for a person."[13]
> "It surely depends upon the person. When the

13 A remark characteristic of the self-made man. In the first chapter, Mr. Touchett attributes Warburton's "boredom" to idleness. "You wouldn't be bored if you had something to do; but all you young men are too idle. You think too much of your pleasure. You're too fastidious, and too indolent, and too rich." Caspar Goodwood is the industrious suitor.

person's good, your making things easy is all to the credit of virtue. To facilitate the execution of good impulses, what can be a nobler act? . . ."

"Isabel's a sweet young thing; but do you think she's so good as that?"

"She's as good as her best opportunities. . . ."

"Doesn't it occur to you that a young lady with sixty thousand pounds may fall a victim to the fortune-hunters?"

"She'll hardly fall victim to more than one."

"Well, one's too many."

"Decidedly. That's a risk, and it has entered into my calculation. I think it's appreciable, but I think it's small, and I'm prepared to take it. . . ."

"But I don't see what good you're to get of it. . . ."

"I shall get just the good I said a few moments ago I wished to put into Isabel's reach—that of having met the requirements of my imagination. . . ."

The differences between Gilbert Osmond and Ralph Touchett are vast, but they are also thin.

Isabel Archer is thus free to try her wings. She is thrown upon the world. She becomes the friend of Madame Merle, "the great round world herself": polished, perfect, beautiful without a fault, mysterious, exciting, treacherous, repellent, and at bottom, like Isabel, identically betrayed; like Isabel again, seeking out of her own ruin to protect Pansy, the new subject, "the blank page," from that same round world that is herself. It is irony of the profoundest sort that "good" and "evil" in their paths should pass so closely. The dark ambitions of Serena Merle are lightened by a pathetic bulb, and it is only those whose eyes are fascinated and convinced by surface who can put their confident finger on the "really good." Ralph Touchett, and we are not meant to miss the appropriateness of his name, has not only failed to respect

Isabel Archer as an end, he has failed to calculate correctly the qualities of his object. Isabel is a sweet, young thing. She is not yet, at any rate, as good as her best opportunities. The sensitive eye was at the acute point blind. Ralph has unwittingly put his bird in a cage. In a later interview, Isabel tells him she has given up all desire for a general view of life. Now she prefers corners. It is a corner she's been driven to. Time after time the "better" people curse the future they wish to save with their bequests. Longdon of *The Awkward Age* and Milly Theale of *The Wings of the Dove* come immediately to mind. Time after time the better artists fail because their point-of-view is ultimately only *theirs*, and because they have brought the esthetic relation too grandly, too completely into life.

In the portrait of Fleda Vetch of *The Spoils of Poynton* James has rendered an ideally considerate soul. Fleda, a person of modest means and background, possesses nevertheless the true sense of beauty. She is drawn by her friend Mrs. Gareth into the full exercise of that sense and to an appreciation of the ripe contemplative life which otherwise might have been denied her. Yet Fleda so little awards the palm to mere cleverness or sensibility that she falls in love with the slow, confused, and indecisive Owen Gareth. Fleda furthermore separates her moral and her esthetic ideals. Not only does she refuse to manipulate others, she refuses, herself, to be manipulated. The moral lines she feels are delicate. She takes all into her hands. Everyone has absolute worth. Scruples beset and surround her and not even Mrs. Gareth's righteousness, the warmth of her remembered wrongs, can melt them through. The impatience which James generates in the reader and expresses through Mrs. Gareth is the impatience, precisely, of his brother: for Fleda to act, to break from the net of scruple and seize the chance. It would be for the good of the good. It would save the spoils, save

Owen, save Mrs. Gareth, save love for herself; but Fleda Vetch understands, as few people in Henry James ever do, the high brutality of such good intentions. She cannot accept happiness on the condition of moral compromise, for that would be to betray the ground on which, ideally, happiness ought to rest. Indeed it would betray happiness itself, and love, and the people and their possessions that have precipitated the problem and suggested the attractive and fatal price.

It is not simply in the organization of character, dialogue, and action that Henry James reveals The Moral Passion, nor is it reflected further only in his treatment of surroundings[14] but it represents itself and its ideal in the increasing scrupulosity of the style: precision of definition, respect for nuance, tone, the multiplying presence of enveloping metaphors, the winding around the tender center of ritual lines, like the approach of the devout and worshipful to the altar, these circumlocutions at once protecting the subject and slowing the advance so that the mere utility of the core is despaired of and it is valued solely in the contemplative sight.[15] The value of life lies ultimately in the experienced quality of it, in the integrity of the given not in the usefulness of the taken. Henry James does not peer through experience to the future, through his future to the future futures, endlessly down the infinite tube. He does not find in today only what is needful for tomorrow. His aim is rather to appreciate and to respect the things of his experience and to set them, finally, free.

[14] When, for instance, in *The Portrait* Gilbert Osmond proposes to Isabel, the furnishings of the room in which their talk takes place seem to Osmond himself "ugly to distress" and "the false colours, the sham splendour . . . like vulgar, bragging, lying talk"—an obvious commentary by the setting on the action.

[15] The ritual function of style is considered at length in "The Stylization of Desire."

THE STYLIZATION OF DESIRE

Why is it that philosophers have always felt obliged to think badly of the basic biological functions? They may believe in a life force; they may even applaud its ferocity; but they do not inquire whether it keeps its chin clean at table. It almost seems as if to come near the breathing, sweating, farting body were an unphilosophical act; and it is certainly true that although the philosopher frequently prefers to begin with some commonplace fragment of experience, ready enough to ponder the lessons of the spider or the problems of the sodden wax, as though to say: "Look, you think I deal with empty abstractions and make my thoughts fly off from daily life like a startled sparrow, but how unjust that is, for as you see I begin by considering the shape and color of this quite ordinary penny, the snowed-on blankness of this simple sheet of writing paper, the course these burning logs are taking, or even the existence of my own well-manicured hand"—he does not deceive us with these subterfuges, since we can also see how carefully he ignores the secretion of saliva, the shaping of dung in the lower intestine, the leap of sperm (indeed the whole history of that brazen nozzle), all our vague internal twinges, heart stops, and bellyaches, though distantly these things are made the subject of denigrating comparisons. Thus from Plato to Tolstoi philosophers have felt that to liken something to the art of cookery was better than an argument against it. Even when Epictetus advised us to behave in life as at a banquet, he did not mean "eat hearty"; he meant "be polite." Had they tongues of leather, these gentlemen (and they were all, all gentlemen), or was it rather that the needs we each share and must daily confess to are uninteresting, unromantic, unsuited to the royal aspirations of so head-proud an animal?

In the West man's sexuality was never the object of any important or prolonged philosophical study before Freud (in Plato, in Saint Augustine, and so on, there are brief sallies), yet of our fundamental occupations only something discreetly called "loving" has received much notice. The reason, I suspect, is that of the lot it is the only one which can be successfully prohibited, and the only one, therefore, it makes sense to condemn. The eighteenth-century version of human nature, for example, constructed with a Johnsonian sense of the decorous, was triumphantly shallow, and it is possibly for this reason that when Hume hunted through his own experience for that constant impression which might be identified as the source of the idea of the self, he never came upon his own breathing, traditionally identified with the soul, and whose regular, unobtrusive rhythms, like those of the heartbeat, accompany all our acts and feelings, and order and qualify them who knows how profoundly—just as profoundly, certainly, as the man whose experience of the world is always accompanied by the grinding of his teeth is affected by *that*.

The Stylization of Desire

We always ski on the higher slopes when we can. Count-less works of rich abstraction have been written about perception. I know none on the subject of chewing.

Now all of us have read of men, and some of us have even seen them—such are the chances for experience in our time—who were by want and ill condition returned into the animals they came from; who fought among themselves and rushed upon their meat (though it were rank, spat on, and cast before them in the dirt) with all the mindlessness of dogs; and it is distressing but necessary to observe that man-ners serve one badly in such circumstances, that civilization is an impediment to life—who holds to it will perish.

The happier case finds us at table. There is fresh water and wine at the points of our silver, and our eye considers whether the colors on the central platter are properly com-posed and if the sauces will be smooth and thoughtful. We listen to a ribald anecdote about Petronius from a scholar on our right, and wish the lady on our left had not employed so vulgar and insistent a perfume, it is ruining the bouquet of the food; and while we damn her in that moment as a savage only lately from the forest, to remember, then, the truly opposite condition I just mentioned is to realize that she has not forgotten her manners altogether, but has merely got her arts confused. Such are the vexations of a civilized existence.

Between these two extremes, as I should like to study them, lie all the stages that must be passed, all the conditions that must be met, if one is to leave one's place among the beasts to someone else. It is fundamentally a process of design, and the advantages of my central situation, as I perceive them, are that its lines are simpler and show them-selves more plainly than the lines of others; that concentrat-ing on the human stomach effectively removes the problem

of style, which is my real subject, from the preconceptions
and confusions that so muddle most examinations of it in the
major arts.

Desires, alas, do not contain their own fulfillment. There
is a necessary incompleteness in them. They must figure to
themselves some end which, lying public, they can reach
for, and in that effort they express themselves. At one end
there is feeling and sensation, hunger's pain and discontent
for instance, while at the other is the set of hunger's objects,
seen one by one and each by each as food, for no desire will
be so foolish as to feed upon a class and miss the nourishment of members. Desire upon its natural base is always general and can be said to have a general aim; we are hardly
born with a passion for cream puffs. Each need has an eye—
a principle—a set of marks—whereby it recognizes something as its own, and in this way desire defines its nature.
Simple hunger asks for any food and since the goal it posts is
broad, the means are many; but its pangs are pangs which
issue from the stomach and only through some great
maliciousness of nature can these signs be so confused that
hunger's pain or hunger's motions seem directed from the
throat or lungs or from the heart or bowels or from the
privy members, though such maliciousness is not unknown.

Suppose we ate through our anus and shat through our
mouth: how much of the world would be turned topsy-
turvy besides ourselves?

Hunger's purpose is to satisfy—that is, destroy—itself,
and it is a matter of the merest chance, to it, that sight and
smell are its most useful instruments, or that the stomach
must be filled through the mouth so that food finally happens on the palate (we can feed through our veins); but
when the desire for food is stylized, it is not hunger which
receives the elaboration, but these instrumental senses, these

accidental ones, and this is always true when a desire is shifted from its natural base and satisfied by symbolic actions. Thus there is a general movement toward sensation, concentrating first of all around the products of the act of eating, certain tastes and odors mainly, swallowing and chewing, and second around the signs of wanted objects, special sounds and colors. This movement, which I've chosen to call the displacement of desire from its natural base, and which is the ground of all such stylization, begins with the association of hunger with something formally higher, something otherwise than blind and random in its effort, something intrinsically aware. As the movement continues, this association becomes so intimate and necessary that, at the end, the values of eating are inverted, and one eats largely to produce a succession of agreeable sensations, and only incidentally, and regretfully, to fill the stomach.

The need for nourishment is very general, but it soon becomes precise. Precision in desire, like the association with it of sensations, defines a rarer, less attainable object, for the gourmet's hunger issues its commands no longer from the stomach, whose chemicals are perfectly indifferent to sauce mornay and truffled fowl, but from the tongue and lips and from the eye and nose, and finally, from imagination. The process whereby desire is made precise depends first of all upon the lessening of its strength through success, and second by the interruption of its haste by forcing choice upon it. The desperately hungry man finds his whole soul filled with pain and incompleteness, his body is aflail for food, every sense and every thought is lost but to that aim, and any object bearing the proper sign will be intently set upon and instantly consumed.

All discrimination thus demands a ground of satisfaction, a blunting of the edge of want which permits the exercise of choice and provides for the leisure of body and calmness of mind essential to contemplation. When rage retires, a man may understand his hate. When emotion leaves the eye, a man may see. So he may be able to express himself with style when the need to express himself at all has passed its adolescence. A man who must choose must reflect upon the nature of his wants and the power objects have to satisfy them. Finally some factor tips the scale, and that factor acts as the principle of preference. The original class of hunger's objects divides. Desires multiply. Where one object was before, soon there are a dozen, then a hundred, then a thousand, so that where the purely hungry man wished food, the mildly hungry man with choice considers vegetables and meats and fruits, considers soups and casseroles and stews, and in the object of each new desire may arrange all its probable representatives according to his preferences. The entire process of precision may be repeated for each fresh division and may continue until the object of each desire is perfectly precise: one individual thing.

The poor man has no such problems. He works; he grows hungry; he eats what he has. His interest in food is specific because his circumstances limit his opportunities. An economy which is devoted to the satisfaction of many, widely varied wants (and even to the manufacture of new ones) can easily be thought to be corrupting, as Tolstoi believed: the simple life of the peasant replaced by the temptations of the supermarket. What happens to the composer of simple tribal songs when set down in the middle of a modern music market? what happens to the painter locked in Malraux's wall-less museum? or the poet caught between the covers of some worldwide anthology? And will straightforward screwing sustain a man in a country where kinds of copulation are canned and merchandised as variously as peas, beans, and carrots are? Soon he will wonder: which brand? Poverty protects the simple man from sin—at least the sophisticated and expensive ones. So it has been frequently argued.

We cannot will an end, Kant said, unless we are prepared to will some way of achieving it, and he separated willing from wishing for us on that basis; for when I merely wish for something—as I might dream of owning a yacht one day or of having peace or marrying a movie star—it can be observed that I never take any effective steps to obtain it. Therefore when desire takes aim at its object, it takes aim also at some means, and the force it has for its object it has also for the means. If I want the bananas, which are yellowing on the tree, I want equally badly the stick which will knock them down. This energy, however—the measure of my need—since in its object it has a single end, and in the means generally a choice of many, cannot stake itself entirely upon one method and so preserve its purity and power, but it must hover, avoiding ultimate commitment, prepared to give way at one point to succeed at another. Stick or ladder, each will serve. I shall not insist on the stick when it is simply the bananas I want. The desire of the end is thus obtained for the means, but ordinarily the desire is disloyal, based upon pure utility.

The most important step in the stylization of desire, as in the stylization of anything whatever, is the amalgamation of a means with its end. This fastens the whole force of desire as firmly on the method as a leech on a leg. Success henceforth requires not only the enjoyment of the end but the use of one path to it. When I want the bananas only if they have been stick-struck; when I want money, power, and the love of women only because I'm the heavyweight champ; when I want my julep in a silver cup; it's clear that I've proposed a new goal for myself, a goal which possesses more than the character of an object of lust, pride, or hunger, but an additional character, a ritual one. My desire has become precise in its object and concrete in its method until the method and the object have merged. And as soon as there is a new object, there is, of course, a new desire. The process of amalgamation, although I have treated it here as if it occurred after the process of precision, is contemporaneous with it and begins, indeed, when desire begins, it is so nearly automatic. A child often fails to distinguish means from ends in any situation, so that Christmas, for example, isn't Christmas without a tree or without a certain cake or a visit to grandmother. The child, who is forever a stylist, identifies the celebration with selected ways of celebrating, and the child may feel, as the primitive man was supposed to, that any kind of success can be guaranteed only by repeating, and by repeating exactly, everything that was done the first time. The aim is good luck and the method is magic, for the actual cause lies unknown in the welter of surrounding conditions. The result is the security that proceeds from repetition, so that if the feeling sought is lost or if the prize is not forthcoming, something in the total order of the acts was wrong—some gesture, some item of clothing, some fragment of the sacred initial occasion left out.

This new end, while a unity, can be mapped. There is an order to its realization. And as each new end, with its corresponding desire, undergoes again the process of precision, it devours further means and swells inside itself until it is constituted by a series of ritual acts. The end is no longer merely had, it is traversed. It is enacted. Each step displaces further the new desire from its natural base. The gourmet's wants become not only precise as to food, but as to service. He envisions glimmering crystal, snowy damask, brilliant talk. Dividing these into ends and means, though it may serve an analytical purpose, is like approximating a curved line by a series of straight ones. The force of the original desire, flowing now through differently ordered channels, animates the whole, and fixes itself successively to various means with all the loyalty of the original desire for its original object.

We should realize that the initial means-ends relation has now been entirely altered. Both have become parts of an active whole in which the former end functions as the final part, like dessert or the eighteenth hole, and the moment the diner takes one bite simply so he may take another, the original amalgamation has been shattered, and dining, as an art, has ceased.

It is necessary to notice, also, that when difficult means are deliberately chosen, and these means ritualized within the end, the end is enriched. The distance at which the pursuer is at first kept encourages contemplation. But all of this supposes an initial ground of satisfaction so that the cat will find it feasible, for example, to play with its food and not swallow it all at once.

Everyone is familiar with the caveman of the popular cartoon who, overcome by desire, goes straight to its object, strikes her over the head with his club and drags her to his cave by the hair. Imagine that we interpose, between the caveman and the object of his lust, a series of formalities: a visit to the father, certain gifts and payments, a gay parade or a ceremonial chase. The object must be contemplated through these difficulties. Admirable points have their chance to be observed. Finally it is forbidden to gain one's bride in the earlier way, and the formalities become essential to the end, an intrinsic part of it. Melodies are strummed under windows, lust is fittingly arrayed, and the woman becomes a lady; she is elevated to a new and more important place. So courtship creates its object, becoming the art of pursuit as running to hounds becomes that of hunting, and love the stylization of carnal desire; while civilized dining, the whole of high cuisine, becomes a transformation of one more vulgar human need into an art.

The amalgamation of means and ends, because it makes for a new aim, clearly shifts the original desire still further from its natural base. The fact that the straight expression of desire is hindered, not by want of objects but by increasing scrupulosity concerning means, makes contemplation possible, and this contemplation discovers what the object is, beyond its mere utility. There is an accompanying rise in value as well as an altered attitude and a changed emotion. Standards, at the same time, make their appearance, for before the only measurements were speed, economy, and success. Now, in addition, there are all those added forms and ceremonies, and judgment frequently turns on them: this gesture has not been made, that rite has been ignored; this sauce employs poor brandy, that caress is crude.

Hunting, having tea, making love, arranging flowers, like so many other minor arts, like gardening, bullfighting, and keeping the sabbath holy, embody ends which might be realized in countless ways. It is often thought, therefore, that those means finally hit upon and combined with the end, so as really to define its nature, have a special affinity the others do not have, some suitability or fittingness, as though the form of the sonnet were somehow metaphysically in harmony with love; and sometimes this is true, and there are what one would normally regard as "good" reasons for the choice of one means rather than another: one is simpler, easier, more economical, cooperates with other customs and with other aims more than another, and so on; but I want to insist that it does not matter. The choices may be whimsical, arbitrary, neurotic, the result of sheerest chance, often like the course a child pursues to school; yet these choices just as thoroughly inform their end with order as any others do. Indeed you often find an artist placing obstacles in his own path out of braggadocio, to show what he can do, or out of self-mortification, because he feels that nothing in the world ought to be easy for him, he is so unworthy. From such a motive is born the penitential style, like the late style of Joyce, and there are many other kinds.

I have been speaking, so far, as if stylization went on in a vacuum, and of course it does not. The gourmet's dinner brings together and satisfies a number of ends in one series of ritual acts, and each of these acts tends to take on a symbolic significance as the art of dining develops. The final limit is reached when the whole performance is so thoroughly conceptualized that the diner (or the hunter or the lover or the keeper of the sabbath, each in his separate way) takes his food not because he is hungry and requires it for life, or because he wishes to indulge himself in certain flavors, but because he wishes, by and through eating, to signify something: safety or social position or breeding or love of neighbor.

There is no lack of Don Juans, either, at the dinner table. There are those, moreover, as we know, who substitute one activity for another and court by cooking; their sensuality sauces the fish; instead of bestowing kisses, they pass a plate of cookies.

The gestures of the actors, the objects in the rite, constitute in this way a language, just as there is, for the composer of flowers, a language of them and their placement. These formalities do not deny the artist any freedom, indeed they make him eloquent, for they are no more confining than any language, and there is always room for an individual use of the given tongue. When such a highly formal language is at large, it makes the most inarticulate and shallow members of society sensitive and expressive, much as the ceremonial rending of clothes and scattering of ashes, for example, gives form and graciousness to what might otherwise be an inelegant spray of feeling.

The final stage in the stylization of desire is reached when the force of the original desire, snipped, as it were, from its natural root, is made to serve another, more elaborate end, an end which only barely contains the original as its final part. The trick, and it is a trick, a process of covering up, of masking and deception, is to retain the force of the original desire without retaining its identity. The danger, and I speak purely from the point of view of the process itself, is that the original end, the culminating act of what has become a rather lengthy activity, may be pushed out altogether, the initial purpose forgotten entirely, and the whole form emptied of significance.

Sterility and confusion of focus—these are the ills which attack style from within, and they are encouraged by the fact that one's attention is naturally directed to the step just ahead, not to the final one, and this becomes more and more the case the further away, by heavy stylization, the end is put. The wooer, delighted by the chase, can forget to possess what at last he's won, and the same mechanism of style that can elevate "woman" from an object of priapic fury to a companion and a wife can lift her also to a pre-Raphaelite cloud, a woman to be pursued and worshiped, and in a sense desired, but never touched—a woman who is always depicted with the reptilian neck of a swan.

Amos reports to us the attitude of God: I spit upon your sacrifices. The Jews, the prophets complained, were merely going through ritual motions; not only had they lost sight of the original aims of these rites, they had made of them ends in themselves.

It is the habit of stylistic formulas to proliferate, new

ones appearing upon the backs of others like the famous fleas, until the weight of the whole becomes intolerable. It is impossible to speak, to eat, to love, or to worship under such circumstances; there is too much to be gone through. The style cannot be called sterile in such a case. It is simply not taken on. It may be abbreviated. The wooer may become a professional slayer of dragons, and it is very likely that hunting, considered as an art, was once a fragment of a larger action that had feasting as its end rather than death or capture or photography. Generally, however, the style is abandoned, and the old end is pursued again in cruder, more direct, more successful ways. Then the process of stylization begins again.

Institutions stress correctness, proper etiquette, righteousness by rule. The revolutionaries are said not to know how to draw, or it is claimed that what they have written are not poems, or that they have made noise, not music; they are ill-mannered boors; they have lost respect for the past, for tradition, hallowed ways; they are, in fact, immoral—objects of scorn and derision, causes of anxiety and apprehension.

While there have always been many individual artists who have seen the danger in an overweight of preparation, ceremony, and ordeal, and have themselves drawn back from it, nevertheless, the form, as if it harbored deadly wishes against itself, goes on to its demise. Artists, on the other hand, can fail a style. Sometimes they lack the wit to grasp the form—a frequent failing; sometimes they cannot keep their will to its work, desire proves the stronger and takes an easier way; sometimes they have too little energy and are discouraged by any obstacle.

And the traditionalist is right: the rebel *does* flounder; he *is* a fool; he does take pride in his ignorance, make a virtue of chaos and disruption, and suppose that he is less a hypocrite for being vulgar; he admires spontaneity and despises effort, thinks sincerity will substitute for skill, allows heat to consume patience, and imagines that his simple presence in the world is cause enough for rejoicing—he need only *be*, and the world will be better. Yet the rebel is right, too. A style can strangle.

We can make an art of anything, but this does not automatically mean it is worth doing. Some arts, like that of dining well, however much they may be a pleasant part of the good life, must remain minor because they have too difficult a struggle to gain the level of concept where really subtle and complicated stylization is possible. A Balinese dance, though it may seem exceptionally mannered to the onlooker, has its every sign writ large, comparatively speaking, giving this impression, while its actual speech is thick, impoverished, and short of breath.

Many of these minor arts have the advantage of a physical concreteness that is close to the desire itself, love and dancing, for instance, eating and the continuance of life; but they have the fatal disadvantage of conceptual inflexibility. The bull is certainly an admirable physical token for a sign of death and love—the noises men make when they make words are not a twelfth as interesting, a lack that poetry always so desperately, by every trick it knows, attempts to overcome—but there is very little you can get a charging bull to say. And this is a disadvantage, not because an art somehow must become symbolic, but because becoming symbolic helps it so much as an art, so immeasurably increases its expressive potentialities.

Finally, I should say that while every ethic involves and specifies a style, stylization alone makes nothing moral. Cruelty can be immensely refined. It can be, in this way, removed from its natural base. It can be associated, as eating is, with accidental qualities, and its general object marvelously split in pieces and precise. Torture can become a ceremony of length and gravity, and of considerable significance for its audience, but however set off from its foundation, however stylized, it must have its victim at last, and for its victim, pleasure in its pain. There is, perhaps, an indirect relation, and it may be this: that such a process as I have here described does the best that can be done with the human nature that it's given, and in that sense, at least, may be, if not the content, at any rate the shape of civilization.

COCK-A-DOODLE-DOO

The couples[1] live in Tarbox.
Come. It is in places marshy. There are trees, lawns of
fine description, bodies, houses like them, banks of purply
flowered scenes, courts for games, arousing speeches, and the
groaning culminations of many amorous machines. That's
because the principal industry in Tarbox is fucking. They
think of it, Elizabethanly, as dying, in Tarbox; descents to
hell are taken every day—through wood-dark poetries un-
warily entered by the middle-aged. No one dies in Tarbox of
too little. Not only the place but the people bear distinguish-
ing names. The heroine is called Foxy by her friends; a
dentist whose tongue is like a dental pick (the souls in Tarbox have teeth) is named Thorne, his wife, Georgene; the
heedless hero (always in dutch) is Piet Hanema; the pairs
most set on swapping are blended prettily together as the
Applesmiths. It is a fortunate thing that a family of sheep
didn't stray into town; the combinations might have proved

[1] *Couples*, by John Updike (New York: Knopf, 1968).

too distracting, especially since this novel is clearly the suburbanite entry in the porno pageant, and I suspect such soft-loaf sophisticates do not delight in the truly unusual: mulogeny or grampalingus, for instance, meatusfoetus or intermissolonghi. Conversant with the modern texts of sexual hygiene, every reader can redream the acts he reads quite guiltlessly. The obscene, sometimes, can even set a standard. Tarbox sex is often oral, but that's the way with writers; the penis was never Nature's purposed instrument of speech.

> Mouths, Piet thought, are noble. They move in the brain's court. We set our genitals mating down below like peasants, but when the mouth condescends, mind and body marry. To eat another is sacred. *I love thee, Elizabeth, thy petaled rankness, thy priceless casket of nothing lined with slippery buds.*

A perfect wedding of style and subject, writing like this is just the love it describes: you must sweep swiftly by in a wash of passion, for if you stop to reflect you may retch with laughter. In order to handle such scenes successfully, the writer must be sure of his own sexuality; otherwise there will be failures of observation and feeling, and he will render them disgusting or ridiculous, attacking indirectly what he thought he wished, so pointedly, to praise. In *Of the Farm*, a far more tightly controlled though less ambitious book, there is only one such passage.

> . . . entered, she yields a variety of landscapes, seeming now a snowy rolling perspective of bursting cotton bolls seen through the Negro arabesques of a fancy-work wrought-iron balcony . . .

and so on. It was an unheeded warning.

The steeple of the Congregational Church in Tarbox is

tipped with a golden colonial rooster, an English copper glinting in its eye. It has already survived several structures which were destroyed or remodeled beneath it.

> Children in the town grew up with the sense that the bird was God. That is, if God were physically present in Tarbox, it was in the form of this unreachable weathercock visible from everywhere. And if its penny could see, it saw everything, spread below it like a living map.

Near the end of the book the church burns, but the weather bird is saved to turn above another building.

> . . . not a restoration but a modern edifice, a parabolic poured-concrete tent-shape peaked like a breaking wave.

The flames which attacked the church were really sexual. The entire book has been that burning. Now book and church and intercourse are charred, as all such customs and competitors, burned out, must end in charring and in ashes. Unaffected as the phoenix, the vane will point the wind again. It is the same with Tarbox couples and their cult of casual coupling, for in the end they give up screwing one another as a principle and take up bridge instead. Communal sex, they argue, will humanize them. Yet it's only another while-a-time game, another dogma ("To eat another is sacred"), another freshly fashioned fad religion which will exempt their lives from the laws of the living.

The novel takes its initial form from the computations of pornography and the conversational bat and catch of Edward Albee . . . much the same. The Appleby-Smiths go through their drills like soldiers. Piet Hanema is carried from one cunt to another like a sea log cresting helplessly. The ladies are strangely worth bedding, and always a pleasure to lay.

The couples' speech is strong, intentions deep, but feeling's weak and meaning shallow. Adultery has no interest as a nervous habit. These people do terrible things to one another, but although their conscience troubles them occasionally, it's only a prick. Everyone is very civilized about his savagery; nobody hits anybody; no one screams convincingly, goes mad, or dies of this contraceptive cruelty. Tarbox, the "post-pill paradise," is a very tepid hell.

Otherwise the novel's form is carelessly old-fashioned. A character is introduced. We pause for his description. Gemlike renderings of nature seldom have a function, unless filling the book is a function, and they shatter the text like a window greeting common stones. The interior monologues seem badly imitated Joyce, and many feats of wit and battle come to nothing more than bluster, smirk, and revengeful tattle. The symbolism is sometimes oppressive ("A condom and candy wrapper lay paired in the exposed gutter"), and the religious parallels aren't convincingly drawn (Piet, the jacket tells us, is a scapegoat, but he is more goat than scape). Then there are those empty expansions of meaning ("Piet felt the fireplace draft on his ankles and became sensitive to the night beyond her hunched shoulders, an extensiveness pressed tight against the bubbled old panes and the frail mullions, a blackness charged with the ache of first growth and the suspended skeletons of Virgo and Leo and Gemini"), unfolding like collapsible tin cups. There's the poetic epithet (for a nipple: "an unexpected sad solidity"; the cat, heaven help us, has a "throaty motor"); there's the uselessly precise fact ("He took his accustomed place in a left back pew"), the fake dislocation of words from their normal positions ("She was in only underwear"), the straining, unsoundable line ("In the liquid a slice of lemon lay at fetal peace"), and overexertions of every other kind ("Her receding hollowed the dull noon. Tipped shoots searched for wider light through entropic gray. The salami he made lunch from was minced death"). In a novel like this there is no point in trying to make poetry out of everything.

In the midst of Tarbox sexual squalor there is a love story lost like a child, and it seems for a time to be part of the author's plan to contrast Piet's and Foxy's adulterous affair, which is beautiful and serious, though carelessly begun, with the empty interlocking of the others. It might have been moving, and the contrast instructive, for Updike can be intense, perceptive, subtle. His prose is musical; his celebration of the female body often glorious and cleansing; and his treatment of the sexual is sometimes delicate and deeply touching, male and female softly enclosed in a fine Japanese line. Many passages, countless details, are nothing less than acts of genius. He can form memorable phrases, and condense an image until it becomes a hard fist of meaning. ("He lay on his back like a town suspended from a steeple." The steeple is Piet's penis, and the whole novel is held in that suspension.) But to turn sex into an ideology is to attack it; to find it always casual in cause and consequence, to separate it from sin and spirit at the same time, as if the spirit were the price, is to attack it; to expose the symbolically sweetest sides of sexual intimacy (as orality sometimes is) to the abuse of words which praise it only out of pride, perversity, and braggadocio, is to attack it centrally, in (as they are felt) the instruments of love itself. Mind and body, value and act, *don't* meet.

Thus despite the pills, coils, diaphragms, and hands and mouths employed, cliché must still be served, and Foxy (whom Piet made love to first when she was freshly pregnant by her husband) later, after the birth of that baby, begins to miss her periods because of Piet's overeager sperm. Now the dirty dentist knows another dentist who will abort our Foxy for a fee, but the villain has his own price: a night with Piet's cold though shapely wife. Naturally Piet has been sleeping with the dentist's sweet frau, too—Georgene—so it's sort of snitch for snatch. All humane considerations gone, it is arranged. Waiting in the living room below, while Dr. Thorne is languid with his prize, Piet decides to give Georgene another whirl. All humane considerations gone, this also is arranged. Besides, downstairs he found it chilly. It's hard to see how anyone could take this diagrammatic melodrama seriously, least of all its author, even though he often seems to. Anyway, it all works out. There are a pair of divorces, and Piet and Foxy marry, move:

> The Hanemas live in Lexington, where, gradually, among people like themselves, they have been accepted, as another couple.

Oh, look out. *Another couple. People like themselves.*

We are promised the weather vane will shine in the sun again. Unreachable, perhaps the bird is God, but I am unpersuaded. It still looks like a cold colonial cock to me.

FROM SOME ASHES
NO BIRD RISES

It was a miserable war, a dirty war, a war fought low in the loins, in his tubercular chest, in the loving, bitter household of himself, the pits, in the flame he liked to fancy was an image of all honest healthy phallic life; his sharply burning beard and head circumnavigated in Brett's paintings of him by a wake of holy light or by the ship of death—it was hard, sometimes, to know which. "Savage," he said (he and Henry Savage were sitting on the edge of a Kent cliff, and Lawrence was striking his chest), "I've something here that is heavier than concrete. If I don't get it out it will kill me." It was Lawrence, of course, who was in there, glaring past the ribs like Rilke's panther past its bars, and there were always other bars before him, colliery chimneys and mother's arms, banning judges, timid editors, teacup society, sycophants and sucking friends, abundant Frieda . . . the menacing female monolith.

His hand was often used to stop his mouth. His cough boiled by his fist. ". . . after our Crucifixion, and the darkness of the tomb, we shall rise again in the flesh, you, I, as we

are today, resurrected in the bodies. . . ." In the physical
sense, what this meant was very simple. The flesh should
rise; it should be swollen with the power of the blood; then,
at last, it should be feasible and safe to enter women. But
there was always that dangerous limpness after, that weakness, that depletion; there was always the fear, in the middle
of success, that this was the end, the sexual ash; there was always in him this awareness, at the very moment of his
exultation, when he had in fact triumphantly come through
it (and a curse upon such consciousness), that the woman to
whom he'd given his seed and feeling had won somehow a
vital battle; that she had brought it off herself, committed
theft, ensnared his soul as she'd enclosed his penis. Presumably, it was *the* great adventure, a fall into the future.

> It is so arranged that the very act which carries
> us out into the unknown shall probably deposit seed
> for security to be left behind. But the act, called
> the sexual act, is not for the depositing of the seed.
> It is for leaping off into the unknown, as from a
> cliff's edge, like Sappho into the sea.

For Lawrence, the green fuse celebrant, sex was suicidal.
"It is so plain in my plant, the poppy," he goes on to say in
his study of Thomas Hardy[1] (which is not a study of Hardy,
but a study of Lawrence, for Lawrence wrote of no one,
ever, nothing, *ever*, in story, tract, or letter, *ever*, but himself) how the life force flows through the stem to flower.

> . . . a little hangs back, in reservoirs that shall
> later seal themselves up as quick but silent sources.
> But the whole, almost the whole, splashes splendidly
> over, is seen in red just as it drips into darkness, and
> disappears.

[1] In *Phoenix*, Vol. I.

The famous doctrine is a futile deception, but the images are honest, and they graphically describe the danger. The poppy blooms, but it bleeds to do so. The snake of the well-known poem, for instance, who comes to drink at the water trough, too, honors the poet with his presence; he induces reverence; and the poet overcomes the voice of an education which tells him the gold snakes of Sicily are venomous and must be killed—he's even grateful to his guest—till the snake puts his head back in that dreadful hole he came from, that entrance to darkness, whereupon the poet throws a stick at the trough and misses his chance, as he says, with one of the lords of life. St. Mawr, the marigold stallion and color of Lawrence, still "don't seem to fancy the mares, for some reason," though he's an animal enfleshment of potency.

There's also a poem about the sex-scream of the tortoise ("half music, half horror"), in which the poet wonders why we were crucified into sex. This seed-fear often fruits in hate: the phallic sacrifice, and the expressionless, hard-eyed Indian who plunges a cold flint knife into a drowsy willing modern woman. "The clutching throb of gratification as the knife strikes in and the blood spurts out!" Sacrifice or crucifixion: were these the sole alternatives to a hermit's isolation and lonely abstinence? Wrestling with his demons, Lawrence wrote of "The Escaped Cock" (a perfect title for him), of Quetzalcoatl, *The Plumed Serpent*, of *The White Peacock*, "The Flying Fish," "The Fox," and also of the almond tree, the gentian, wild animals, reptiles, bullfights, birds, neutering women and neutered men, the red geranium and other flowers, flowers which were, significantly, mostly male, except the snapdragon, which was not, and then of farms and mining towns and seaports, peasants, mating elephants, gamekeepers, Indians, rectors, whales, of hillsides terraced with flowers, of deserts redeemed by flowers (he wrote endlessly of flowers, as, everywhere, the weather: sun, moon, stallions, stars), and found his safest and most hopeful symbol finally in the figure of the phoenix, bird of burning and rejuvenation.

The first volume of Lawrence's posthumous papers was published thirty-two years ago, and now, with yet another volume to companion it, this important collection has been handsomely reissued. There are no letters, poems, or plays, but otherwise the total range of Lawrence's writing is represented: articles, reviews, translations, travel sketches, stories, religious and philosophical effusions, prefaces to his own poems, autobiographical snippets, forewords and fragments, from every period and of every quality except flat. Lawrence may weary his reader with his railing, but his work is never lifeless; he is fully there in every line, for they are cries of his, these lines, and they *are* as he *is,* and go as he goes, whether well or ill, precisely. Nowhere in these pieces does he touch bottom as he does in parts of *Kangaroo* or *The Plumed Serpent*; nowhere is he as sick as he was when he wrote "The Woman Who Rode Away"; seldom is he as silly as when he did parts of *The Fantasia of the Unconscious*, though portions of his book on Hardy are; rarely, also, did he write with such luminous and original beauty as he manages in "Flowery Tuscany," or "The Flying Fish," or display his remarkable powers of characterization more completely than in his Preface to Maurice Magnus' *Memoirs of the Foreign Legion*, and never, I think, is he as sane and cogent in argument as in the essay "A Propos of *Lady Chatterley's Lover*." The set is certainly superbly titled, for Lawrence lives, as the kids say: bright, burning, acrid, and smoky.

Lawrence dreamed of black beetles. "You must leave these friends," he commanded Garnett, "these beetles, Birrell and Duncan Grant are done forever." Bloomsbury gave him nightmares. How the name would have chilled him, like a piece of ice, had he bitten it in half! Beetles, he said, live and feed in a world of corruption; their knowledge ends in the senses, with decay. The force of his fears was so great that the pages of his work, especially these in the volumes of *Phoenix*, are like shouts he's raised up in his sleep, and we are bothered when such insistent realities seem to issue from a distant, dreaming mouth. Cuddling was decay; doting, cooing was decay; it was licking out the bowl before spooning out the porridge. This seemed impossible and sickening to Lawrence. The mind, he claimed, had become a servant of abstraction, industry, and sensuality.

Thus there is less kissing in the later novels: neither Mellors nor Cipriano is inclined to woo; and though the flint knife phase finally passed (he even considered calling *Lady Chatterley's Lover*, in a woeful moment, *Tenderness*), he never allowed love to become an individuating matter. "You can't worship love and individuality in the same breath," he writes in ". . . Love Was Once a Little Boy." Petting is personal; fucking is not. And he goes on in this essay to admire the impassivity, the separateness, of Susan, his cow. So what does tenderness turn out to be? "dirty" words spoken softly? a gentle pat on the ass? a phallus girt with flowers like a filling station ringed with flapping plastic celebrational pennants? The lady's satisfaction was to come from the size of her master's passion (spiritually speaking), and the completeness of her submission to it: "Ah! and what a mystery of prone submission, on her part, this huge erection would imply!" It's felt by Kate, by Alvina, by many other heroines, to be a form of death. Well—better a she than a he.

Such lovemaking is ultimately abstract: Man coming to

Woman. Me Tarzan. You Jane. And part of its primitive quality is due to its generality, the alleged universal sameness of instinct. The id has no personality; it doesn't take snuff or wear spats; it entertains no opinions; it is utterly without eyes; and every expression of it that isn't straight is bent, and bent perversely, mainly by the mind. It's this lovemaking mush that's sex in the head. So every act of intercourse involves a risk, a loss of individuality, of separateness. Yet the dark gods of the mines provide the fuel for life, for the vital burning of the bird; the descent must then be risked, however dangerous or humiliating; even if Tarzan is tiny, with a sunken chest; even if he's the smaller of the two tortoises in those revealing poems.

Much of Lawrence's writing, it seems to me, is symptomatic speech, controlled only by his inner reality, and measurable by little else. His work cries out to the world: accept me! and sotto voce: maybe then I can accept myself. And just as Nietzsche, sick too, overwomaned, powerless to put into the world the power he knew, within, he had, was driven to work his will, instead, with words; so Lawrence wrote novels, stories, essays of challenge and revenge, composed elaborate and desperate daydreams, disposing of his problems and his friends, recreating himself, rewriting his forlorn history. Still, at night he had other dreams. "I hate your love," he once shouted at Murry, "I *hate* it. You're an obscene bug, sucking my life away."

Life was daily to be started in a new spirit. Lawrence would found a colony, Rananim. Bertrand Russell could be president. In Florida. In, perhaps, New Mexico. On the Marquesas. It would be a place "apart from civilization" where he'd have a few other people by him "who are also at peace and happy, and live, and understand," and where he'd "be *free*." Free. With Mansfield, with Murry and

Frieda and Brett, with Campbell, the Cannans, Koteliansky, and Gertler . . . peaceful, happy, kindred spirits all.

If he could only live in his dream. And it seemed so reasonable. He asked only to be free, free of himself, free and proud, a man. Then, and only then, would his agony be ended, Lawrence would enter his nature, enter into a nature in a way no animal had to, for no animal was separate from itself in this fashion, no animal had to knock on the door of its being and ask for entrance, no animal had, malformed, alone, to struggle toward itself. Even a rose, moving out from its stem and flowering finally, did it all easily, thoughtlessly, according to harmonious law. Oh, to be shed of this Protestant skin, this shame, this hesitation, these many weaknesses, these phallic inadequacies!

Lawrence among the flowers and the animals: how free he felt, how accepted, how alive—until he returned to Frieda, who stood in the doorway, absorbing the light. Behind her: publishers, reviewers, judges, critics, Bloomsbury. When the rabbit wrinkled its nose it was wondrous; when Lytton did it, it was not. This human world attacked him, robbed him of his manhood, reminded him constantly of his background, his social origins, his shortcomings, his inability to reason off the cuff. Consumed with rage—impotent rage —he felt himself superior yet cut down, a genius made a fool of, a prophet mocked, while St. Mawr burned like a jewel in his paddock, and the stars burned in the skies like the eyes of wild animals. Meanwhile Lawrence burned with fever, his soul consumed itself, his body wasted, and the only place it was cool was in the sun, in the rarer airs, in the burned dryness of the desert. Rejected by publishers and the public, harried out of Cornwall like a spy, sick, he writes an utterly hateful note to Katherine Mansfield: "I loathe you. You revolt me stewing in your consumption. . . . The

Italians were quite right to have nothing to do with you."
From some ashes no bird rises.

This restless, articulate, flashing, impassioned man mistook
taciturn, slow-spoken, stupid, selfish, stubbornly absorbed,
immovable types—tenders of horses, gamekeepers, Indians
(the one in "St. Mawr" is called Phoenix)—the touch-me-
nots, those who seldom "came to women," who held themselves aloof or lived alone like the wooden heroes of the
West, in whom there seemed to remain something wild and
untamed as their origins or surroundings were—he mistook
these for the true Males of Nature, representatives of (may
some god aid us!) the "twilit Pan." Earlier, before he'd
begun to think of himself as the Nottingham Indian, he carried on, with the farmer, a similar romance. For example,
in *The Rainbow*. Incredibly (unless we understand the myth
he'd thrown up like a barricade), what he admired were
amputees; but Lawrence could not—he dared not—see the
missing member.

So while the public Lawrence cooked, and cleaned, and
kept house, and was sweet and gentle with the sick, and
leaned against women, and railed against them like a woman,
too, and fought with his tongue and threw crockery (and
was cracked in the head from behind once by Frieda—with
a plate), and was mean and cruel as a squaw in a home where
harpy often flew at harpy; the private Lawrence knew his
acts were passive, his love was passive, his rages, too, were
passive, and he hated his life, and regarded it as essentially
unmanly, a life lived at low wick.

> ". . . there is no real truth in ecstasy," he informed
> Gordon Campbell. "Ecstasy achieves itself by virtue
> of exclusion; and in making any passionate ex-
> clusion, one has already put one's right hand in the
> hand of the lie."

But Lawrence's life was built on passionate exclusion, and every book was a battle, vast lines of good and evil rushing pell-mell at one another . . . fanatics of the single sword. And this is the Lawrence we are asked to admire, Lawrence the warrior, the champion of sexual apartheid. Well, minds with sore teeth prefer their foods soft boiled. Certainly, it is no service to an author to admire him for his moments of disaster. Driven by his demons to write about sex, he was prevented by the animosity among them to write well about it; for when Lawrence wishes to render these feelings, he turns to an abstract, incantational shorthand, often full of biblical overtones and antique simplicities, phrases which are used like formulas, reiterated until they become meaningless: hearts grow bitter and black and cold, souls melt or swoon, bodies freeze or burn, people are rapt or blind, they utter strange cries, their feelings ebb and flow (much, indeed, is watery), they are rigid or languorous, they "go mad with voluptuous delight," they overmaster or submit, bowels move poignantly (with sentiment enough to fertilize the earth), and their eyes sing, laugh, dance, stab, harden, burn, flash, seize, subside, cool, dim, and die. One lust could do for another, angers are peas, nothing is clearly envisaged, nothing is precise, and we pass through them soon in a daze.

Yet when Lawrence felt he *could* go unprotected, when he allowed things, landscapes, people, to enter *him*, when he didn't befog them first with his own dark dreams, but took his feeling naked through his eyes, alert in all his senses as an animal, then there was no greater sensualist, no more vital, free, and complete a man, no more loyal and tender a lover. How remarkably he renders the rabbit, "Adolf," or the dog, "Rex"; how perfectly, in a few pages, he puts "The Miner at Home" before us; while books like *Sea and Sar-*

dinia are perfect miracles of living form and sensuous language.

Even at his best, though, his mind is held back, for the mind is memory and argument, the mind is self-awareness, the mind is guilt, and the mind is that which looks down when you are crossing a high place; it puts all in confusion, doubt; and many of his essays reprinted in the *Phoenix* are efforts made by his feelings to harness reason, to make it serve him, and then he takes nothing in, sees nothing but himself. There is no landscape, there are no hills, no stones; there are only sermons, defenses, wailing, and gnashing of teeth, only enemies, and agony of spirit, whittling him, paring him, cutting him down. Lawrence was right, there was a lover living in him, a great one, an *übermensch*, a celebrator of life, a healthy soul; but there was also Lawrence the weasel, the little frightened mama boy, the death seeker, the denier, the sick and terribly weak one, opening his coat to flourish before us a phallus in the form of a flower.

Still, life was daily to be started in a new spirit. Letters, essays, bubbled by his fist. Tolstoi has wet on the flame of life! A new spirit . . . a rabbit held trembling in the hand of his father. Men must have the courage to draw near women, expose themselves. Lawrence grew a beard: "behind which I shall take as much cover henceforth as I can, like a creature under a bush." So to found Rananim. "I shall die of a foul inward poison." The rabbit's white tail, as it flees, is a flag of spiteful derision. *Merde*, it says: *merde! merde! merde!* A new spirit . . . "I curse England, I curse the English, man, woman, and child, in their nationality let them be accursed and hated and never forgiven."

From such ashes no bird rises.

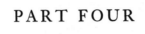

PART FOUR

THE CASE OF THE
OBLIGING STRANGER

Imagine I approach a stranger on the street and say to him, "If you please, sir, I desire to perform an experiment with your aid." The stranger is obliging, and I lead him away. In a dark place conveniently by, I strike his head with the broad of an ax and cart him home. I place him, buttered and trussed, in an ample electric oven. The thermostat reads 450° F. Thereupon I go off to play poker with friends and forget all about the obliging stranger in the stove. When I return, I realize I have overbaked my specimen, and the experiment, alas, is ruined.

Something has been done wrong. Or something wrong has been done.

Any ethic that does not roundly condemn my action is vicious. It is interesting that none is vicious for this reason. It is also interesting that no more convincing refutation of any ethic could be given than by showing that it approved of my baking the obliging stranger.

This is really all I have to say, but I shall not stop on that account. Indeed, I shall begin again.

2

The geometer cannot demonstrate that a line is beautiful. The beauty of lines is not his concern. We do not chide him when he fails to observe uprightness in his verticals, when he discovers no passions between sinuosities. We would not judge it otherwise than foolish to berate him for neglecting to employ the methods successful in biology or botany merely because those methods dealt fairly with lichens and fishes. Nor do we despair of him because he cannot give us reasons for doing geometry which will equally well justify our drilling holes in teeth. There is a limit, as Aristotle said, to the questions which we may sensibly put to each man of science; and however much we may desire to find unity in the purposes, methods, and results of every fruitful sort of inquiry, we must not allow that desire to make mush of their necessary differences.

Historically, with respect to the fundamental problems of ethics, this limit has not been observed. Moreover, the analogy between mathematics and morals, or between the methods of empirical science and the good life, has always been unfairly one-sided. Geometers never counsel their lines to be moral, but moralists advise men to be like lines and go straight. There are triangles of lovers, but no triangles in love. And who says the organism is a state?

For it is true that the customary methods for solving moral problems are the methods which have won honors by leaping mathematical hurdles on the one hand or scientific and physical ones on the other: the intuitive and deductive method and the empirical and inductive one. Nobody seems to have minded very much that the moral hurdle has dunked them both in the pool beyond the wall, for they can privately laugh at each other for fools, and together they can exclaim how frightfully hard is the course.

The difficulty for the mathematical method is the discovery of indubitable moral first premises which do not themselves rest on any inductive foundation and which are still applicable to the complicated tissue of factors that make up moral behavior. The result is that the premises are usually drawn from metaphysical speculations having no intimate relation to moral issues or from rational or mystical revelations which only the intuiter and his followers are willing to credit. For the purposes of deduction, the premises have to be so broad and, to satisfy intuition, so categorically certain that they become too thin for touch and too heavy for bearing. All negative instances are pruned as unreal or parasitic. Consequently, the truth of the ultimate premises is constantly called into question by those who have intuited differently or have men and actions in mind that they want to call good and right but cannot.

Empirical solutions, so runs the common complaint, lop off the normative branch altogether and make ethics a matter of expediency, taste, or conformity to the moral etiquette of the time. One is told what people do, not what they ought to do; and those philosophers who still wish to know what people ought to do are told, by some of the more uncompromising, that they can have no help from empiricism and are asking a silly question. Philosophers, otherwise empiricists, who admit that moral ends lie beyond the reach of factual debate turn to moral sentiment or some other *bonum ex machina,* thus generously embracing the perplexities of both methods.

3

Questions to which investigators return again and again without success are very likely improperly framed. It is important to observe that the ethical question put so directly as "What is good?" or "What is right?"[1] aims in its answer not, as one might immediately suppose, at a catalog of the world's good, right things. The moralist is not asking for a list of sheep and goats. The case of the obliging stranger is a case of immoral action, but this admission is not an answer, even partially, to the question "What is wrong?"

Furthermore, the ethical question is distressingly short. "Big" questions, it would seem, ought to be themselves big, but they almost never are; and they tend to grow big simply by becoming short—too short, in fact, ever to receive an answer. I might address, to any ear that should hear me, the rather less profound-sounding, but nonetheless similar question "Who won?" or perhaps the snappier "What's a winner?" I should have to ask this question often because, if I were critical, I should never find an answer that would suit me; while at the same time there would be a remarkable lot of answers that suited a remarkable lot of people. The more answers I had—the more occasions on which I asked the question—the more difficult, the more important, the more "big" the question would become.

If the moralist does not want to hear such words as "Samson," "money," or "brains," when he asks his question, "What is good?" what does he want to hear? He wants to hear a word like "power." He wants to know what is good in the

[1] The order in which these questions are asked depends on one's view of the logical priority of moral predicates. I shall not discriminate among them since I intend my remarks to be indiscriminate.

things that are good that makes them good. It should be perfectly clear it is not the things themselves that he thinks good or bad but the qualities they possess, the relations they enter into, or the consequences they produce. Even an intuitionist, who claims to perceive goodness directly, perceives a property of things when he perceives goodness, and not any *thing*, except incidentally. The wrong done the obliging stranger was not the act of cooking him but was something belonging to the act in some one of many possible ways. It is not I who am evil (if I am not mad) but something which I *have* that is; and while, of course, I may be adjudged wicked for having whatever it is I have that's bad, it is only because I have it that I am wicked—as if I owned a vicious and unruly dog.

I think that so long as I look on my act in this way, I wrong the obliging stranger a second time.

The moralist, then, is looking for the ingredient that perfects or spoils the stew. He wants to hear the word "power." He wants to know what is good in what is good that makes it good; and the whole wretched difficulty is that one is forced to reply either that what is good in what is good makes the good in what is good good, or that it is, in fact, made good by things which are not in the least good at all. So the next question, which is always "And why is power good?" is answered by saying that it is good because it is power and power is good; or it is put off by the promise that power leads to things worth much; or it is shrugged aside with the exclamation, "Well, that's life!" This last is usually accompanied by an exhortation not to oppose the inevitable course of nature.

You cannot ask questions forever. Sooner or later the questioning process is brought up short by statements of an apparently dogmatic sort. Pleasure is sought for pleasure's sake. The principle of utility is susceptible of no demonstration. Every act and every inquiry aims at well-being. The non-natural property of goodness fastens itself to its object and will remain there whatever world the present world may madly become. Frustrated desires give rise to problems, and problems are bad. We confer the title of The Good upon our natural necessities.

I fail to see why, if one is going to call a halt in this way, the halt cannot be called early, and the evident, the obvious, the axiomatic, the indemonstrable, the intrinsic, or whatever one wants to name it, be deemed those clear cases of moral goodness, badness, obligation, or wrong which no theory can cloud, and for which men are prepared to fight to the last ditch. For if someone asks me, now I am repentant, why I regard my act of baking the obliging stranger as wrong, what can I do but point again to the circumstances comprising the act? "Well, I put this fellow in an oven, you see. The oven was on, don't you know." And if my questioner persists, saying, "Of course, I know all about *that;* but what I want to know is, why is *that* wrong?" I should recognize there is no use in replying that it is wrong because of the kind of act it is, a wrong one, for my questioner is clearly suffering from a sort of *folie de doute morale* which forbids him to accept any final answer this early in the game, although he will have to accept precisely the same kind of answer at some time or other.

Presumably there is some advantage in postponing the stop, and this advantage lies in the explanatory power of the higher-level answer. It cannot be that my baking the stranger is wrong for no reason at all. It would then be inexplicable. I do not think this is so, however. It is not inexplicable; it is transparent. Furthermore, the feelings of elucidation, of greater insight or knowledge, is a feeling only. It results, I suspect, from the satisfaction one takes in having an open mind. The explanatory factor is always more inscrutable than the event it explains. The same questions can be asked of it as were asked of the original occasion. It is either found in the situation and brought forward to account for all, as one might advance pain, in this case, out of the roaster; or it resides there mysteriously, like an essence, the witch in the oven; or it hovers, like a coil of smoke, as hovers the greatest unhappiness of the greatest number.

But how ludicrous are the moralist's "reasons" for condemning my baking the obliging stranger. They sound queerly unfamiliar and out of place. This is partly because they intrude where one expects to find denunciation only and because it is true they are seldom if ever *used*. But their strangeness is largely due to the humor in them.

Consider:

My act produced more pain than pleasure.

Baking this fellow did not serve the greatest good to the greatest number.

I acted wrongly because I could not consistently will that the maxim of my action become a universal law.

God forbade me, but I paid no heed.

Anyone can apprehend the property of wrongness sticking plainly to the whole affair.

Decent men remark it and are moved to tears.

But I should say that my act was wrong even if my stranger were tickled into laughter while he cooked (though the absence of pain *would change the nature of the case*); or even if his baking did the utmost good it could; or if, in spite of all, I could consistently will that whatever maxim I might have had might become a universal law; or even if God had spoken from a bush to me: "Thou shalt!" How redundant the property of wrongness, as if one needed *that*, in such a case! And would the act be right if the whole world howled its glee? Moralists can say, with conviction, that the act is wrong; but none can *show* it.

Such cases, like that of the obliging stranger, are cases I call clear. They have the characteristic of moral transparency, and they comprise the core of our moral experience. When we try to explain why they are instances of good or bad, of right or wrong, we sound comic, as anyone does who gives elaborate reasons for the obvious, especially when these reasons are so shamefaced before reality, so miserably beside the point. What we must explain is not why these cases have the moral nature they have, for that needs no explaining, but *why they are so clear*. It is an interesting situation: any moralist will throw over his theory if it reverses the decision on cases like the obliging stranger's. The most persuasive criticism of any ethical system has always been the demonstration, on the critic's part, that the system countenances moral absurdities, despite the fact that, in the light of the whole theoretical enterprise, such criticisms beg the question. Although the philosopher who is caught by a criticism of this sort may protest its circularity or even manfully swallow the dreadful conclusion, his system has been scotched, if it has not been killed.

Not all cases are clear. But the moralist will furrow his brow before even this one. He will pursue principles which do not apply. He does not believe in clear cases. He refuses to believe in clear cases. Why?

4

His disbelief is an absolute presupposition with him. It is a part of his methodological commitments and a part of his notion of profundity and of the nature of philosophy. It is a consequence of his fear of being arbitrary. So he will put the question bravely to the clear cases, even though no state of fact but only his state of mind brings the question up, and even though putting the question, revealing the doubt, destroys immediately the validity of any answer he has posed the question to announce.

Three children are killed by a drunken driver. A family perishes in a sudden fire. Crowded bleachers collapse. Who is puzzled, asking why these things are terrible, why these things are wrong? When is such a question asked? It is asked when the case is not clear, when one is in doubt about it. "Those impious creatures! . . . At the movies . . . today, . . . which is the Lord's!" Is that so bad? Is being impious, even, so bad? I do not know. It is unclear, so I ask why. Or I disagree to pick a quarrel. Or I am a philosopher whose business it is to be puzzled. But do I imagine there is nothing the matter when three children are run over by drunkenness, or when a family goes up in smoke, or when there is a flattening of people under timbers under people? There is no lack of clarity here, there is only the philosopher: patient, persistent as the dung beetle, pushing his "whys" up his hillocks with his nose. His doubts are never of the present case. They are always general. They are doubts in legion, regiment, and principle.

The obliging stranger is overbaked. I wonder whether this is bad or not. I ask about it. Presumably there is a reason for my wonderment. What is it? Well, of course there is not any reason that is a reason about the obliging stranger. There is only a reason because I am a fallibilist, or because one must not be arbitrary, or because all certainties in particular cases are certain only when deduced from greater, grander certainties. The reason I advance may be advanced upon itself. The entire moral structure tumbles at once. It is a test of the clarity of cases that objections to them are objections in principle; that the principle applies as well to all cases as to any one; and that these reasons for doubt devour themselves with equal right and the same appetite. That is why the moralist is really prepared to fight for the clear cases to the last ditch; why, when he questions them, he does so to display his philosophical breeding, because it is good form: he knows that if these cases are not clear, none are, and if none are, the game is up.

If there are clear cases, and if every moralist, at bottom, behaves as if there were, why does he still, at the top, behave as if there were none?

5

He may do so because he is an empiricist practicing induction. He believes, with Peirce, that "the inductive method springs directly out of dissatisfaction with existing knowledge." To get more knowledge he must become dissatisfied with what he has, all of it, by and large, often for no reason whatever. Our knowledge is limited, and what we do know, we know inexactly. In the sphere of morals the moralist has discovered how difficult it is to proceed from facts to values, and although he has not given up, his difficulties persuade him not that no one knows but that no one can be sure.

Do we not frequently find him, even when he is swimming in his own pool, doubting the wetness of the water, the buoyancy of his own body, the presence of his bathing suit? He is not sure I am writing these words now, and believes I should be equally skeptical. Perhaps I am dreaming? perhaps I am drunk? perhaps I am under hypnosis or suffering from theology? And perhaps he is bathing in the belly of a whale.

The Case of the Obliging Stranger

Above all, the empiricist has a hatred of certainty. His reasons are not entirely methodological. Most are political: certainty is evil; it is dictatorial; it is undemocratic; all cases should be scrutinized equally; there should be no favoritism; the philosopher is fearless. "Thought looks into the pit of hell and is not afraid."

The moralist may behave as if there were no clear cases because he is a rationalist practicing deduction. He knows all about the infinite regress. He is familiar with the unquestioned status of first principles. He is beguiled by the precision, rigor, and unarguable moves of logical demonstration. Moreover, he is such an accomplished doubter of the significance of sensation that he has persuaded the empiricist also to doubt that significance. He regards the empiricist as a crass, anti-intellectual booby, a smuggler where he is not an honest skeptic, since no fact, or set of facts, will account for the value we place on the obliging stranger unless we are satisfied to recount again the precise nature of the case.

The rationalist is a man in love, not with particular men or women, not with things, but with principles, ideas, webs of reasoning; and if he rushes to the aid of his neighbor, it is not because he loves his neighbor, but because he loves God's law about it. He treats his children justly, as blind to them as persons as the statue—even, but empty, handed. He has a military mind, and he obeys.

Suppose our case concerned toads. And suppose we were asking of the toads, "Why? Why are you toads?" They would be unable to reply, being toads. How far should we get in answering our own question if we were never sure of any particular toad that he was one? How far should we get with our deductions if we were going to deduce one from self-evident toadyisms? What is self-evident about toads except that some are toads? And if we had a toad before us, and we were about to investigate him, and someone doubted that we had a toad before us, we could only say our creature was tailless and clumsy and yellow-green and made warts. So if someone still wanted to doubt our toad, he would have to change the definition of "toad," and someone might want to do that; but who wants to change our understanding of the word "immoral" so that the baking of the obliging stranger is not to be called immoral?

The empiricist is right: the deductive ethic rests upon arbitrary postulation. The rationalist is right: the inductive ethic does not exist; or worse, it consists of arbitrary values disguised as facts. Both are guilty of the most elaborate and flagrant rationalizations. Both know precisely what it is they wish to save. Neither is going to be surprised in the least by what turns out to be good or bad. They are asking of their methods answers that their methods cannot give.

6

It is confusion which gives rise to doubt. What about the unclear cases? I shall be satisfied to show that there are clear ones, but the unclear ones are more interesting, and there are more of them. How do we decide about blue laws, supposing that there is nothing to decide about the obliging stranger except how to prevent the occurrence from happening again? How do we arbitrate conflicts of duty where each duty, even, may be clear? What of principles, after all? Are there none? Are they not used by people? Well, they talk about them more than they use them, but they use them a little—often to hide behind, like the bureaucrat does, or that just father I mentioned.

I should like to try to answer these questions another

time. I can only indicate, quite briefly, the form these answers will take.

I think we decide cases where there is some doubt by stating what it is about them that puzzles us. We hunt for more facts, hoping that the case will clear:

"She left her husband with a broken hand and took the children."

"She did! the ungrateful bitch!"

"He broke his hand hammering her head."

"Dear me, how distressing, but after all what's one time?"

"He beat her every Thursday after tea and she finally couldn't stand it any longer."

"Ah, of course. But the poor children."

"He beat them, too. On Fridays. And on Saturday he beat the dog."

"My, my—such a terrible man. And was there no other way?"

"The court would grant her no injunction."

"Why not?"

"Judge Bridlegoose is a fool."

"Ah, of course, poor thing, she did right, no doubt about it. Except—why didn't she also take the dog?"

If more facts do not clear the case, we redescribe it, emphasizing first this fact and then that until it is clear, or until we have several clear versions of the original muddle. Many ethical disputes are due to the possession, by the contending parties, of different accounts of the same occasion, all satisfactorily clear, and this circumstance gives the disputants a deep feeling for the undoubted rightness of each of their versions. Such disputes are particularly acrimonious, and they cannot be settled until an agreement is reached about the true description of the case.

And I don't like descriptions which embarrass me morally.

Do you? So I'm inclined to resist them. Naturally I want the facts to support me, my ego, and its interests.

There are, of course, conflicts of duty which are perfectly clear. I have promised to meet you at four to bowl, but when four arrives I am busy rescuing a baby from the jaws of a Bengal tiger and cannot come. Unclear conflicts we try to clarify. And it sometimes happens that the tug of obligations is so equal as to provide no reasonable solution. If some cases are clear, others are undecidable, and moral tragedies can ensnare the most righteous.

It is perfectly true that principles are employed in moral decisions—popular principles, I mean, like the golden rule and the laws of God. Principles really obscure matters as often as they clear them. They are generally flags and slogans to which the individual is greatly attached. Attack the principle and you attack the owner: his good name, his reputation, his sense of righteousness. Love me, love my maxims. People have been wrongly persuaded that principles decide cases and that a principle which fails in one case fails in all. So principles are usually vehicles for especially powerful feelings and frequently get in the way of good sense. We have all observed the angry arguer who grasps the nettle of absurdity to justify his bragging about the toughness of his skin.

Distances are great, human affairs can be complex, essential data may be missing. We cannot argue every case on its merits. Most of our lives we are morally in the dark, yet, because we must move about, we like to act as if we had invented light. Love, for instance, is meaningless apart from those small communities which make a constant, close communication possible. Where we cannot offer love, we've at least justice. So we resort to abstractions, to the rule of law, to the ideal of equality, and notions of fair play and benevolence. Principles may be makeshifts; they may be, in the facile, empty grandeur of their claims, even lies; but our duty to those we do not know: how else can we conceive it except through ardent generalities?

I should regard useful principles as summaries of what may be present generally in clear cases, as for instance: cases where pain is present are more often adjudged bad than not. We might, if the reverse were true for pleasure, express our principle briefly in hedonistic terms: pleasure is the good. But there may be lots of principles of this sort, as there may be lots of rather common factors in clear cases. Principles state more or less prevalent identifying marks, as cardinals usually nest in low trees, although there is nothing to prevent them from nesting elsewhere, and the location of the nest is not the essence of the bird. When I appeal to a principle, then, the meaning of my appeal consists of the fact that before me is a case about which I can reach no direct decision; of the fact that the principle I invoke is relevant, since not every principle is (the laws of God do not cover everything, for instance). In this way I affirm my loyalty to those clear cases the principle so roughly summarizes and express my desire to remain consistent with them.

7

Insofar as present moral theories have any relevance to our experience, they are elaborate systems designed to protect the certainty of the moralist's last-ditch data. Although he may imagine he is gathering his principles from the purest vapors of the mind, the moralist will in fact be prepared to announce as such serenities only those which support his most cherished goods. And if he is not careful to do just this, he will risk being charged with irrelevancy by those who will employ the emptiness and generality of his principles to demonstrate the value of trivialities: as for example, the criticism of the categorical imperative that claims one can universally will all teeth be brushed with powder in the morning, and so on in like manner.

Ethics, I wish to say, is about something, and in the rush to establish principles, to elicit distinctions from a recalcitrant language, and to discover "laws," those lovely things and honored people, those vile seducers and ruddy villains our principles and laws are supposed to be based upon and our ethical theories to be about are overlooked and forgotten.

Postscript

Esthetics is in an analogous fix. If anything, its fix is worse. Philosophers distrust the subject. It has always been a stepchild, a kind of after-error, offspring of the menopause. Metaphysicians have swept it up with the rest of the dust, and nowhere can you find better examples of ignorance and arrogance cooperating against a subject than in many of their writings about art. Landscape gardening is a higher form of art than architecture, Schopenhauer says. Animal training is even more expressive. There is no end.

They distrust the subject, not themselves. Everyone has seen a painting. And no one imagines they lack the requisite sensitivity, any more than they fancy themselves without a sense of humor.

From an account of my baking the obliging stranger, any reader can soon form an opinion of the ethical value of the act reported. From a comparable description of the *David* or *Desire Under the Elms*, nothing about the artistic worth of these works can rightfully be concluded. Our knowledge of other things by the same artist, and our acquaintance with present efforts of the same kind, often allows us to make reasonable predictions, but such judgments rest on externals, and are clearly not judgments of the work itself.

It is certainly not the function of esthetics, or even of criticism, to inform us once again that *King Lear* is a great play. *King Lear*'s greatness is clear—clear as the case of the obliging stranger. Nor can we get anywhere by deriving, from Shakespeare's practice, principles of judgment or rules of composition. Neither keeping the unities nor dissolving them is of any use, nor is loyalty to symmetry, harmony, balance, or coherence. A consistent image can be dull, and an inconsistent one both noble and exciting. You have to taste to tell.

In the search for beauty-making properties, it is not surprising that the philosopher has most frequently found them living elsewhere, at strange addresses, and under assumed names—names like "knowledge" and "salvation." It is not merely that the esthetician doubts the existence of clear cases; he doubts the existence of esthetics. The enjoyment of beauty simply as beauty is an intolerable frivolity. And in a world of function, purpose, and utility—this world of the drone, the queen bee, and the hive—so it is. So it is.

RUSSELL'S MEMOIRS

Ghostly, like a slow sea fog, religious doubts and vague metaphysical disquiets began to darken Bertrand Russell's mind, and when, at eighteen, he read a refutation of the First Cause Argument in Mill's *Autobiography*, he became an atheist. He was somewhat puritanical and priggish in his views, but a day of constant kissing altered that. His first wife, Alys, intellectually freer about sex than Russell was, emotionally had the same beastly Victorian attitudes. In their relationship, she'd decided intimacy would, by preference, be rare. "I did not argue the matter," Russell says, adding smugly, "and I did not find it necessary to do so." Happy in his marriage, Russell had been leading a calm and superficial life: an imperialist in politics, an empiricist in philosophy, he had scrubbed his mind through mathematics until its surface shone with analytical clarity. One day a witness to the agonies of an attack of angina in Mrs. Whitehead, he changes again, this time going further, faster (in five minutes), and concluding that "the loneliness of the human soul is unendurable," that only intense love can "pene-trate" it, that "whatever does not spring from this motive is harmful," that consequently "war is wrong," public school education "abominable," the use of force as well, and "that in human relations one should penetrate to the core of lone-liness in each person and speak to that." Not commonplace sentiments then, as inferences they were even more remark-able; but logic's hold on Russell has always been precarious.

Happy and *superficial*: these are constantly conjoined in Russell's life; only pain and controversy give his mind its weight; only then does it sink out of sight in the loneliness he speaks of. Is it, for all of us, the same? Once, bestriding his bike, he realized he no longer loved his wife. A grave, tumultuous insight suddenly possesses the rider of the ma-chine. Of course he finds his reasons, but the page is plainer than he is. Over the years he had floated to the surface of Alys; he could no longer penetrate her; and no longer touch-ing bottom there, he could not confront more than the fore-head of himself either. For renewal, Russell needed another love affair. The rider would like to be running, feeling his own feet lifting him forward as he had, in the depths of his love, once before.

The first volume of Russell's *Autobiography*, from which these incidents have been taken, shows him to be a man of fairly shallow calculation, cold, and capable of the cruelty of indifference, using his mind as a weapon and a cover; but it shows him also periodically and quite irrationally shaken by instinct and impulse, warm and generous sometimes, noble and fine, or charmingly foolish. Gradually, through-out this brilliant second volume,[1] we see these hidden forces, appearing in his life in bursts, move his heart to the right

[1] *The Autobiography of Bertrand Russell, 1914–1944* (Boston: Atlan-tic/Little, Brown, 1968).

place, allowing him to speak for peace and gentleness and love—often eloquently, with force, and at great personal sacrifice; but we see, too, that he hasn't yet ceased to simplify, to reduce, as though the weight of experience were mostly fatty excess to be sweated away by a series of vigorous mental exercises. His feelings may run deep, but his view of life remains naïve, and he is constantly surprised, sometimes desperately disappointed, driven to the edge of suicide.

Whitehead once complained of some of Russell's preliminary work for *Principia Mathematica* that "Everything . . . has been sacrificed to making proofs both short and neat." In youth, for a period, a materialist, he nevertheless found consciousness an irreducible datum; still, as this second volume shows, he has continued to feel his self, his inward person, to be like a ghost in some alien, indifferent, Cartesian machine. To touch. To be touched! But you cannot touch a ghost, nor can a ghost touch. *Ghost.* Over and over, unconsciously, he uses this word to describe himself, both in his present account and in the letters he wrote at the time. And the God he seeks vainly for is also a ghost, as is the love he needs.

Russell is forty-two when this volume begins, and a well-known philosopher, yet he is astonished to find that most people are delighted at the prospect of war. He had, he says, to revise his views on human nature; but he merely swings from one facility to another, and blithely compares his simplistic views with Freud's. He dreads failure, and has an unwholesome tendency to recant. Even D. H. Lawrence's furious, sick, sadistic, Fascist rant derails him momentarily; for passion appeals to him, as does Lawrence's cult of the deep core. Russell throws off this illness, although from it, slowly, he learns a little more. He honestly wants to be an impulsive man. We find him planning to be impulsive, and congratulating himself afterward for acting in the moment, heedless of consequence, as he does so often in his love affairs. This leads him to mistake the suddenness of his thoughts sometimes for cachets of their truth, though his intellect insists upon a thorough investigation.

Still, he never is able to commit his mind to social issues with the rigor and severity he allows it in logic and epistemology. There is not a little, in Russell, of the scholar's wistful love of power ("Power over people's minds is the main personal desire of my life . . ."), as if, through social action, he could finally penetrate others, materialize his ghost.

Throughout the First World War he carries his pacifism bravely, and there is a fine account of his imprisonment for it. There are also excellent descriptions of his trips to Russia (which he hated) and China (which he loved). With Dora Black, his second wife, he founds an experimental school for children. It swallows much of his money, while thought and theory, like bubbles of air, carry him soon from its depths, as he is carried gradually from Dora's, too. The freedom he wishes to give his pupils, as well as the freedom he wishes to give his wife, both have to be modified, the one in the practice, the other in the hope. "Anybody else could have told me this in advance, but I was blinded by theory." The Nazis then give his pacifism too stiff a test. Nonviolent resistance, he decides, "depends upon the existence of certain virtues in those against whom it is employed." This volume concludes with an account of his trip to the United States with his third wife, Patricia Spence, his teaching and writing here, and especially the (for us) shameful contretemps concerning his appointment at City College.

Clear, incisive, frequently witty, as honest as his inner check and the law will allow, Russell has written the history of an emblematic life: exemplary in its devotion to both

emotion and truth, triumphant in its dedication to our freedom to decently pursue them, and symptomatic of the consequences of their separation in its sometimes painful failures.

A MEMORY OF A MASTER

Professor Gregory Vlastos had completed his paper on Reinhold Niebuhr. The paper was excellent but the discussion had swallowed itself as such things sometimes do (one was only inclined to cough), and even the effort to be brilliant at someone's expense seemed no longer worth the trouble, when the funny, shabby man began speaking. At least he seemed shabby, though I remember giving him small notice at first. Old, unsteady, queerly dressed, out of date, uncomfortable in space, he struck me as some atheistical, vegetarian nut who'd somehow found his way to this meeting of the Cornell Philosophy Club and would, at any moment, heatedly, endlessly, support and denounce with wild irrelevance whatever simple, single thought was burning him up. But he'd been silent and I'd forgotten about him. Now he spoke, clearly yet haltingly, with intolerable slowness, with a kind of deep stammer involving not mere sounds or words but yards of discourse, long swatches of inference; and since these sentence lengths, though delivered forcefully, indeed with an intensity which was as extraordinary as it was quiet, were always cut short suddenly—in midphrase, maddeningly incomplete—and then begun again, what you heard was something like a great pianist at practice: not a piece of music, but the very acts which went into making that performance.

Thus in this sudden, silly way began what was to be the most important intellectual experience of my life, yet it was an experience almost wholly without content, for it was very plainly not just what the old man said that was so moving, it was almost entirely the way in which he said it, the total naked absorption of the mind in its problem, the tried-out words suspended for inspection, the unceasingly pitiless evaluation they were given, the temporarily triumphant going forward, the doubt, despair, the cruel recognition of failure, the glorious giving of solutions by something from somewhere, the insistent rebeginning, as though no one, not even the speaker, had ever been there. Without cant, without jargon, and in terms of examples, this abstract mind went concretely forward; and is it any wonder that he felt impatient with twaddle and any emphasis on showy finish, with glibness, with quickness, with polish and shine, with all propositions whose hems were carefully the right length, with all those philosophies which lean on one another, like one in a stupor leans against a bar? No wonder he was so jealous of his thoughts, no wonder he so entirely hated those who seized on his results without the necessary labors, as one might who'd sacrificed himself for summits only to await there the handclasps of those who had alighted from helicopters he'd designed; for he felt philosophy to be an activity, this very activity he was entering on before us, exactly as Valéry had felt concerning the creation of poetry, where every word allowed to remain in a line represented a series of acts of the poet, of proposals and withdrawals which, in agony, at last, issued in this one, and how no one word was final, how the work was never over, never done, but only, in grief, abandoned as it sometimes had to be, and so, in the manner of the poet, each line of thought was a fresh line, each old problem no older than the sonnet, invented today, to be conquered again for the first time, never mind if you've written a thousand; and a murmur ran round the seminar table, heads turned toward Malcolm, his student, who'd brought him, but I don't know for how many this movement was, as it was for me, a murmur, a movement, of recognition.

I was also amused. Malcolm's mannerisms were like his master's, and nearby sat Nelson, one of Malcolm's students, whose own mannerisms, in that moment, seemed to me but one more remove from the Form. The three men had fashioned, whether through affinity or influence, a perfect Platonic ladder.

Wittgenstein spoke very briefly, then. He produced an example to untie the discussion. A few weeks later he met with us, the graduate students there in philosophy, for two two-hour sessions. Monologues they were really, on the problems of knowledge and certainty, but since it was his habit merely to appear—to appear and to await a question—it was we who had to supply the topic, and for that delicate mission one of us was carefully briefed. G. E. Moore had once asked, staring, I suppose, at the end of his arm (and with what emotion: anguish? anxiety? anger? despair?): how do I know that this is a hand? and it was thought that the opening question might properly, safely, touch on that. Not all of us were primed, though, and before anyone realized what was happening a strange, unforeseen and uncalculated question had rolled down the table toward the master. Aristotle? Had it to do with Aristotle? And Wittgenstein's face fell like a crumpled wad of paper into his palms. Silence. Aristotle. We were lost. He would leave. In a moment he would rise and shuffle out, pained and affronted. Then Paul Ziff put his question—ours—for it was he who had been the student appointed; and after a terrible empty moment, Wittgenstein's head came up, and he began.

I thought, at the time, I'd undergone a conversion, but what I'd received, I realize now, was a philosophy shown, not a philosophy argued. Wittgenstein had uttered what he felt could be uttered (and it was very important), but what he had displayed could only be felt and seen—a method, and the moral and esthetic passion of a mind in love. How pale seems Sartre's *engagement* against the deep and fiery colors of that purely saintly involvement. It now seems inevitable that the *Tractatus* should have stressed, so much, the difference between what can be *said* (and anything that can be said can be said clearly), and what can only be *shown*, and it is completely proper that Engelmann should stress this himself in his memoir.[1]

However, the letters which comprise this volume, and the recollections which follow them (by an architect and friend during the time of the *Tractatus*), are almost entirely empty of interest. "I have received X, for which I thank you; I wish you would send me Y at once; my train will arrive in Z at T, and I feel ill and morally awful." You have now read the letters. Engelmann's little history gives us no more of the man than they do, and if we want to sense this unusual philosophical presence, we must still go to Malcolm's lovely and delicate account. Engelmann's pre-

[1] Paul Engelmann, *Letters from Ludwig Wittgenstein with a Memoir*, trans. L. Furtmuller (New York: 1968).

occupied with himself. He is full of wind-up, but has little pitch, and his discussions of the *Tractatus*, though he mentions some unarguably important things, are incomplete, vague, and misleading. A statement like this: ". . . an understanding of this philosopher will encourage the true believer to be undismayed in the face of the advancement of enlightenment and science, however successful they may be in their proper field; because their range stops short where that which alone matters to him begins . . ." will demonstrate, to anyone who knows Wittgenstein's work at all, how much Engelmann's emotional inclinations have got the better of him. His claim is that Wittgenstein's work has been generally misunderstood (which is easy enough to understand by itself), and that, as in Kant, the emphasis should fall upon the restrictions he places on reason, upon what can be meaningfully said, and that this leaves metaphysics open to be enjoyed, provided it remains mute (indeed the only way metaphysics *can* be enjoyed sometimes; the silence is wonderful when it occurs). Yet even if we make the distinction between saying and showing as simply as Engelmann does, we are, it seems to me, constrained to see that, in Wittgenstein, the world we cannot speak of can be very precisely *expressed*. Whereof we cannot speak, the philosopher has famously remarked, we must remain silent; but does it follow from this that we must not show what can only be shown by speech of Wittgenstein's kind? Or that showing is now something beyond the reach of reason, as Engelmann seems to imply? As every poet knows, the relation is rigorous. Nevertheless, Engelmann is right to call attention to the moral and esthetic side of the *Tractatus*, for these things have not received the attention they deserve.[2] The following strange line appears in this

---

2 Now, every day, this becomes less true.

beautiful poem: ethics and esthetics are one. I think Engelmann glosses it correctly, for I feel I saw it *shown* in those three evenings with the genius, and he quotes Karl Kraus appropriately:

> I cannot get myself to accept that a whole sentence
> can ever come from half a man.[3]

Both poet and logician have an equal interest here. Showing has several dimensions. Wittgenstein's propositions are complete, and therefore baffling to the wrong minds because they record the struggles of one who as a day-to-day human was only a half, no more, but who, as a philosopher, was considerably greater—perhaps a man and a half.

[3] The last essay in this book, "The Artist and Society," might be considered to be a gloss upon these words.

THE EVIL DEMIURGE

The neck, Plato tells us in the *Timaeus*, was fashioned by the Demiurge as a kind of isthmus between the head, which houses the higher soul, and the damper, softer regions given to the appetites and passions. This was done in order to protect the mind from their pollutions. Since then we have had nothing but complaints about the arrangement. That sovereign light, we hear, is a sly beguiler, a false leader, creator of gods and myths, an envious organ of denial, and a professional instrument of deceit. Long have the liver and the lungs, the bowels, heart, and privy members, languished out of sight in the ghettos of the body—becoming more resentful, more impoverished, more maligned, and more embittered every age.

A revolution is finally under way: not one merely which will deliver single bodies to them, some minuscule psychologies (that's happened often enough), or even one which will turn over to these vital but barbaric powers an entire state (that's also occurred occasionally), but one which will catch the whole declining West in its paws, and incidentally demonstrate the parallel which Plato drew between the condition of the soul and the corresponding health of society. Now, everywhere, in the name of Priapic Power, there is a rising against that absent landlord, Monsieur Teste, and his chief work, our civilization. "Whenever I pronounce the word 'civilization,' " Gauguin cried, "I spit." And M. Cioran writes: ". . . everything is virtue that leads us to live against the stream of our civilization, that invites us to compromise and sabotage its progress . . ."[1]

Yet cliché—and Cioran is, like Pope, a polisher of commonplaces, a recutter of old stones, though he would disapprove of any comparison with so classical a poet—cliché informs us (doesn't cliché tell us everything we know?) that every revolution is betrayed from the beginning—the ground of its spring is always spongy—and we have good reason to be sorry for this one, good *reason*. For what ruler has pleaded for his overthrow with greater eloquence and poetry, provided better demonstrations of his own unfitness, or supplied deadlier weapons to his enemies; who has spoken with more bitter poignancy of the ruler's isolation, the burdens of such office and the emptiness of its outward show, protesting "what have kings, that privates have not too, save ceremony," and exclaiming against all deeper differences, "if pricked, do I not bleed?"; who has represented more honestly the claims of the viscera to rule, then, than the mind-weary philosopher and king of the necktie tower,

[1] Although *The Temptation to Exist* is the first of E. M. Cioran's books to be translated into English (and beautifully, by Richard Howard [Chicago: Quadrangle, 1968]), six of his essays have been published by the *Hudson Review* since 1962: "A Bouquet of Heads," several snippets from this *Temptation;* "A Portrait of Civilized Man," from which this quotation is taken; "The Ambiguities of Fame," "The Snares of Wisdom," "The Evil Demiurge," and, most recently, "The New Gods."

who now divides his realm to rally opposition and lead it, howling, against the head? But why? why, except to restore the intellect to greater health, serener power?

The guts give the mind its strength; certainly the isthmus must be crossed, and ditched up after; but we should not, out of bad conscience, as Nietzsche warns us, Oedipus our eyes out, trade scepter for staff, or kingship for a beggar's tatters. The mind is the only claw a man has. Cioran, least of all, wants men harmless; he admires them when they're most wild . . . barbaric . . . mad. "Reason: the rust of our vitality," he writes, using a plumber's phrase. And were the Vandals thoughtless? were the Medici? Or was their reasoning new and fresh instead, unweary, full of force and optimism; weren't they led on by what they thought they could *become,* so that they drove themselves like warriors into change?

Change, however, is a curse. Concentrating on it deprives us of the present; we become a slave of time. "*Doing* is tainted with an original sin from which Being seems exempt."[2] The beggar, on the other hand, by cultivating his impoverishment, gains his freedom. "He *has* nothing, he *is* himself, he endures: to live on a footing with eternity is to live from day to day. . . ." Like Yeats's old men and his mendicants, like Shakespeare's fools, and Beckett's often crippled outcasts, these beggars are purely imaginary. The mystic, too, seeks Being, but through ecstasy, "the wreck of consciousness." With the magisterial myth of final nothingness, they lift themselves out of ordinary fictions. Fiction for fictions? Knowing this, we cannot follow them. Mystic, beggar, and barbarian: all tempt him, but only temporarily. Like a ball which can't escape its court, Cioran

---

[2] "The Ambiguities of Fame."

is volleyed from one racket onto the unyielding strings of another, his thought continuously describing the hopeless parabolas of paradox. Zeno's arrow, we all remember, either occupies successively each place in its path, thus is stationary there, and its movement, made of an infinity of stills, is mere illusion; or else it does not pass the points at all, is never anywhere, and its movement, as it's fallen altogether out of space, is, once again, a mere illusion.

Each of Cioran's essays adopts the tone of the dilemma, even if none has Zeno's unflinching elegance of form, for Zeno was rapacious, the Attila of logic, and wished to win; he strove always for conclusions. Conclusions? Cioran seems to say, they are only vanities, and he repudiates them all . . . but again, not absolutely. Although he seems to have taken his aphoristic style from Nietzsche, as well as many of his ideas, he is never as wild or bold or positive as Nietzsche was. His work drones with disillusion. His complaints about the intellect, his stress on instinct, his references to time, remind one of similar attitudes in Schopenhauer and Bergson, as well as some of the moods of the existentialists; nor can one escape the feeling that he's been kissed, immoderately, by Spengler. However, principally he is a Platonist unsure of which horse he should allow to lead, and regrets sometimes that the dark horse of desire has been tamed. Being, Non-Being, and Becoming: these ghosts haunt him, as do those ancient Greek divisions of the soul. His essays are exemplifications of the disease he says we suffer from: superbly written, economical, concerned with the very foundations of thought and being, they are nevertheless extraordinarily careless pieces of reasoning, travel from fallacy to fallacy with sovereign unconcern, deal almost wholly with borrowings, and spider down from dubious premises thick threads of purely *historical* associations. So evenly is

Cioran divided against himself, on irony's behalf, that there is scarcely a line which does not contain truth by precisely a half. Yet it is the conditions these pieces reveal which justifies their claim (strong, though implicit) to picture our contemporary mind. What one essay says of Meister Eckhart perfectly applies to Cioran himself:

> Even in the Middle Ages, certain minds, tired of sifting the same themes, the same expressions, were obliged, in order to renew their piety and to emancipate it from the official terminology, to fall back on paradox, on the alluring, sometimes brutal, sometimes subtle formula . . . his style, rather than his ideas, gained him the honor of being convicted of heresy. . . . Like every heretic, he sinned on the side of form. An enemy of language, all orthodoxy, whether religious or political, postulates *the usual expression.*

Thus, as Susan Sontag points out in her exemplary Introduction, there is nothing fresh about Cioran's thought . . . except its formal *fury*. His book has all the beauty of pressed leaves, petals shut from their odors; yet what is retained has its own emotion, and here it is powerful and sustained. *The Temptation to Exist* is a philosophical romance on modern themes: alienation, absurdity, boredom, futility, decay, the tyranny of history, the vulgarities of change, awareness as agony, reason as disease.

E. M. Cioran is, in every way, an alien; he has no home, even in his own heart. Born in Roumania, that nebbish among nations, he was exiled from it before he left, though now he bitterly pretends to have come to terms with its history of failure and its Balkan sense of fatality: ". . . would I have been able, without my country, to waste my days in so exemplary a manner?" Living in Paris since 1937, he has abandoned his native language (alien, now, to that, too), and composes his tight little essays in French; essays which he has no home in either, for he distrusts even his occupation ("To write books is to have a certain relation with original sin"[3]), since a concern with the Word withdraws us from the World—we vanish inside our syllables. "At least," he addresses a prospective author, "I have the excuse of hating my actions, of performing them without believing in them," and although he loathes his own self-loathing, he often regards this emotion as the only way to redemption. Are we to take all these repudiations seriously? Not a bit. Just a little. Yes and no. Truths he utters ironically to expose the falsehood in them, while falsehoods receive the same treatment, so what soundness they have will shine through. He seems really to think that if he writes his lies *like* lies, that will excuse them, but what he risks by this tactic is revealing an essentially frivolous mind. At his worst he appears a world-weary wit out of Oscar Wilde, no more: "Self-doubt worked on human beings to such a point that they invented love as a remedy, a tacit pact between two unfortunates to overestimate and praise each other shamelessly."[4] Consciousness, itself, he's quite alone in. Thought, as well—his sole addiction—takes him even further from the sources of vitality, and ruthlessly discloses its own futility—so much so that he says, "our strength can be measured by the sum of beliefs we abjure," and "each of us should wind up his career a deserter of all possible causes."[5]

What Cioran would do without his belief in alienation, disease, and decline is not clear; yet surely these ideas should

---

[3] Cioran has sinned, so far, six times.
[4] "The Ambiguities of Fame."
[5] "The Snares of Wisdom."

be abandoned, unless he is willing to qualify them until they lose their usefulness to poetry. Indeed, all his causes are in the same sinking boat. He tells us that the only minds which intrigue us "defend indefensible positions," and that "the only minds which seduce us are the minds which have destroyed themselves trying to give their lives a meaning" (note how we are dragged by the *us* out to these extremities); yet there are other minds, other styles, which risk more (one essay is titled "Style as Risk"), those which dare to replace flamboyance with responsibility. If we ask ourselves soberly what such remarks mean, or what amount of truth they contain, mustn't our answer honestly be: very little, and not much?

Although his treatment of the doctrine of Destiny is acid, and his feelings about determinism in general more than skeptical, the opposition between reason and instinct, between civilization and vitality, between time and freedom —the whole lot—is presented as inescapable; and he regularly throws his thought, which he properly describes as autobiographical (and which has only a subjective, a psychological validity), into the first person plural, where it obtains the abstractness and rigidity of a mathematical model. Theories of decline and decay require a belief in Necessity as much as those which naïvely predict Progress; they both lean on history (which Cioran sourly regards as "man's aggression against himself"), and both depend heavily upon the use of terms (like "instinct," "intellect," "civilization") which facilitate equivocation, and produce in the reader that effortless sense of depth and subtlety which is so rewarding and so inexpensive. Finally, both need eyes which blaze at the oncoming of contrary facts, and dazzle them into the ditch.

Nietzsche, who made so many of the same observations Cioran does, was altogether wiser: the Apollonian and Dionysian principles are only *possible* enemies; the health he was after required their unity, not their opposition. Cioran suffers from what Nietzsche called

> the greatest and most disastrous of maladies, of which humanity has not to this day been cured: his sickness of himself, brought on by the violent severance from his animal past, by his sudden leap and fall into new layers and conditions of existence, by his declaration of war against the old instincts that had hitherto been the foundation of his power, his joy, and his awesomeness.

Cioran's diagnosis is the same, but he regards, even a little smugly (a condition, of course, he also recognizes), this disease as incurable; and therefore—some think bravely— perseveres in it, aggravates it, champions it.

We no longer remember the trouble we took to walk. It did not come so easily as sprouting for a seed. Now, when we learn to drive a golf ball or a car, some notion of the effort we took returns to us. Our body was our enemy at first, a foreign thing, an uncustomary country. We were forced to tackle the problem in a series of steps, mechanically; commands were issued from the head to the head, to the torso, to the legs, the arms, but they did not immediately obey us, nor were our orders clear. Like a cage of big cats, we frightened our limbs into obedience, into a semblance of order. How arbitrary, too, the aims of the vaulter, how artificial his grip, how unnaturally he must move to scramble up the sky, how out of reach his achievement is for most of us, how against Nature; yet how easily, how thoughtlessly, how beautifully he finally does it. For at the moment of his mastery, the vaulter and his pole, the bar he is overing, the pit below, the medium he moves through: all of these are extensions of his will. We ought to understand these powers, this expanded condition, for we did learn walking once, and overcame similar handicaps, and now we stroll, or run, or dance, or speak as simply as we see when we open an eye. The world is there; we need not issue commands to it: let there be horns, hills, houses, intransitive verbs; let there be strolling: left, right, left, right; let there be rhymes. Yet these trained athletes are animals. Where is the severance in them? They are well with regard to their activities. Should thoughtfulness, the moves of the mind, and its relation to its objects, be any different?

To feel at home in our body, to sense the true *nostos* of it, is to have it move to our will so smoothly we seem will-less altogether. The will of God, Kant thought, might be that holy with respect to the Good. We take walking for granted, elementary seeing for granted, yet we find we cannot feel. Thought seems to remove us; we cannot enjoy life; the mechanics of the car are so demanding, we cannot have the pleasure of the ride. Beckett's men on their bicycles, or with their cripples' sticks, point the analogy in the other direction. We have fallen out of our bodies like a child from a tree; bruised, forlorn, we bellow at the foot of it and wish we were back there among the leaves, and wish at the same time never to suffer such risks again.

Love is an achievement like the achievement of the vaulter; it's to rise as expertly and naturally as he does. One fundamental remedy for alienation is mastery—the incorporation of skill. Rightly chosen, such skills liberate desire, empower it; only when, for whatever reason, we no longer bring into our bodies the forms of civilization are these felt as frustrating obstacles and enemies of want. Civilized dining, to name a lowly instance: in what ways do its rites demean us, and leave our stomachs empty, our natures unfulfilled?[6] As Marcuse writes: "The power to restrain and guide instinctual drives, to make biological necessities into individual needs and desires, increases rather than reduces gratification. . . ." But such considerations have no place in the myth of alienation.

Our minds can grow their own bodies, become body, play a different Demiurge. We can swell with the world we take in. Otherwise we shrink and wrinkle like a prune. In the prune, contracting on its core, I sense small temptation, little reason to exist.

[6] The previous points are developed in "The Stylization of Desire."

THE IMAGINATION OF
AN INSURRECTION

History may not be, as Stephen Dedalus thought, a nightmare, since we are murdered in our beds of sleep quite bloodlessly; but dreams are part of history, although all images, apparitions, fits, illusions, myths, the mind's confusions, trances, dreams, even history books themselves, and poetry, are frequently ignored because they seem unlike most facts: so many shot on this date, so many starved on that, so many neighbored by the graves and cried a lot. Indeed, the failure of history seen as a kind of science is its stubborn externality; it follows the course of human behavior as the eye might follow sliding rocks, and never feels the avalanche, never gains admission to events, in the belief (an important myth itself) that they have no historically significant inner life. We comprehend insanity still less, standing, as we like to think, safely high on shore. The river is simply discarding its banks (also a seasonal thing with snakes). We label it a flood and warn the town: what more? Causes we examine, yes, but seldom the quality of the experience. There is a silly grin upon the madman's face. Is there another silly grin inside? If not, what? It's possibly all that matters to the madman, and it's he who may decide on doing divination with your bowels.

If behavior alters consciousness, as it surely does, consciousness alters behavior; and no one supposes, now, that consciousness is just a simpleminded mirror of the world. These facts, indeed, these hard realities, often find no reflection there. Yet history may be a nightmare (appear, that is, fundamentally incomprehensible like the actions of the mad when merely observed) if we do not understand men more completely than hitherto we have. We must try to understand, for instance, how a man's own image of himself can take hold of him as powerfully as a spinning wind, and whirl him off to a land like Oz, which might be Berlin on the Night of the Crystal, or Dublin entering the Troubles.

Mr. Thompson's imaginatively conceived, carefully researched, and beautifully written book[1] concerns the impact of imagination on events, and although the moment he has chosen (the Easter Rebellion) is perfect for him, allowing him to match two important literary and political movements, he is at all times aware of parallels among the acts of the French in 1789, the Germans in 1844 (and again, alas, later), the Irish in 1916, and the American Negro now. These comparisons are tactfully made, nowhere insisted on, and Mr. Thompson's argument does not require them; yet despite the great interest which his development of the Irish case has, it is the theoretical pattern which emerges that is most exciting; though it is curious, in this connection, that Mr. Thompson overlooks such a book as Tolstoi's *What Is Art?* since it expresses so perfectly the same attitudes and dreams as the Irish rebel poets.

[1] *The Imagination of an Insurrection* (New York: Oxford University Press, 1967).

For a long time Irish society dawdled through the stages of decay as though it suffered from a drawn-out illness. The well-intentioned and well-educated were quite guiltily aware of their advantages. The sensitive deplored the conditions of the peasants, but they also lived in fear of urbanization and the machine. It is easy to sympathize, hard to give up privilege; thus the nicer members of the aristocracy dreamed that like a loving father they would move from hut to manor, elevating, educating, bettering lots, as though the evils everyone endured could be picked out like weevils in a biscuit, leaving the remainder palatable, fresh, and even sweet. Shame and contradiction were the basis of these liberal beliefs, because if you are going to give your poor niggers a hand up, you must always stand higher than they. Desiring the impossible, both to retain and to change, and unable to achieve either for themselves as long as Ireland stayed an English fief, they began to express their national aspirations by cultural rather than political means. They liked to feel it wasn't they who'd rendered Ireland impotent or enslaved its peasantry, and when they cast out evil from themselves, they extended this purification to the whole people. Scholars slowly discovered, as Mr. Thompson relates so brilliantly, a national past—the heroes, the glory, of an ancient age. But if the Irish soul is basically pure, why hasn't it triumphed? Where is the source of this corruption? Clearly it was contained in that imported English culture which had created the Irish scholars and artists themselves, the very men who came forward finally to condemn it.

Thus imagination enters Irish history; henceforth everything's reseen. Since the accepted religion is "foreign," the new one will be different, incorporating superstition in the guise of mysticism. Business should be honest barter based on agriculture. And a real morality is needed, one to accompany innocence like mint jelly and its lamb. Literary styles and canons, subject matters, themes, are made over to the ancients. Myths and fairy tales jet from the Folk like a fountain. But no tale the poets are able to take away from time is more remarkable than the two they make up themselves: that of Ireland's glorious heroic age, and the goodness and beauty of the common way. They found that the peasant (Irish peasants, German peasants, Russian peasants, Negroes) sang; led simple lives; spoke poetry; were near the elemental things; had deeper personal ties than they had; loved, slept, worked, and died in the rhythms of the seasons; possessed natural piety, sexual potency, and a unity of instincts which could only have been a gift flown straight from the gods. Their art was simple, crude—yes; but it was sincere, fundamental, moving; and it promoted that collective unity which present poets ought to strive for themselves. The past, in short, was good; the present, awful.

Of course what Yeats (and Tolstoi) wanted was to keep the huts and manor: they would move among their peasants like the liberal moves among his Negroes, patting them on the head, giving them instruction, and admiring, in turn, the beautiful life, the rich culture, they had built out of ignorance, poverty, and servitude. In the face of such accomplishments, one no longer needs to feel guilty; one can even feel proud. The effect of these delusions on consciousness is catastrophic, and the effect on poetry equally ruinous (Yeats is driven away), for they oversimplify experience dangerously, and finally deny that very poverty, ignorance, and general suffering which they were intended to alleviate in the first place.

Nevertheless, so great is the need to believe these confusions, so flattering, at first, do they seem, that the people seize on them greedily; ideas have their edges rounded, become slogans with wheels, ready to roll into action. Yet the myth is incomplete without martyrs, and the martyrs must be real. Plunkett. Pearse. MacDonagh. The world which they imagine weighs upon the world they act in as substantially as shadows on a street. The poet is a dreamer in this dream, and drawn to politics, remaking the nature and identity of the nation, he steps inside his own mythology; not to disappear as the legendary painter disappears in his painting, but, a saint of the ridiculous, to die of Easter in an Irish place.[2]

Mr. Thompson not only examines the images which helped shape the Rising, he investigates with equal skill the way in which the rebellion was retained and construed by Yeats, A.E., and O'Casey. This is history, too. "The consequences of an event take place in the mind, and the mind holds on best to images." His book is a fine example of imagination working on imagination: instance and theory, scholarship and history, criticism and poetry are woven in a single spell. Mr. Thompson spells quite beautifully. I hope everyone will read him.

2 See "The Artist and Society."

EVEN IF, BY ALL THE OXEN
IN THE WORLD

Consciousness comes too easily. We did not learn it like a language. It leaps to its work like a mirror. Yet consciousness can close and open like an eye; its depths are not illusory, and its reflection on itself is not mechanical. It's something won, retrieved, conserved, as love is, and as love should be. It is with regard to consciousness, and the consciousness of consciousness, that I wish to examine popular culture in this country; and I shall simply suppose that cultural objects are created so we can become aware of them, and that those which are popular are so in a double sense: because they are widely approved and widely employed.

Imagine that a mirror, nothing falling into it, began reflecting itself: what a terrifying endlessness and mockery of light—merely to illuminate its own beams. You might think that an empty consciousness, like a vacuum, would immediately fill; that the nerves would pour in their messages like so many spouts from the roof of the skin, but sensing is not so simple as we sometimes suppose. Like falling, descent is easy only once we've jumped. Every consciousness has its rainless lands and polar wastes, its undiscovered and unventured countries. And there are simply boring stretches, like the Western Plains or the dry mouth's taste. Certainly consciousness is capable of subtle, wonderful, and terrifying transformations. After all, it is the dream we live in, and like the dream, can harbor anything. Although we are alert to changes in our physical and mental health, and have catalogued their causes and conditions, little has been done to describe adequately states of consciousness themselves or evaluate their qualities. Nonetheless, it is the whole of all we are at any time. At any time, if it is thrilling, we are thrilled; if it is filled with beauty, we are beautiful. It is our only evidence we live. Yet nothing seems more obvious to me than the fear, hatred, and contempt men have for it. They find it useful (an electric map of tracks and trains); otherwise it is embarrassing at best, or boring; at worst, it's threatening and horrible. Indeed, it's so much worse than simple black oblivion that only an obstinate, foolish will to live, the simple insistence of the veins which leaves have, cowslips, oxen, ants have just as well, can account for most men's going on, since such a will moves blindly, in roots beneath the ground, in bottle flies and fish, and our feelings are the price we pay for being brained instead of finned. Perception, Plato said, is a form of pain.

The working consciousness, for instance, is narrow, shuttered by utility, its transitions eased by habit past reflection like a thief. Impulses from without or from within must use some strength to reach us, we do not go out to them. Machines are made this way. Alert as lights and aimed like guns, they only see the circle of their barrels. How round the world is; how like a well arranged. Thus when desire is at an ebb and will is weak, we trail the entertainer like a child his mother, restless, bored, and whining: what can I do? what will amuse me? how shall I live? Then

> L'ennui, fruit de la morne incuriosité,
> Prend les proportions de l'immortalité.

The enjoyment of sensation as sensation, a fully free awareness, is very rare. We keep our noses down like dogs to sniff our signs. Experience must *mean*. The content of an aimless consciousness is weak and colorless; we may be filled up by ourselves instead—even flooded basements, some days, leak the other way—and then it's dread we feel, anxiety.

To tie experience to a task, to seek significance in everything, to take and never to receive, to keep, like the lighter boxer, moving, bob and weave, to fear the appearance of the self and every inwardness: these are such universal characteristics of the average consciousness that I think we can assume that popular culture functions fundamentally with regard to them.

But "before Plato told the great lie of ideals," Lawrence wrote, "men slimly went like fishes, and didn't care. . . . They knew it was no use knowing their own nothingness. . . ." Nothing keeps us back from nothingness but knowing; knowing, now, not necessarily in the sense of squeezing what we know into a set of symbols and understanding those; but knowing in the sense of seeing—seeing clearly, deeply, fully—of being completely aware, and consequently of being perfectly ourselves; for Lawrence lets his pagans speed to their mark as thoughtlessly as arrows.

Must we be drunk or doped or mad, must we be dunced and numb to feed our animal halves? So it appears. The average man does not want to know how he looks when he eats; he defecates in darkness, reading the *Reader's Digest;*

his love has an awkward automatic metal brevity, like something sprayed from a can, and any day his present sex may be replaced with plastic; his work is futile, his thought is shallow, his joys ephemeral, his howls helpless and agony incompetent; his hopes are purchased, his voice prerecorded, his play is mechanical, the roles typed, their lines trite, all strengths are sapped, exertion anyhow is useless, to vote or not is futile, futile . . . so in almost every way he is separated from the centers of all power and feeling: futilely he feeds, he voids, he screws, he smokes, he motorboats, he squats before the tube, he spends at least a week each year in touring and a month in memorizing lies—lies moral, religious, and political—he beats the drum or shouts hurray on cue, he wears a neon nightie, swallows pills, and chews his woman's nipples now because a book he's read has told him that he ought to; my god, he jigs, he swigs, he sings the very latest tra-la-las and sends his kids to scouts and all-white schools, he rounds his bottom to a pew, loves pulpitry, and contributes yearly to a cause; with splendid sexlessness he breeds—boards receive their nails with greater sensitivity— he kites the lies he's learned as high as heaven where they sing like toads in trees, yet he sickens just the same, and without reason, for he's been to bridge and bingo, said his rahs as well as anyone, never borrowed on his insurance, kept his car clean, and put his three sons twice through Yale; but age, which is not real, hangs like a dirty suit inside his freshly pressed tuxedo; thus he fails, assumes another slumber, and dies like merchandise gone out of season.

Imagine for a moment what would happen if the television paled, the radio fell silent, the press did not release. Imagine all the clubs and courses closed, magazines unmailed, guitars unplugged, pools, rinks, gyms, courts, stadia shut up. Suppose that publishers were to issue no more dick, prick, and booby books; movies were banned along with gambling, liquor, and narcotics; and men were suddenly and irrevocably alone with themselves . . . alone only with love to be made, thought, sense, and dreadful life. What would be the state of our nature, then, Mr. Hobbes?

It is the principal function of popular culture—though hardly its avowed purpose—to keep men from understanding what is happening to them, for social unrest would surely follow, and who knows what outbursts of revenge and rage. War, work, poverty, disease, religion: these, in the past, have kept men's minds full, small, and careful. Religion gave men hope who otherwise could have none. Even a mechanical rabbit can make the greyhounds run.

People who have seen the same game, heard the same comedians, danced to the same din, read the same detectives, can form a community of enthusiasts whose exchange of feelings not only produces the most important secondary effect of popular culture (the culture hero and his worship services), but also helps persuade people that their experiences were real, reinforces judgments of their values, and confirms their addiction. Popular culture occurs in public; it is as much an event as an experience; and it is reported on in the same spirit. There are therefore both participants and spectators, and in much of popular culture a steady drift toward voyeurism and passivity. As culture rises, it shatters; nothing remains in what were formerly the highest cultural realms but isolated works; isolated now by their character, which repels all but the most devoted and cultivated love, and by the divisive nature of society which sets them apart in order to destroy them if possible. The objects of popular culture are competitive. They are expected to yield a return. Their effect must be swift and pronounced, therefore they are strident, ballyhooed, and baited with sex; they must be able to create or take part in a fad; and they must die without fuss and leave no corpse. In short, the products of popular culture, by and large, have no more esthetic quality than a brick in the street. Their authors are anonymous, and tend to dwell in groups and create in committees; they are greatly dependent upon performers and performance; any esthetic intention is entirely absent, and because it is desired to manipulate consciousness directly, achieve one's effect there, no mind is paid to the intrinsic nature of its objects; they lack finish, complexity, stasis, individuality, coherence, depth, and endurance. But they do possess splash.

It's in a way unfair to popular culture to compare it with the workmanships of artists since they do perform such different functions; nevertheless, this kind of comparison is not entirely unjust. Both shape a consciousness, but art enlarges consciousness like space in a cathedral, ribboned with light, and though a new work of art may consume our souls completely for a while, almost as a jingle might, if consumption were all that mattered, we are never, afterward, the same; we cannot unconsciously go on in the old way; there is, as in Rilke's poem "Torso of an Archaic Apollo," no place that does not see us, and we must change our life. Even Arnold Bennett noticed that we do not measure classics; they, rather, measure us. For most people it is precisely this that's painful; they do not wish to know their own nothingness—or their own potentialities either, and the pleasures of popular culture are like the pleasures of disease, work, poverty, and religion: they give us something to do, something to suffer, an excuse for failure, and a justification of everything.

If sixty percent of the people of a country are addicts of opium, then we are not rash in inferring there a general sickness of spirit; if alcoholism is epidemic, or suicide, or gambling, still another spiritual malaise can be confirmed; and if a great portion of any population is spending many hours every day driving all life from the mind, in worship of low-cost divinities like the goddess of the golden udder, there's been another plague in spirit, and there are deaths to show for it, and endless deformities. Art does not, I hasten to say, have a hortatory influence; it's not a medicine, and it teaches nothing. It simply shows us what beauty, perfection, sensuality, and meaning are; and we feel as we should feel if we'd compared physiques with Hercules.

None of these complaints is new, and there would be little point in repeating them except that from time to time one senses an effort to Hitlerize the culture of the Folk; make it somehow spring from some deep well of human feeling, as if art were ever the triumph of sincerity over ineptitude, as if passion were a substitute for skill, as if, indeed, its gaucheries were not only charming, but *esthetically* so . . . this, in order to put out those high and isolated fires, those lonely works of genius which still manage, somehow, amazingly, now and then, to appear. There is no Folk, of course; there are no traditions; fine moral sentiments improve no lyrics, nor beautify their song; the occasional appearance of splendid exceptions does not soften, excuse, or justify anything; popular culture is the product of an industrial machine which makes baubles to amuse the savages while missionaries steal their souls and merchants steal their money.

How romantically he talks about it, you may say; what wretched little dramas he's made up—these wee morality plays from wild exaggerations. "High and isolated fires" indeed. Anything which surrounds us like the air we breathe, with which like wives and husbands we're easy and familiar, can't be so poisonous; we are alive, aren't we? Well no, if you ask me, we aren't, or only partially. This muck cripples consciousness. Therefore no concessions should be made to it; and those who take their pleasure there should not be permitted to appear to lift those tastes to something higher with scholarly hypocrisy and philosophical pretense. The objects of popular culture are not art; their success or failure should not be judged as art's is; and the pleasures they provide, among goods, come last, even if, as Plato says, they are asserted to be first by all the oxen in the world.

THE ARTIST AND SOCIETY

The tame bear's no better off than we are. You've seen how he sways in his cage. At first you might think him musical, but the staves are metal, and his movements are regular and even like the pulses of a pump. It's his nerves. Even when he claps his paws, rises like a man to his hind feet and full height, he looks awkward, feels strange, unsure (his private parts and underbelly are exposed); he trembles. Smiling (you remember the fawning eyeshine of the bear), he focuses his nose and waits for the marshmallow we're about to toss, alert to snap up the sweet cotton in his jaws. There's something terrible about the tame caged bear . . . all that wildness become marshmallow, terrible for his heart, his liver, his teeth (a diet so sugary and soft and unsubstantial, the bowels seek some new employment), and terrible for us—for what we've lost. His eyes, too, are filled with a movement that's not in the things he sees, but in himself. It is the movement of his own despair, his ineffectual rage.

The Artist and Society

My subject is the artist and society, not the tamed, trained bear, but in many ways the subjects are the same. Artists are as different as men are. It would be wrong to romanticize about them. In our society, indeed, they may live in narrower and more frightened corners than most of us do. We should not imitate their ways; they're not exemplary, and set no worthy fashions. Nor does the artist bear truth dead and drooping in his arms like a lovelorn maiden or a plump goose. His mouth hasn't the proper shape for prophecies. Pot or bottle ends or words or other mouths—whole catalogs of kissing—noisy singing, the folds of funny faces he's created and erased, an excess of bugling have spoiled it for philosophy. In the ancient quarrel between the poets and philosophers, Plato was surely right to think the poets liars. They lie quite roundly, unashamedly, with glee and gusto, since lies and fancies, figments and inventions, outrageous falsehoods are frequently more real, more emotionally pure, more continuously satisfying to them than the truth, which is likely to wear a vest, fancy bucket pudding, technicolor movies, and long snoozes through Sunday.

W. H. Auden remarked quite recently, when pestered, I think it was, about Vietnam:

> Why writers should be canvassed for their opinion
> on controversial political issues I cannot imagine.
> Their views have no more authority than those of
> any reasonably well-educated citizen. Indeed, when
> read in bulk, the statements made by writers, in-
> cluding the greatest, would seem to indicate that
> literary talent and political common sense are rarely
> found together. . . .

Israel makes war, and there are no symposia published by prizefighters, no pronouncements from hairdressers, not a ding from the bellhops, from the dentists not even a drill's buzz, from the cabbies nary a horn beep, and from the bankers only the muffled chink of money. Composers, sculptors, painters, architects: they have no rolled-up magazine to megaphone themselves, and are, in consequence, ignored. But critics, poets, novelists, professors, journalists—those used to shooting off their mouths—they shoot (no danger, it's only their own mouth's wash they've wallowed their words in); and those used to print, they print; but neither wisdom nor goodwill nor magnanimity are the qualities which will win you your way to the rostrum . . . just plentiful friends in pushy places and a little verbal skill.

If it is pleasant to be thought an expert on croquet, imagine what bliss it is to be thought an authority on crime, on the clockwork of the human heart, the life of the city, peace and war. How hard to relinquish the certainty, which most of us have anyway, of *knowing*. How sweet it is always to be asked one's opinion. What a shame it is, when asked, not to have one.

Actually Auden's observation can be spread two ways: to include all artists, not writers merely, and to cover every topic not immediately related to their specialized and sometimes arcane talents. It's only the failed artist and his foolish public who would like to believe otherwise, for if they can honestly imagine that the purpose of art is to teach and to delight, to double the face of the world as though with a mirror, to penetrate those truths which nature is said to hold folded beneath her skirts and keeps modestly hidden from the eyes and paws of science, then they will be able to avoid art's actual impact altogether, and the artist's way of life can continue to seem outrageous, bohemian, quaint, a little sinful, irresponsible, hip, and charming, something to visit like the Breton peasants on a holiday, and not a challenge *to* and denial *of* their own manner of existence, an accusation concerning their own lack of reality.

Yet the social claims for art, and the interest normal people take in the lives of their artists, the examinations of the psychologists, the endless studies by endlessly energetic students of nearly everything, the theories of the philosophers, the deadly moral danger in which art is periodically presumed to place the young, unhappily married women, sacred institutions, tipsy souls, and unsteady parliaments, and all those nice persons in positions of power: these claims and interests are so regularly, so inevitably, so perfectly and purely irrelevant that one must begin to suspect that the tight-eyed, squeeze-eared, loin-lacking enemies of art are right; that in spite of everything that's reasonable, in spite of all the evidence, for example, that connoisseurs of yellowing marble statuary and greenish Roman coins are no more moral than the rest of us; that artists are a murky-headed, scurvy-living lot; that if art told the truth, truth must be polkadot; in spite, in short, of insuperable philosophical obstacles (and what obstacles, I ask you, could be more insuperable than those), art does tell us, in its manner, how to live, and artists are quite remarkable, even exemplary, men. We are right to keep them caged.

Thus I begin again, but this time on the other side.

Ronald Laing begins his extraordinary little book *The Politics of Experience*[1] by saying:

> Few books today are forgivable. Black on the canvas, silence on the screen, an empty white sheet of paper, are perhaps feasible. There is little conjunction of truth and social "reality." Around us are

[1] (New York: Pantheon, 1967).

pseudo-events, to which we adjust with a false consciousness adapted to see these events as true and real, and even as beautiful. In the society of men the truth resides now less in what things are than in what they are not. Our social realities are so ugly if seen in the light of exiled truth, and beauty is almost no longer possible if it is not a lie.

You can measure the reality of an act, a man, an institution, custom, work of art in many ways: by the constancy and quality of its effects, the depth of the response which it demands, the kinds and range of values it possesses, the actuality of its presence in space and time, the multiplicity and reliability of the sensations it provides, its particularity and uniqueness on the one hand, its abstract generality on the other—I have no desire to legislate concerning these conditions, insist on them all.

We can rob these men, these acts and objects, of their reality by refusing to acknowledge them. We pass them on the street but do not see or speak. We have no Negro problem in our small Midwestern towns. If someone has the experience of such a problem, he is mistaken. What happened to him did not happen; what he felt he did not feel; the urges he has are not the urges he has; what he wants he does not want. Automatically I reply to my son, who has expressed his desire for bubble gum: Oh, Peppy, you don't want that. Number one, then: we deny. We nullify the consciousness of others. We make their experiences unreal.

Put yourself in a public place, at a banquet—one perhaps at which awards are made. Your fork is pushing crumbs about upon your plate while someone is receiving silver in a bowler's shape amid the social warmth of clapping hands. How would you feel if at this moment a beautiful lady in a soft pink nightie should lead among the tables a handsome poodle who puddled under them, and there was a conspiracy among the rest of us not to notice? Suppose we sat quietly; our expressions did not change; we looked straight through her, herself as well as nightie, toward the fascinating figure of the speaker; suppose, leaving, we stepped heedlessly in the pools, and afterward we did not even shake our shoes. And if you gave a cry, if you warned, explained, cajoled, implored; and we regarded you then with amazement, rejected with amusement, contempt, or scorn every one of your efforts, I think you would begin to doubt your senses and your very sanity. Well, that's the idea: with the weight of our numbers, our percentile normality, we create insanities: yours, as you progressively doubt more and more of your experience, hide it from others to avoid the shame, saying "There's that woman and her damn dog again," but now saying it silently, for your experience, you think, is private; and ours, as we begin to believe our own lies, and the lady and her nightie, the lady and her poodle, the lady and the poodle's puddles, all *do* disappear, expunged from consciousness like a stenographer's mistake.

If we don't deny, we mutilate, taking a part for the whole; or we rearrange things, exaggerating some, minimizing others. There was a lady, yes, but she was wearing a cocktail dress, and there was a dog, too, very small, and very quiet, who sat primly in her lap and made no awkward demonstrations. Or we invert values, and assume strange obligations, altogether neglecting the ones which are obvious and demanding: we rob the poor to give to the rich rich gifts, to kings their kingdoms, to congressmen bribes, to companies the inexpensive purchase of our lives. We rush to buy poodles with liquid nerves—it has become, like so much else, *the rage*. Teas are fun, we say, but necking's not nice. Imagine. We still *do* say that. Or we permit events to occur for some people but not for others. Women and children have no sexual drives; men don't either, thank god, after fifty—sixty? seventy-five? We discredit events by inserting in otherwise accurate accounts outrageous lies. It was the lady who made the mess, not the poodle. In short, we do what we can to destroy experience—our own and others'. But since we can only act according to the way we see things, "*if our experience is destroyed, our behavior will be destructive.*" We live in ruins, in bombed-out shells, in the basements of our buildings. In important ways, we are all mad. You don't believe it? This company, community, this state, our land, is normal? Healthy, is it? Laing has observed that normal healthy men have killed perhaps one hundred million of their fellow normal healthy men in the last fifty years.

Nudists get used to nakedness. We get used to murder.

Why are works of art so socially important? Not for the messages they may contain, not because they expose slavery or cry hurrah for the worker, although such messages in their place and time might be important, but because they insist more than most on their own reality; because of the absolute way in which they exist. Certainly, images exist, shadows and reflections, fakes exist and hypocrites, there are counterfeits (quite real) and grand illusions—but it is simply not true that the copies are as real as their originals, that they meet all of the tests which I suggested earlier. Soybean steak, by god, is soybean steak, and a pious fraud is a fraud. Reality is not a matter of fact, it is an achievement; and it is rare—rarer, let me say—than an undefeated football season. We live, most of us, amidst lies, deceits, and confusions. A work of art may not utter the truth, but it must be honest. It may champion a cause we deplore, but like Milton's Satan, it must in itself be noble; it must be *all there*. Works of art confront us the way few people dare to: completely, openly, at once. They construct, they comprise, our experience; they do not deny or destroy it; and they shame us, we fall so short of the quality of their Being. We live in Lafayette or Rutland—true. We take our breaths. We fornicate and feed. But Hamlet has his history in the heart, and none of us will ever be as real, as vital, as complex and living as he is—a total creature of the stage.

This is a difficult point to make if the reality or unreality of things has not been felt. Have you met a typical nonperson lately? Then say hello, now, to your neighbor. He may be male, but his facial expressions have been put on like lipstick and eyelashes. His greeting is inevitable; so is his interest in the weather. He always smiles; he speaks only in clichés; and his opinions (as bland as Cream of Wheat, as undefined, and—when sugared—just as sweet) are drearily predictable. He has nothing but good to say of people; he collects his wisdom like dung from a Digest; he likes to share his experiences with "folks," and recite the plots of movies. He is working up this saccharine soulside manner as part of his preparation for the ministry.

These are the "good" people. "Bad" people are unreal in the same way.

Nonpersons unperson persons. They kill. For them no one is human. Like cash registers, everyone's the same, should be addressed, approached, the same: all will go ding and their cash drawers slide out when you strike the right key.

So I don't think that it's the message of a work of art that gives it any lasting social value. On the contrary, insisting on this replaces the work with its interpretation, another way of robbing it of its reality. How would you like to be replaced by your medical dossier, your analyst's notes? They take much less space in the file. The analogy, I think, is precise. The aim of the artist ought to be to bring into the world objects which do not already exist there, and objects which are especially worthy of love. We meet people, grow to know them slowly, settle on some to companion our life. Do we value our friends for their social status, because they are burning in the public blaze? do we ask of our mistress her meaning? calculate the usefulness of our husband or wife? Only too often. Works of art are meant to be lived with and loved, and if we try to understand them, we should try to understand them as we try to understand any-one—in order to know *them* better, not in order to know something else.

Why do public officials, like those in the Soviet Union, object so strenuously to an art which has no images in it—which is wholly abstract, and says nothing? Because originals are dangerous to reproductions. For the same reason that a group of cosmetically constructed, teetotal lady-maidens is made uneasy by the addition of a boozy uncorseted madam. Because it is humiliating to be less interesting, less present, less moving, than an arrangement of enameled bedpans. Be-cause, in a system of social relations based primarily on humbug, no real roaches must be permitted to wander. Be-cause, though this may be simply my helpless optimism, your honest whore will outdraw, in the end, any sheaf you choose of dirty pictures.

Pornography is poor stuff, not because it promotes lascivious feelings, but because these feelings are released by and directed toward unreal things. The artist, in this sense, does not deal in dreams.

Of course there are many objects labeled works of art, I know, which are fakes—the paint, for instance, toupeed to the canvas—but I am thinking of the artist, now, as one who produces the honest article, and obviously, *he* is valuable to society if what he *produces* is valuable to it. He is presently valuable because in his shop or study he concocts amusements for our minds, foods for our souls—foods so purely spiritual and momentary they leave scarcely any stools. However, I wanted to say that despite the good reasons for wondering otherwise, the artist could be regarded an exemplary man— one whose ways are worthy of imitation. How can this be? The fellow sleeps with his models and paint jams the zipper on his trousers.

I think we can regard him as exemplary in this way: we judge it likely that a man's character will show up some- where in his work; that if he is hot-tempered and impetuous, or reckless and gay . . . well, find somebody else to be your surgeon. And we regularly expect to see the imprint of the person in the deed, the body in the bedclothes. I think it is not unreasonable to suppose, too, that the work a man does works on him, that the brush he holds has his hand for its canvas, that the movements a man makes move the man who makes them just as much, and that the kind of ideals, dreams, perceptions, wishes his labor loves must, in him, love at least that labor.

Often enough we lead split lives, the artist as often as anybody; yet it isn't Dylan Thomas or D. H. Lawrence, the drunkard or sadist, I'm suggesting we admire, but the poets they were, and the men they had to be to be such poets. It would have been better if they had been able to assume in the world the virtues they possessed when they faced the page. They were unable. It's hard. And for that the world is partly to blame. It does not *want* its artists, after all. It especially does not want the virtues which artists must employ in the act of their work lifted out of prose and paint and plaster into life.

What are some of these virtues?

Honesty is one . . . the ability to see precisely what's been done . . . the ability to face up . . . because the artist wants his every line to be lovely—that's quite natural—he wants to think well of himself, and cover himself with his own praise like the sundae with its syrup. We all know that artists are vain. But they're not vain while working. We know, too, that they're defensive, insecure. But they dare not be defensive about a bad job, explain their mistakes away, substitute shouting for skill. If a runty tailor dresses himself in his dreams, he may measure for himself the suit of a wrestler. You can fill yourself with air, but will your skin hold it? They don't make balloons with the toughness and resiliency of genius.

Presence is one. The artist cannot create when out of focus. His is not another theatrical performance. There's no one to impress, no audience. He's lived with his work, doubtless, longer than he's had a wife, and it knows all about him in the thorough, hard-boiled way a wife knows. No poseur wrote "The Ballad of Reading Gaol." Presence is a state of concentration on another so complete it leaves you quite without defenses, altogether open; for walls face both ways, as do the bars of a cage. Inquire of the bears how it is. To erect bars is to be behind them. Withholding is not a requirement of poetry.

Unity is another. The artist does not create with something special called imagination which he has and you haven't. He can create with his body because that body has become a mind; he can create with his feelings because they've turned into sensations. He thinks in roughness, loudness, and in color. A painter's hands are magnified eyes. He *is* those fingers—he becomes his medium—and as many fingers close simply in a single fist, so all our faculties can close, and hold everything in one clasp as the petals close in a rose or metal edges crimp.

The Artist and Society

Awareness is another. Honesty, concentration, unity of being: these allow, in the artist, the world to be *seen*—an unimaginable thing to most of us—to fully take in a tree, a tower, a hill, a graceful arm. If you've ever had an artist's eyes fall on you, you'll know what I mean. Only through such openings may the world pass to existence.

Sensuality is another. Painting and poetry (to name just two) are sexual acts. The artist is a lover, and he must woo his medium till she opens to him; until the richness in her rises to the surface like a blush. Could we adore one another the way the poet adores his words or the painter his colors— what would be the astonishing result?

Totality is still another. I mean that the artist dare not fail to see the whole when he sees with the whole of him. He sees the ant in the jam, yet the jam remains sweet. He must fall evenly on all sides, like a cloak. If he stops to sing a single feeling, he can do so well because he knows how feelings move; he knows the fish is offset from its shadow; knows the peck of the crow does not disturb the beauty of its beak or the dent it makes in the carrion. There is, it seems to me, in the works of the great, an inner measure, wound to beat, a balance which extends through the limbs like bones, an accurate and profound assessment of the proportion and value of things.

Naturally the artist is an enemy of the state. He cannot play politics, succumb to slogans and other simplifications, worship heroes, ally himself with any party, suck on some politician's program like a sweet. He is also an enemy of every ordinary revolution. As a man he may long for action; he may feel injustice like a burn; and certainly he may speak out. But the torn-up street is too simple for him when he sculpts or paints. He undermines everything. Even when, convinced of the rightness of a cause, he dedicates his skills to a movement, he cannot simplify, he cannot overlook, he cannot forget, omit, or falsify. In the end the movement must reject or even destroy him. The evidence of history is nearly unanimous on this point.

The artist's revolutionary activity is of a different kind. He is concerned with consciousness, and he makes his changes there. His inaction is only a blind, for his books and buildings go off under everything—not once but a thousand times. How often has Homer remade men's minds?

An uncorrupted consciousness . . . what a dangerous thing it is.

One could compile, I do not doubt, another list. These are examples, although central ones. I could so easily be wrong that no one's going to pay me any mind, and so I shall suggest most irresponsibly that we and our world might use more virtues of this kind—the artist's kind—for they are bound to the possibility of Being itself; and occasionally it strikes me as even almost tragic that there should be artists who were able, from concrete, speech, or metal, to release a brilliant life, who nevertheless could not release themselves, either from their own cage, or from ours . . . there is no difference. After all, we are—artists and society—both sway-ing bears *and* rigid bars. Again, it may be that the *bars* are moving, and the bears, in terror—stricken—are standing be-hind them . . . no, in front of them—among them—quite, quite still.